FICTION
True, False and Fantastical

BOTSOTSO 19

First published by Botsotso in 2018

Box 30952 Braamfontein 2017
Email: botsotso@artslink.co.za
Website: www. botsotso.org.za

ISBN 978-0-9947081-3-7

Editors:
Allan Kolski Horwitz, Siphiwe ka Ngwenya, Mboneni Ike Muila
Design, layout and make up: Vivienne Preston

Botsotso would like to thank the National Arts Council of South Africa for
supporting the publication of this anthology.

NATIONAL ARTS COUNCIL
OF SOUTH AFRICA

an agency of the
Department of Arts and Culture

Behind joy and laughter there may be a temperament, coarse, hard and callous. But behind sorrow there is always sorrow. Pain, unlike pleasure, wears no mask. Truth in art is not any correspondence between the essential idea and the accidental existence; it is not the resemblance of shape to shadow, or of the form mirrored in the crystal to the form itself; it is no echo coming from a hollow hill, any more than it is a silver well of water in the valley that shows the moon to the moon and Narcissus to Narcissus.

Truth in art is the unity of a thing with itself: the outward rendered expressive of the inward: the soul made incarnate: the body instinct with spirit. For this reason there is no truth comparable to sorrow. There are times when sorrow seems to me to be the only truth. Other things may be illusions of the eye or the appetite, made to blind the one and cloy the other, but out of sorrow have the worlds been built, and at the birth of a child or a star there is pain.

Oscar Wilde ('De Profundis')

Contents

EDITORIAL

IT'S ALL ABOUT LANGUAGE

"The historical consciousness, through the feeling that it creates, constitutes the safest and most solid shield of the cultural security of a people. This is why every people seeks only to know and to deeply live their true history, and to transmit its memory to their descendants. The most essential thing is for people to rediscover the thread that connects them to their ancestral past."

Cheikh Anta Diop

"Most South African students of applied language agree that the most difficult obstacle in the way of the rapid development of the African languages is what Ngugi wa Thiong'o has called "the colonised mind" — that is to say, the fact that the vast majority of black people simply do not believe that their languages can or should be used for higher-order functions even though they cherish them and are completely committed to maintaining them in the primary spheres of the family, the community and the church."

Neville Alexander

Are we all agreed that language is the key means for human communication? And that being able to use a common language is vital in terms of generating, understanding and participating in the worldviews and value systems that societies create in order to satisfy individual and collective needs. And that, because this is the case, language choice, knowledge and status are critical in giving expression to the development of human culture and in so doing make possible the exchange of ideas and the spread of economic trade.

Now in Africa alone there are more than 2,000 languages with several being spoken in more than one country viz Swahili (the main language of Kenya, Tanzania, the Democratic Republic of Congo, Rwanda and Uganda) and Arabic (spoken all over north and some of central and east Africa). Other languages spoken by many millions include Berber and Somali (north and east Africa), Oromo and Am-

1

haric (Ethiopia), Yoruba, Hausa and Igbo (Nigeria), Manding and Fulani (west Africa), Shona (Zimbabwe), IsiZulu (South Africa) and Wolof (Senegal). However, it is significant that "twelve dialect clusters (which may group up to a hundred linguistic varieties) are spoken by 75% and fifteen by 85% of Africans as a first or additional language. Although many mid-sized languages are used on the radio, in newspapers and in primary-school education, and some of the larger ones are considered national languages, only a few are official at the national level." (Wikipeadia).

And why is this the case? The former colonial powers continued control of the 'commanding heights' of 'post' independent economies and the arbitrary nature of the 'countries' they created (which combined innumerable tribes/peoples), meant that each new state had many contending languages with no natural way to select one over the other for 'official' business. The result was that, in the political, academic, cultural and economic spheres, the colonial languages – English, French and Portuguese – retained their pre-eminence. Today this means that most government documents, trade relations, literary production and scientific research are written and conducted in these languages. And, as a consequence, indigenous languages struggle to develop vocabularies that are adequate to these spheres and remain marginalised while the elite, which controls the state apparatus and enters into business relations with foreign corporations, communicates in a colonial language. In turn, this de facto 'low' status inevitably forces the new generation to view mastery of the colonial languages as the key to self-advancement and participation in the 'global village' and so the situation is self-perpetuating.

But, the 'realist' will ask, is this not dialectically as it should be? Is this not a phenomenon to be expected? The 'strong will overcome the weak', the "more developed, the primitive'. Were not the vast majority of African languages framed by 'hunting and gathering' and by subsistence agriculture and herding, modes of production that produced very basic systems of philosophy, science and technology – whereas the European languages were the tools and vessels of far more complex and advanced civilizations that had enabled them to conquer the world? In addition, these African languages were, by and large, first codified and reduced to writing by those very European missionaries and administrators so that their rules (incorporating vocabulary, syntax, pronounciation and idioms) were set by foreign experts rather than by the speakers themselves – and that this was a blessing: better that those who already have the skills perform such an important task than 'beginners'.

The above view, is, of course, the classic colonial denigration of all African knowledge systems; and reflects the racist assumptions that rationalised the greed and inhumanity that subjugated and obliterated so many African cultures. Moreover, this rule of overlords instilled a certain fear and hesitancy to challenge so that the language of the conqueror became the vehicle for expressing the inherently unequal relationships between master/mistress and slave/servant and over time forced the slave/servant to surrender his/her innermost self to the thoughts and feelings generated by the master/mistress's sensibilities – and, in so doing, destroying the slave/servant's sense of self-worth and thus any possibility of equality. And so the colonists ruled, not just subjugated African bodies, but our minds.

But again why be surprised? (As this line of thought continues.) It is natural for the conqueror to impose his/her cultural/ideological rule as much as he/she needs to impose it in the military and economic spheres – and language is the key means for the transfer of orders as much as beliefs. Let us look at the Roman empire as a prime example. Rome, a small city-state, conquered the 'barbarian' Germanic tribes of Europe so that a whole continent became their vassals, paid tax and served as their mercenaries and slaves. This rule lasted several centuries but eventually contradictions emerged, and these same barbarians, having absorbed the key features of Roman civilization (its engineering techniques, its legal and taxation systems, its medicine and art) were over time able to successfully challenge the metropolis and slowly shift the centre of power and influence away from the Mediterranean to northern Europe.

However, what was the result of this political victory on language use? Ironically, most tribes retained the imperial language, Latin, as their language of government and commerce as well as for other intellectual and clerical purposes, including social use by the elite. With regard to its penetration among the peasants, artisans and slaves, it took several more centuries to 'bastardize' Latin sufficiently to create new dialects – which today we call the Romance languages (French, Spanish, Italian, Portuguese and Rumanian). And so, whole new literatures developed and millions of people embraced these new languages and allowed their vernaculars to die.

Another factor to consider is that past cultural constructions and practices (including the languages that communicate them) are not necessarily without limitations and may in fact discriminate against sections of a society and act as brakes on enlightenment. Indeed, they may limit life opportunities – particularly for women and those whose sexual/gender orientations are not conventionally heterosexual – and exersize censorship with regard to scientific enquiry and artistic expression. So was this extinction really such a loss? Of course, we cannot know what might have been had they survived. But new challenges transform everything we create, and now, in the twenty-first century, faced by paradigm shifts in information sharing which, in turn, are connected to the need for standardized means of global understanding (including the setting of global production/quality standards), new modes of communication are required. The result is widespread global acceptance that a single dominant language is a necessary condition for a globalised world to function effectively – and that, largely due to the economic and military power of the United States and western Europe, this language, certainly for the present and the near future, is English.

Now how should we, as Africans, relate to this global choice? Should we embrace it wholeheartedly? Or should we decry it as the language of slave masters, of genocidists, of empire builders, of monopolists, of warmongers? After all, is the history of Europe not drenched in blood, in endless wars that terrorised its own population as well as others so that all the major European languages carry the stains of Europe's imperialism? Surely, at the very least, the world should adopt a neutral language, one that does not bear the weight of this past.

Now such an argument is theoretically sound but the current balance of global power militates against it being a practical option. The invention of Esperanto (an artificially constructed language) in 1887 by Zamenhof, a Polish-Jewish ophthalmologist, was a remarkable feat but only some two million people have to date mastered it and it continues to be just a curiosity rather than a day-to-day reality. As such, it would be self-defeating for Africa to try and ignore the colonial languages. We must use them, appropriate them with flair but at the same time nurture and expand our own languages and their rich heritage. Africans want to be part of the global whole and not be peripheral. We have much to offer and share. And so, the youth, in looking for effective tools to advance their personal and public objectives, correctly aspire to maximum proficiency in English so that they will keep Africa abreast of global standards and trends and unlock powerful synergies.

And in this regard, if Africa wishes to participate on an equal footing with the rest of the world, we must industrialise and massively expand the local manufacture of what we consume. How can this come about? A new leadership must rise; a leadership that will offer political and moral direction without being arrogant and that will see through the bankruptcy of the western consumer society that is controlled by a small number of corporations across the different economic sectors. And in order to achieve this, this new leadership will truly seek engagement with those they represent, so that their conduct befits the responsibility.

For what does the post-independence African generation largely see in our societies? State capture by corrupt interests; state agencies that struggle to carry out their functions; the continued supremacy of white capitalist formations (joined now also with Chinese and Indian ones); the tensions of mass unemployment and general economic stress. Undoubtedly all these negative features are highly significant but there is also a new individual freedom, a freedom 'to be who you want to be', to realise potential and break through all the barriers to personal fulfilment and ambition that stood in the way of previous generations.

And even if this freedom, that excites many young people, comes with the responsibility of the 'black tax' (the maintaining of family networks, both materially and emotionally) there is more mobility than ever before now that direct colonial rule is over. Moreover, internal continental migration (as existed before the colonial period) has resumed so that millions of Africans now do not live in the countries of their birth. This has brought other issues to the fore: xenophobia towards fellow Africans and a confused response to the rights of refugees and economic migrants. But it is also helping to forge a new Pan-African identity which is a prelude to continental rebirth.

How does language fit into all this? Any student of human civilization will know that in order to effectively (that is, accurately and authentically) convey the nuances and rhythm of a people's life, the language used to convey that uniqueness has to be the language of the people themselves – their very words must carry their feelings, their dreams, their ideas and their reflections and this includes their past history as well as their present realities. Such a vehicle must surely contain (as the colonial languages do not) their essential spirit (elan) formed over generations thus giving expression to something far deeper than the alienated colonial object or client relationship which neo-colonial capitalist/bureaucratic systems lead to. For this deeper consciousness is the imagination of a collective spirit that stretches back in time and includes oral history and tradition. And if we agree that there is something palpable in historical memory, alive yet veiled from those who scoff at such a dimension, then we will realise that if one does not use such a local language, one is *translating* as opposed to expressing and embodying its essence. And so, if one desires authentic expression, the continuing dominance of colonial languages in Africa is highly problematic.

Another aspect is that it is largely only after the first phase of a national liberation struggle (namely, the attainment of political power) that 'decolonization of the mind' can gather momentum and influence a significant number of the newly liberated majority. The struggle to gain political independence certainly kickstarts the process but it is only the new government that will generally have the means to shape the form and content of education, manage a process for deciding on the official language(s) and allocate sufficient resources for indigenous language use and development. To carry this out, a revolutionary layer of activists in the social and education spheres is necessary. This vanguard must lead a consciousness raising movement of the working class, in particular its youth, who will then organise on a grassroots level with the assistance of government though retaining the right of co-planning and implementation.

The words of Neville Alexander (political activist and student of language policy) are instructive: "It is not clear to them (viz the ruling Black African elite), to take a few random examples, that an English-only or even an English-mainly policy, prevents the majority of the people from gaining access to vital information and, therefore, from full participation in the democratic political process. This undermines the self-confidence of second-language speakers and, even more so, of those for whom English is effectively a foreign language; and by the same token smothers the creativity and the spontaneity of people who are compelled to use a language of which they are not in full command and at the economic and workplace levels causes major avoidable blockages that have significant negative impacts on productivity and efficiency." Alexander went on to suggest that the Nguni languages and the Sotho–Tswana complex be restandardized and unified (that is harmonised) to form one new language. Sadly there has not been much support for this and the South African language board has not pursued this option with any vigour.

But, if we agree with this perspective, and it is a very persuasive one, the first need is for at least one local language to be elevated to official status – that is, use in actual government business and at the highest levels of commerce, art and science. In general, such a choice will be based on the number of speakers and on their regional spread. In South Africa, isiZulu would seem to be the best candidate. However, in addition to this national indigenous language, children from the very start of their schooling and up until matric should learn English and the main language of the province in which they reside. In the Eastern Cape this would be isiXhosa; in the Western Cape, Afrikaans; in the North West, Tswana and so on. Having said this, the overwhelming consensus of pedagogical experts is that from at least grade 1 to grade 5 the first and main language of instruction be the child's home language so that learning is associated with the familiar and is a natural and comfortable process.

The tables below bear out the practicality of this arrangement. The 2011 census recorded the following distribution of first language speakers:

Language name		Speakers as a 1st language	
English	Endonym	Count	% of popu.
Zulu	isiZulu	11,587,374	22.7
Xhosa	isiXhosa	8,154,258	16.0
Afrikaans	Afrikaans	6,855,082	13.5
English	English	4,892,623	9.6
Northern Sotho	Sesotho sa Leboa	4,618,576	9.1
Tswana	Setswana	4,067,248	8.0
Sesotho	Sesotho	3,849,563	7.6
Tsonga	Xitsonga	2,277,148	4.5
Swazi	siSwati	1,297,046	2.5
Venda	Tshivenda	1,209,388	2.4
Ndebele	isiNdebele	1,090,223	2.1
SA Sign Language		234,655	0.5
Other languages		828,258	1.6
Total		50,961,443	100.0

Language	% in 2011	% in 2001	Change (pp)
Zulu	22.7	23.8	-1.1
Xhosa	16.0	17.6	-1.6
Afrikaans	13.5	13.3	+0.2
English	9.6	8.2	+1.4
Northern Sotho	9.1	9.4	-0.3
Tswana	8.0	8.2	-0.2
Sesotho	7.6	7.9	-0.3
Tsonga	4.5	4.4	+0.1
Swazi	2.5	2.7	-0.2
Venda	2.4	2.3	+0.1
Ndebele	2.1	1.6	+0.5
SA Sign Language	0.5		
Other languages	1.6	0.5	+1.1
Total	100.0	100.0	

Now all the above relates to the individual country level. What of the need to promote a Pan–African language that will assert a continental African identity? Such a language will facilitate cultural and economic relations and restore self-confidence to Africans in a world in which we are dominated by foreign economic interests and overwhelmed by foreign cultural icons. Fortunately in this regard we already have strong examples of regional languages that are rooted in Africa and are relatively accessible in terms of syntax, spelling and pronounciation.

East and central Africa have long embraced Swahili with very positive results whilst still recognising other minority languages; North Africa has long had Arabic as its dominant and commonly accepted language whilst (admittedly after a long fight) recognising Berber and Somali. As such, movement towards a Pan-African language is possible but the political leadership has to spearhead this with energy and resources. In selecting one of them, Swahili must be a favourite because of its Bantu and Arabic roots, and the large land mass it already covers. If it is next introduced into southern Africa, west Africa would slowly also be drawn into its use. In this organic way, a United States of Africa would slowly emerge with all the benefits of economic, scientific and cultural exchange.

In conclusion, it must be emphasized that these are complex issues that require both fundamental shifts in consciousness and substantial financial resources to carry out concrete campaigns. In this regard, writers, educators and all other activists in these fields need to finalise a plan of action and then revive and capacitate state institutions like the Pan South African Language Board so that there is a serious and ongoing focus on mapping out a new direction.

ALEXANDRA WALLACE

Abigail George

Left behind, out on the edge, to smile with all walls closing in on me, interiors seeking closure, comfortable borderlines distinct and pretty, infinite and mapping out a precariously wacky, sweet, precocious personality.

Talking to yourself again?

Just thinking out loud, musing, writing. It must be anticipatory nostalgia.

And what exactly are you thinking about?

I'm thinking of Kerry Cohen's Loose Girl. In fact, I just finished it. Have you given up on The Bell Jar, Girl Interrupted and Marya Hornbacher's Wasted? I do not want to talk, debate and argue about the take on female promiscuity in modern literature this evening. Can we just watch the news or a show in peace? You read too much. You think too much. You should start saving some of the stuff you make a point of throwing away as if it isn't good enough. It is good enough. It is more than good enough. You should save it.

You should stop interrupting me when I am trying to make a point, when I'm writing and trying to watch you, watch you breathe, the light catch your hair, your neck, your eyes – I wanted to say all at the same time. What's on your itinerary for today?

You are on my itinerary.

You're going to ruin your posture forever if you're going to persist in lying on the sofa like that. What do you want to eat? Shouldn't I just order something? We had the white fish, hake, and pasta this week already, a summer soup, pie and mash, and chicken wings with peppers that came out really pretty on the plate. But that's enough chit-chat. Did anyone who has ever left this country forsake us and when they came back were they looking for salvation?

I really don't know the answer to that question.

Do you think I am a good woman?

You want to be celebrated.

All women want to be celebrated. Shut up now I'm trying to follow the dialogue.

You started the conversation.

It was an advertisement.

All women dumb themselves down at some point in their lives.

I can't believe that you of all people just made that statement! Is it in response to what I am watching on the television?

I am a man who believes in the greater good of the feminist movement but it has also caused a lot of harm.

Women, thinking they can be independent, believe in equality when it comes to defining their relationships with men. They want to be free-spirited thinkers and have it all. Isn't every mother in love with the son that she's created and the man he later becomes? If women don't dumb themselves down or stop themselves from doing what their mothers did in response to their fathers not demonstrating paternal love towards their children, they are going to burn themselves out.

Waiting, watching, watching and waiting for him, always for him to make a mark. I study him as he makes his way from room to room. I'm a learner again making acute observations.

You want it all.

I could feel his eyes on me like his hands. I felt his hand on my breast, my shoulder, it lingered on my neck, and then on my mouth.
Leaving so soon.

You forgot to wake me up.

Don't leave me to drown.

I want to be an instrument of change and of reconciliation, so many defining roles. Is that too much to ask from the universe? No, seriously, I want you to answer me. I want to be an instrument of change like Arthur Nortje, George Botha, Dennis Brutus, Zakes Mda, Mxolesi Nyezwa, Mzi Mahola, Nadine Gordimer (what a pretty name, Nadine!), Fugard, Coetzee, Richard Rive, Dambudzo Marechera. And perhaps be as relevant as Antjie Krog. White is the sun of my homeland. But the sunlight is black.

You want it all don't you? You want everything.

I know what you're thinking.

So you can read minds now too and be a brilliant teacher?

You can't give me everything.

You're insatiable. You're insatiable, courageous, beautiful and determined.

I'm not beautiful. My mother is.

You're lovely in a different way though. Yes, I've seen your mother's picture. The photograph you keep on your desk of your parents on their wedding day outside the church.

My sister is striking. All the women in our family are. My Aunt Joan was beautiful, too. They have spitfire personalities. You all know about my hurried notes, the journals I've kept from childhood, the rejected novel, the poems I've scribbled and that time and energy and ego forgot. Then there're the black Croxley notebooks I'm determined to keep away from you and the rest of the world for good.

He wounds me/them like an animal. His women, women, women, he winds them up as if they're electric dolls. I heated up the liver, mushrooms and bacon, the leftovers, scrambled the eggs and listened to the morning news on the radio. The bus coming in from Port Elizabeth to Johannesburg had flipped into the air off the highway. There were no fatalities. The plums were juicy and sweet. I saved some for lunch. I sat at the kitchen table, buttered my toast, drank my lukewarm coffee, crossed my legs, scratched my knee absentmindedly and stared out of the window. The breakfast's grease was stuck to the pan. I could forget about it. And the more aware I became of the sky, and the internal environment, the more aware I became of who created this invention, vision, dream, goal, and end of this line of sky, of blue, of this writer, this tortured poet, this bird?

If I painted your soul a million times would you promise to come back?

This alchemist, magician, illusionist, artist and dream catcher; this older man who was different in so many ways from anyone I'd ever met.

You're also different from anyone I've ever met, he said.

Smile.

And I welcomed the warmth, movement and space and curled up under the blankets.

The soup nourished our souls like a meditation on Bach.

I stared at the fable unfolding in front of me, forgetting the angels under the table.

She hung up on me. In the silence that followed I realized I had never felt anything like this before. I miss my sister.

You don't have a sister.

I miss clouds dancing across the sky, being filled with courage and the white light of the afternoon sun, our almost telepathic connection from childhood.

You don't have a sister.

I am not so good with friends (one part saint, one part devil). But I can still remember you speaking of the gems in my chromosome pool, my mitochondria, and my bilateral symmetry. And that you said you were not good with people. You said you had 'poor social skills'. You said you were 'vulnerable' and that you became more aware of it when you were with me.

I felt his hand and then nothing.

She doesn't love me.

Your mother never loved you?

Yes, she never loved me.

I don't believe you.

But it's true.

You're making it up.

And then I felt ashamed. Then I watched him walk away from me. I watched him close the door on me.

The dream girl after leaving Johannesburg turned into a woman. She returned to the coast, to her father's house, her mother's kitchen, her mother's wisdom and the thrones of her childhood and to the art of a heart undone. She returned to the coast where water could be found in wild places, where tides were subject to change, to the place where she spent blue hours staring up at the sky. She had her books. Her index finger would linger on the spines in her father's grand study, his library, and his 'London experience'. The house was dilapidated, tiles falling off the wall in the kitchen. The walls needed paint. The dream girl had returned. The dream girl was also determined to change. She wanted to be heroic and magical.

Writing about grief is one of the most difficult things I have ever had to do. Nerves I could fathom as I stood in front of them but what I really wanted to do was escape. Everybody always speaks about the miracle of life at a funeral. When death pays a visit there is no apprehension about discussing what music to play when the coffin is lowered, what hymns will be played, what verse will be read out of the bible, and who will make the potato salad.

What is it about the past that haunts you so?

In this picture I am the birthday girl with the red balloons; in the next, a bird with a broken wing; then one with the frosting of her cake on her hands in a place in time, a moment of reflection; fleeting sadness, on the verge of tears – a nervous breakdown? Nobody wanted me. Nobody wanted to speak to me, take responsibility for me, pick me up, and drive me anywhere.

It hurt you?

Yes, it did hurt me. It hurt me and that is why I am and always will be the bird with the broken wing.

Then let it go.

Why? Why should I do that?

Because the people who did that to you have moved on with their lives – they're living in the present while you're stuck in the past. When they were hurting you, what they wanted to see was your spirit crushed and your mind's eye immovable. They don't have your intellect, your psyche. All they have is ego.

They were unkind.

Yes, I agree. They were unkind to you.

Blow me a kiss.

Here's a kiss from me to you. Is this enough?

What do you mean?

Is this enough for you?

For now it is enough for me.

You mean for the time being.

What is this machinery you've put in place?

I've put it in place to spy on you. You won't able to handle it. Can you handle it?

I'm a professional. Of course I'll be able to handle it.

Your skin is so golden, your eyes so bright. You're a golden/brown paradise road in a lover's country under a ripple of pale moonlight with the texture of water against my fingertips. You smell like pineapple scented soap and the afternoon sun – sunlight, vanilla, powder and salt.

It's the new shampoo I've been using.

It's the scent of a woman.

The wind here resonates with the euphoria I feel inside my heart; the heat, the colour of the day and its song chills me to the bone. I feel as if the wind is in pursuit of something; I am in pursuit of something. The flowers are dead. I must rinse the vase out and fill it with fresh water. Nasturtiums. Violets. The violets are the color of his eyes and the colour of the day.

Your feet are cold. What are you reading?

Oh, this. African stories.

What are you reading?

I am reading about the growing intimacy between a man and a woman. It's a kind of ballad.

Is it hectic?

Yes, hectic. Intense.

Am I welcome?

Yes, yes, you're welcome.

Read me something.

Anything?

Yes, read me anything. Read me what you like.

I can hear the two them talking, laughing, drinking wine while circling love's world, temptation's country. But then there's the split personality, the mushroom of black light.

The silent treatment again . . .

I'm reading. Don't be a spoilsport.

I watched you swimming today.

You did?

I was proud.

Yes. It was a very big first step. It was my giant leap back into the world, the planet, humanity and soul-defying gravity, as it were.

It was the first time you'd been out since your aunt's death.

Are you sending me a secret message from the divine? I thought I would never feel connected to the world again.

You're a big girl now. I think you know what I am trying to say. You know I'm trying to tell you that I love you. I love you very, very much.

KILLING THE GOAT

David Kerr

At that time human beings, god and animals all lived in peace, living off what the forest provided for them. Nor was there any distinction between wild and domestic animals.

Sitting on a mattress in the back of the 4 x 4 gave you such a stupid sense of freedom. Even at 9.30 the sun was fierce and Deirdre, who was wearing shorts, had to cover her legs with a kitenge. Kagiso seemed to be enjoying the ride as the breeze-block suburbs of Gaborone sped past. He peeped through the cab window and indicated that she should also look. In the front seat, Brian was driving with one hand, while his other stroked Mildred's thigh. The car CD-player was banging out a reggae number. Deirdre turned away, with a smile she hoped wasn't too prim.

Soon after Molepolole they turned off along a dirt road. Villagers stood outside their houses to stare at these symmetrically inter-racial couples. Before long the houses thinned out and eventually disappeared altogether. The sun was beginning to be uncomfortable and Deirdre put on her straw hat, securing it with a ribbon under the chin. Mildred wriggled her eighteen-year-old torso out of the window, letting beaded dread-locks fly in the wind.

'We're free now,' she yelled as she bounced to the music, 'No cops here, we're in the bush.' She asked for some beer. Kagiso crawled to the plastic cooler box and took out a six-pack of Hansa. He tore at the plastic wrapper and pulled two cans off, giving the remainder to Mildred. Deirdre peeped through the cab window as Mildred opened two cans, gave one to Brian, snuggled against his shoulder and swigged at her own.

Kagiso opened a can and offered it to Deirdre. She hardly ever drank beer but she felt she had to now. She wanted to quell the queasiness she felt over Brian and Mildred's lust. She didn't want to seem abnormal. The remorseless sunshine was making a small fire crackle in her head. She needed to latch onto the freedom of the journey, the escape from library chores of learning Setswana, reading anthropology books and making sense of her research notes.

After some time man became dissatisfied. He wanted to control everything. He found a way of making fire. One day man's fire set the bush ablaze.

Brian was a fast driver; orange dust plumed out behind the bakkie. Occasionally they plunged jerkily down slopes to cross dried up river beds. Otherwise the landscape was utterly flat. There was nothing to look at but blue sky, a few, stunted white-thorn trees and the trail of dust.

Kagiso swigged at the beer.

'I didn't know you drank,' Deirdre said.

'I don't usually. Today's special.'

He hardly looked like a neophyte. Deirdre liked him. He had a more mature attitude than the usual university student and was a patient Setswana teacher who seemed to have some genuine interest in her research plans to catalogue Tswana folklore. If, as she suspected, he had romantic designs on her, he disguised them well.

Deirdre gulped at the beer, out of thirst, not desire for alcohol. A particularly hard bump sent liquid spurting out of the can onto the mattress. She mopped it up with her kitenge.

Kagiso opened a small pack of biltong. He chewed at a piece contentedly.

'Not much use offering you this, I suppose?'

She shook her head.

'Or there are peanuts.'

She accepted these. Kagiso had once told her that Botswana, where cows outnumbered people, was the worst place for her to come and do research. He dismissed her theories of meat-as-oppression-ecological-degradation, pointing out that she would have to develop some sympathy for a cattle culture if she was to penetrate Setswana mythology.

'How did you get to know Brian?' Kagiso asked.

'He doesn't seem my type?'

'You're a real academic –truly interested in your research and village life. He's just an engineer.'

'It's true,' she said, smiling at this snobbery. 'He's not my type. When I first arrived, we went out together a couple of times. But it didn't work.'

The problem wasn't that Brian was much older and divorced but that he was too wrapped up in cars, booze and chasing women.

'But we still get on okay.'

'Besides, he's got the bakkie.'

'Right,' she laughed. 'It's torture trying to get transport out of UB'.

The animals began to flee in panic, running from the flames. It became total confusion. There was a stampede of hooves and paws as the forest blazed more fiercely.

She winced as she saw Brian throw his empty beer can into the bush. A solitary red-throated bird lit up the landscape for a second, then was gone. On their first date Brian had taken Deirdre to a notorious Gaborone pub. There were a lot of busy pool tables, thick smoke and a hubbub of music interrupted by arguments or screaming laughter. At the bar were middle-aged white men quaffing drinks and pawing at pretty Batswana teenagers. Deirdre had felt sick.

The memory prevented her from finishing the beer, which was rapidly getting warm. She threw the dregs over the side and kept the can tucked next to the mattress. She felt a stuffiness which sometimes coalesced as a head ache. The open plains and vast blue sky, which had seemed to generate freedom, were beginning to be oppressive.

The bakkie came to a halt. They were at a cross roads. Three dust roads lay available – all deserted, stretching straight, apparently going nowhere. Brian kept the engine running but got out of the cab.

'I think you'd better drive, china,' he said to Kagiso. I don't know the way. Me and Mildred can get in the back. You guys could do with a bit of comfort, anyway.'

The couples swapped places. The cab shade was welcome. A compilation of old 80's rock hits was playing.

'Do you really want this on?' Deirdre asked.

'Yes,' Kagiso replied, though turning the volume down.

He led the car down the right-hand track, humming to the music.

'Do you think we might find anyone as good as that old Shakawe man?' Deirdre asked.

'The one who told us the story about the fire?'

'Yes, I'm keen on teleological narratives. I'd like to reconstruct a whole Tswana creation mythology'.

'I doubt it. My uncle's cattle-post is too westernized.'

Deirdre couldn't help thinking the car stereo and beer cans were somehow chasing away the myths. She looked back through the glass.

Despite the heat, Mildred and Brian had disappeared under a blanket.

God became afraid and asked help from a spider. The spider built a swift web. She built it higher and higher until god reached the clouds and took up residence there.

Kagiso pointed out a dilapidated grocery, well off the track; its Coca Cola and Rooibos adverts incongruously garish against the semi-desert landscape. There was no sign of either proprietor or customers. Soon afterwards a jumble of ramshackle homesteads appeared on the right. Kagiso pipped the horn as he drew the bakkie to a halt outside the wire fence. A young barefooted boy ran elatedly and opened a contraption of bark strips and thorn branches which served as a gate.

An old woman came out of a hut and ululated when she saw the vehicle entering the compound. Two middle-aged men, who were sitting under a thatched shelter also stood up as the bakkie came to a halt. Deirdre stepped out of the cab with the feeling of anticipation and tension which she always experienced when she went to a village. Maurice, her PhD supervisor back at SOAS, always emphasized the importance of first impressions in field work. She saw the old woman's eyes looking at the back of the vehicle. To Deidre's horror, she realised that Mildred and Brian were still under the blanket. Even the ever-cool Kagiso seemed embarrassed.

'Why didn't you tell us we were nearly there?' Brian's voice moaned.

The blanket seethed with bumps, the occasional limb protruding, as the couple got their clothes back on. Deirdre felt a flame of nausea. She was angry that the lovers might have spoiled the planned story collection.

At last Mildred and Brian emerged, still adjusting zips and buckles. Looking half-guilty, half-defiant, they jumped down and the introductions could begin. In addition to Kagiso's two uncles and his step-grandmother, there were various cousins and step-cousins. This was not the main branch of Kagiso's family.

Deirdre tried to make amends by being as polite as possible, gripping her right wrist with her left hand as she shook each person's hand. But Brian went straight to the back of the vehicle to pull out the cooler box.

The children brought stools, benches and old Chibuku crates for everyone to sit on. Despite the shade of the tree, the noon heat made

Deirdre's head throb. Brian pulled out some beers. Kagiso and Deirdre refused theirs. Mildred, ripping off her ring-pull, started to ask the older uncle about buying the goat. Kagiso had already sent word the previous week, so the subject wasn't a surprise. Mildred needed the goat to make biltong as her contribution to a stokvel being organised at her sister's house the following Friday.

When the fire burned itself out the whole world looked just like charcoal. The animals were very angry with man, and most of them declared him their enemy.

After agreeing on the price, the two uncles rose and stood aside to talk. The elder, Reuben, returned to the group, while the younger, Kelebogile, went outside the stockade to where the goats were grazing. Brian put an extension cable from the battery so the CD player could be brought outside. He put on a CD of Country and Western music. Deirdre complained about the disturbance to her anthropology work. Brian shrugged and switched the tape off. Reuben muttered to Kagiso who explained that Reuben and his mother liked the music. Brian triumphantly switched the CD back on.

Reuben went outside the stockade to look at the dappled, brown goat which a young boy was dragging with a twine halter. Mildred also rose, and Deirdre, not wishing to be left with Brian and Dolly Parton, followed. Mildred pretended to complain that the goat was too small, but finally accepted it. The goat was leaping, kicking and bleating frantically, as if aware of its fate.

Mildred went across to Brian.

'Darling, don't you want to see them kill the goat.'

'No, thanks. I don't like blood.'

'But you like meat.'

'That comes from supermarkets, darling.'

'But they still kill the cows.'

'No,' Brian joked, 'they buy it from a meat factory.'

Mildred went to the bakkie and took out her camera. Deirdre was dizzy with the sounds of the goat, but felt, as part of her induction into the culture, she ought to be there. Reuben, with a self-important manner, collected his knife from one of the houses. Kagiso and Kelebogile dragged the struggling animal to a tree where the boy had tied a rope from a branch. The tree, sand, hangman's noose and noon sun had all the simplicity of a nightmare ritual. Reuben's knife flashed swiftly. A few drops of blood fell on the sand. Deirdre twisted her face away and held onto the tree. Dust on the floor of the Camden attic, where, at the age of twelve, she had been deflowered by her step-father, had also absorbed such slowly dripping blood.

When the forest began to grow again with the coming of the rains, man began to hunt the animals and, whenever the opportunity arose, the animals in turn attacked man.

The drops were followed by a stream, and the screams became a gurgle, then silence, though the kicking continued. Reuben made a neat aperture, so that the goat's head fell half away from the body. Kelebogile tied one leg into the noose, and with Kagiso's help they hoisted the carcass, so its head just cleared the ground.

Mildred stood next to the swaying goat and asked Deirdre to take her photograph. She must have realised that Deirdre was feeling unwell, because she quickly turned to Kagiso, who took the snap, while Mildred made a silly pose of triumph.

The boy collected a plastic bucket and Reuben made an incision in the goat's belly. The entrails slithered out in a mass of black and yellow slime, the boy catching them in the bucket. Reuben began cutting away at the skin, starting with the legs. Kagiso held onto a corner, so that Reuben's skilful knife could dislodge the pelt from the still quivering muscles.

Even before she fainted Deirdre knew it was happening. She could feel her back go cold and her legs shivery. She was aware of the sand twisting from horizontal to vertical as she crashed down, but there was no pain – only darkness. It seemed a mere second, but must have been longer, because when she recovered she was lying on the mattress in the bakkie, and Kagiso was fanning her with a Bona magazine. Mildred brushed sand from Deirdre's shoulder and Brian was looking on with concern.

Deirdre could feel her heart beating wildly, and the claustrophobia of the Camden dust was still choking. She got up on one elbow, desperate to see the pure expanse of semi-desert. Kagiso propped her head on the blanket. Mildred gave him an already-opened can of Coke and Deirdre sipped it thankfully. As the palpitations went down she felt well enough to step out of the bakkie. She sat on one of the stools under the tree.

She couldn't help looking at the other tree where the goat, now completely skinned, was being hacked down the spine into two pieces. Kagiso went to help his uncles. Mildred and the old woman talked in hushed tones about Deirdre's swoon. Brian put on the reggae CD again.

'Are you okay?' he asked.

'Yeah, I'll be fine.'

Man had to build villages protected by fences. Only a few animals such as dogs and goats remained loyal to man and stayed in the villages in fear of the wild animals.

Mildred got a couple of beers from the cooler for herself and Brian. She put her arms around his neck, and whispered into his ear. Brian went to the cab and fished out a gas container and cooker. Mildred found the frying pan, and took the chicken pieces and boerwors from the cooler box. She began cooking. Brian took out the bread and the plastic container of salad. Mildred left the cooking for a minute while she whispered to Brian again. They stole some kisses.

Brian went to the cab and took out a large bottle of Mainstay from behind the seat. Kagiso, who had returned from his goat duties, took the remaining beers and soft drinks out of the cooler and poured out the slush of icy water. Reuben and Kelebogile brought one half of the goat each and squeezed them into the cooler box. Kagiso put the remaining block of ice on top and replaced the cans of beer and softies. Mildred offered the Mainstay to the two men. They thanked her profusely and sent a girl to collect two plastic mugs.

Mildred offered soft drinks to the old woman and the children. Kagiso opened a beer for himself. The two uncles refused any mixer, preferring to drink the mainstay neat. Mildred asked Brian to look after the meat so she could dance to the reggae; she dropped her shoulders and the dreadlocks fell shaking over her face. Brian switched off the gas cooker and announced that the meat was ready. Mildred served it up on plastic plates. Deirdre refused hers but nibbled at some remaining peanuts so that she shouldn't seem to be excluding herself from the meal.

After they'd cleared up the food and were all into another round of drinks, Kagiso brought up the topic of the old stories, explaining that Deirdre wanted to collect them for her research. The uncles, who had seemed so self-assured when working on the goat, were suddenly reduced to incoherence as if the Mainstay had instantly taken away their dignity; but they encouraged the old woman, into whose Coke they had reluctantly allowed a tot of liquor, to think of stories though she too seemed to have a total memory failure.

God was also angry with man and made him work hard cultivating the land for his living. Man had to pray to god so rain could fall and irrigate the fields.

Kagiso shrugged at Deirdre. She stood up and whispered in his ear.
  'Don't worry. I can see we'll get nowhere. Let's just leave it.'
  'It seems a waste.'
  'There'll be other villages.'
  'Are you sure you're okay?'
  'Yeah, I think I want to go for a walk – before we have to set off.'
  Kagiso stood up to accompany her. They went out of the stockade past some spinach being grown under a shelter of straw. The sun was getting low and a different young boy was whistling and cracking a whip to lead a large herd of cows back to the kraal. They walked across the track and into the scrub, treading carefully to avoid large thorns. Kagiso held her hand. She looked at him, not sure whether he was doing it out of solicitation for her health or to press the friendship towards romance. They stopped walking and she disengaged her hand. Kagiso finished his beer, looked as though he was about to toss the empty can away but changed his mind.
  'I think I want to be alone, Kagiso.'
  'Are you sure you're alright?'
  'There aren't any wild animals here are there?'
  'No... but...'
  'I'm fine. I want to think.'
  'Okay. I'll check you after half an hour, if you don't come back. We'll want to leave then anyway.'
  He started walking towards the houses. She turned and looked at his progress in time to see him drop the beer can in the sand. Deirdre walked further away from the homestead till it was a mere speck on the horizon. There were no cans or torn plastic bags, not even cow plats – only the sand, bird song and thorn trees, their shadows lengthened by the late afternoon sun. On the far horizon, plumes of smoke arose from a bush fire.

From that time, every year after harvest, men and women burnt the fields in remembrance of the first conflagration and poured libations so god could forgive their sins.

She found a slightly bigger tree than the others and stood under its shade. There was a flat stone which she sat on. Deirdre could hear her heart still pounding. She leaned back till her hands took the weight of her body and her head hung loose. She looked at the pattern of white thorns, astonishingly brilliant and complex against the blue sky. The prickly earth felt warm and reassuring. For the first time since they'd left Gaborone, the stuffy feeling in her head was easing away. Even the birdsong began to fade and the lulling silence was replaced by a low rumble. She closed her eyes and the ground trembled minutely. The rumbling got louder and she saw in her mind the lovely leaping herds of buffalo, kudu, wildebeest, impala and springbok, thundering closer.

She stood up and walked calmly away from the homestead towards the approaching stampede.

A LETTER TO THE SAAD FAMILY

Habib Ahmadzadeh

The first finder or finders of this letter are kindly requested to deliver its contents in any way possible to the family of 'Saad Abd al-Jabbar,' a member of the 23rd Battalion of the Special Republican Guard Forces of Iraq; the letter is from the forces under control of the Third Army of Basra.

Esteemed Family of Soldier Saad

Greetings,

I don't know whether sending this letter is the right thing or proper under the circumstances but it seemed necessary to write it and then entrust it to your son, and, in this unorthodox way, have it reach you.

The subject of the letter is the mysterious manner in which I became acquainted with your son. Eleven years have now passed and this enigmatic acquaintance has to be explained and I feel compelled, in order to eliminate any doubt or misunderstanding on your part as regards the lamentable incident, to provide you with an exact and detailed account of how we met and the circumstances surrounding our meeting.

Right now your son Saad is standing beside me and is no doubt waiting impatiently for me to finish the letter so that he can be the bearer of the facts to you. This is the last time we will see each other, and certainly it will be our last goodbye! But let me not digress – I know that it would be best to get to the point.

The incident took place ten years ago: on the morning of 28 September 1981, to be exact. That was the first time I saw your son. During the morning of that day I was returning from the banks of the Karun River to our rear. Major operations had taken place in the sector the night before. The operations were intended to break the siege of our city. By morning we had fought our way to the area around the river.

This was the first time during the one-year siege of the city that our forces were able to recapture the sector. Delighted to take part in these pivotal operations and wanting to make a record of my participation, I had brought with me an expensive camera, but the intensity of the fighting did not allow me to use it.

Until this moment everything that could have happened took place as they did in other operations; with the leaden skies of pre-dawn, fresh forces took the place of the tired fighters and everyone but me took advantage of the cover of night to return to the rear. I had the urge to tour the newly liberated areas to see what had befallen the region. Having skirted a minefield, I came upon a road made of packed sand that the Iraqis had constructed. This was to join up with the main asphalt road. I followed this sand road until it came to the intersection of two roads. I was now face-to-face with a causeway that I had hoped to reach for a year so I could use it to go on leave. The road still hadn't been cleared of mines, booby traps, and barbed wire; nevertheless it was a freeway to me.

As I walked along it, I remember clearly that the sun was rising. I let out several loud cries and, without paying attention to the sur-roundings, started to prance around, happily waving my weapon up and down. I was overjoyed. At that time I was sixteen – about two years younger than your son was at the time.

This marked the beginning of the incident. I didn't know what hit me, but for a moment I turned, and was abruptly stunned: while I was dancing on the asphalt road, an Iraqi soldier was sitting watching me from behind. Automatically assuming a defensive position, I dived to the ground then scrambled behind the shoulder of the road and released the safety on my weapon. Why hadn't he fired at me? There could be only one explanation: he was totally alone, abandoned in the newly liberated territory, and now wanted to surrender.

The sum of these thoughts gave me the nerve to try to get behind him. After briefly hesitating, I ran to the other side of the hill and was about to shout 'Hands up!' in Persian. Now that you have the letter, of course, everything to an extent will be obvious.

That's right: I came face to face with your son's corpse, which had been put on the ground in a kneeling position; his neck and both wrists had been tied from behind to the crossroad sign with the kind of telephone wire they use in the desert. Blood had pooled under his feet.

The weapon went limp in my hands. As I got closer I noticed they had tied your son up in such a way that the wounds on his neck and wrists made a horrible sight. After the shock of seeing him like this wore off, I became aware of the sounds of exploding shells and mortar rounds that were coming at every moment towards our sector.

I looked at his face; his eyes were wide open and startled. I don't know why it occurred to me to take a picture of your son's face, but I took it. Maybe it was just because I wanted to use the camera. As I was putting it back in my pack, the explosions became more distinct as did the barking of stray dogs behind the Baathist lines; these dogs would generally whine every night before operations. This also reminded me of what would happen to your son's corpse if it remained out there.

I looked into his open eyes, and, to escape the urgings of my conscience, I said to him, 'I know, but I swear to God if I had a shovel I would definitely bury you' – just like any other person who uses an excuse to avoid doing something important. Then I got going trying to escape the explosions which were increasing by the minute. But I hadn't gone a hundred meters when I saw a large shovel buried up to the handle sticking out of a pile of dirt next to a bunker.

I stopped, stood still, deeply undecided. But, having made an irrevocable promise to your son, I had no choice. Despite great difficulty, I managed to pull the shovel out and went back to him. Showing him the shovel, I said, 'Here it is,' and began to dig in front of him. I dug so close to him that after a while a stream of blood appeared in the hole. As I dug, I would keep one eye on your son and one eye on the stream of blood, and move the shovel around lest it leave bloodstains on the heels of my boots. I would also talk to your son, but to keep this letter short I can't set down everything we spoke about; besides the subjects are without doubt not worthy of your attention.

Briefly then: when the job was nearly over, it occurred to me to ponder, given my short life as gravedigger, whether I had oriented the hole properly, that is, according to the direction of prayer. But suddenly there was this immense explosion and the next thing I was in the grave along with your son Saad on top of me. Would there be no end to these shocks? Here I was in a sector with nobody from our side, now thrown into a pit, face-to-face with a corpse.

The bombardment continued. I used all my strength to push your son aside and climb out. I realized that the situation had come about as a result of an explosion that had occurred behind your son. When I looked closer, I noticed there was a fresh stream of blood flowing down his overcoat, and that he had taken several pieces of shrapnel in the head; in other words, he was positioned exactly between me and the explosion or, said in a more precise way, between me and death.

It was at this point that my interest in your son increased several times over. I quickly finished digging the grave and was about to put

Saad in it, when I figured that I shouldn't allow his face to touch the ground. So I took his long coat off and covered his head with it and having wrapped his head in the coat, found his ID card and a letter in one of the pockets. Then I untied his hands and began to shovel dirt on him. And as I was doing this, I noticed four spent cartridges inserted into his mouth. Of course this bothered me but there was no time to spare for yet another matter had struck me: this stranger, who was far from his family, should be buried in a grave over which someone should recite the Q'uran. I was really going to do the right thing! But my head was spinning as the bombs began falling even faster. And it was with a bitter feeling that I continued shovelling, covering him with earth as I filled the grave. Anyway, having marked the grave with the same signpost that had hung from his neck, I got away as fast as I could.

Later on, during my first leave away from the front, I had his picture developed. I put it in my album. And when leafing through the album, I would think of him as the corpse that had saved my life, and, despite the fact that I knew his name was Saad from the ID card, I still thought of him as an Iraqi soldier.

Eleven years passed; the whole incident became an incidental memory. But one day I became acquainted with some fellow countrymen whose job it was to exchange the bodies of Iraqi soldiers for those of our own dead. These exchanges took place on the border between the two countries. Anyway I brought up the subject of Saad with them, and today was the day we had arranged for me to show them his grave.

When we were there, I realized that I shouldn't rely too much on the signpost to find the grave, but that the intersection where the two roads crossed would be of some help. After excavating at two different locations, we managed to dig up your son; finding him in the same condition in which you will possibly observe him when this letter reaches you. But the real reason why I am writing you this letter has nothing to do with these matters. It relates to the secret discovery that we made after we had dug him up.

When the fellows unwrapped the overcoat around his head, they looked at one another knowingly.

'What's the problem?' I asked.

'Another deserter,' they said.

Their experience in finding and examining bodies told them that

Saad was a deserter because the Iraqis would first execute deserters, then clamp their jaws shut with four bullets between the teeth to serve as a warning to others. After I explained the way in which Saad had been kneeling on the ground, they said that before execution, he had probably been shot in the knees. A further examination confirmed this truth which, at the time of my burying him, his clothing and flesh had kept hidden from me.

Please do not think me unfeeling. As I write this, I know that these facts are brutal and upsetting, especially since they concern your child. Indeed, my emotional and psychological state is no less affected than yours although I must admit that over the last eleven years, despite my travelling that road out of the city many, many times, even when passing the crossroads, it never crossed my mind to say a prayer for your son. For this omission I hope God will forgive me. Furthermore, come to think of it, I could have written to you years ago and sent the picture that I had taken of your son's body. And please forgive me for the unorthodox material on which this letter is being written: it is only because I have no other that I am using the back of the forms describing the particulars of the body. (On the other hand, perhaps what one of the disinterment fellows said is right – that it is better to let the truth remained buried under the ground; that way I will not be the cause of so much pain and discomfort to you. There is also the added risk that the letter might fall into the wrong hands who would prevent you from even taking possession of your son's body. On this account you will be pleased that I have used this extraordinary method and thereby decreased to a considerable extent the chances of it's detection.) Lastly, you will note that I have written my address at the bottom so that you can contact me if you see fit. I don't know how you feel about my hiding the letter in the broken bone of your son's leg. Hopefully this method of concealment will prevent the authorities from noticing it, but if they do, and it is buried with Saad, then you will remain ignorant of his fate and the apologies will not be necessary.

Am I still grappling with myself about why I am writing this? It is only in these last lines that I will be able to express why this is the case. As you know, for many years the thought of writing such a letter would never have crossed my mind. But now that I have a son of my own, I can see that it is the absolute right of every family to know how their child spent his last minutes on earth.

And so the time for saying my last goodbye has come. I know that in future whenever I leave the city and pass the crossroads, as I stare at his empty grave, my heart will feel the anguish of his fate. Forgive me for closing now but the fellows are complaining about how long this letter is taking. I entrust you and Saad to that same God who caused me to take a different path that day, who allowed me to see him and find a shovel, and to now uncover an eleven-year-old secret. And, may that same God allow this letter to reach you.

LELIK

Jolynne Philips

The dog just arrived here one day. No one knew where he came from and I don't think anyone was looking for him. I mean, he looked brandsiek; a real pavement special. A mix between a poodle and a husky, his hair looked like sun rays, wild, more like a wild dog's. Shame, the poor thing was ugly and that was the end of it. I felt so sorry for him, let him sleep in my yard and gave him bones and lefto-vers to eat, but he stayed thin. Later on we got used to each other. He never listened to my commands, but he would walk all the way to the stop sign at the end of our street and wait there for me until I returned from the shop. Later on I thought: give the poor thing a name. I started calling him Snuffels, Fluffy, then Ore, but he never responded when called until that day when old Hennie came over for coffee and a few ginger cookies. Hennie actually lives here but sometimes he forgets. He doesn't remember who he is or where he came from, so I will treat him like he is a long lost cousin, or someone visiting from a faraway country, but he changes his role every day.

'Shu, but that is a bloody ugly dog!'

Suddenly the dog gets up, waves his tail excitingly and runs to-wards Hennie. That's it! The blerrie dog's name is 'Lelik'! Old Hennie is a strange oomie, a wanderer. He has nine fingers and an Afrikaans accent that sounds like skop, skiet and donner American movies but heaven knows where he got it, and now that I think about it, I never cared to ask,

Years ago he worked in a butchery, next to Susan's in town. One day he wanted to steal meat; he had to close the shop that evening but he was too drunk and ended up cutting off his middle finger. Today he is almost sixty and I, who is not even his child, has to look after him because he murders all his brain cells with the papsak. Now the other day I am at home hanging over the gate watching him come down the road just like an ou roeker. He stands there with a businessman smile and asks me very politely.

'Do you know where Josephine Fielies lives?'

I burst out laughing. I laugh until it feels like my stomach muscles pull together, until I find myself crying, 'Hennie just ask me where Josephine Fielies lives!' I take him by the arm and give him a cup of coffee. It's still hot. He drinks it like it's cooldrink in one go. It's as if his body forgets to react to the pain. He has forgotten how to be human.

He would go and rest after his third cup, and today he seems a bit weak. I guess it's back to changing his nappies 'coz his body weakens by the day. Sometimes he sits there like he's dead and he just mumbles things like, 'Spider webs, spider webs, spider webs . . .' and goes back to looking like a zombie. Once I was busy making cabbage stew. I didn't hear him come to the kitchen and screamed, 'Spinnerakke!' when he stuck his face in front of me. The Lord must forgive for my language, but ek het my binne in my moer geskrik. All you saw was a wooden spoon, flying in the air. Hygend! The focking jong.

Lately he and Lelik became best friends, where Hennie was, so was Lelik. Old Hennie couldn't walk so fast anymore, that's why he walked behind, and if you dared touch him, Lelik would vreet your ankles. So at least I didn't worry too much, Lelik was there to look after him. That's why today it was strange seeing Lelik come home without him, but I thought to myself, maybe it's because he's walking slower, or visiting a neighbour. Later I checked again – maybe he was sitting on the street made from concrete, it was his usual spot to smoke his pipe. But Hennie was nowhere to be seen.

When the street lights began to light up I became really worried. I walked over to his elder son's house, that one has a car now, and we drove to the police. The police officer told us to come back in 72 hours, only then can they declare him as a missing. I swear it was the longest 72 hours of my life. So eventually they declared him missing and they took tracker dogs and, whole bunches of cops were searching, and the local newspaper asked the community to be on the lookout. Everyone searched, except for Lelik. That damn hond wouldn't lift a paw and go out and find his master. No matter what we tried, he wouldn't budge.

Meanwhile the eldest son took over the main house, and shamelessly put his two brothers out. Man, he couldn't wait to turn the house into a hotel, for him and his family. Now Tikitoi, his younger brother, lives with me in the old caravan in the backyard. Skerul, the second oldest, sleeps with his meide – he has one in almost every part of Gansbaai. Why they let the eldest keep the house is a mystery. When I ask they just say, we don't want to talk about it now. I let it be now because I take pride in keeping my nose out of other people's noses. To think the eldest brother didn't give me a blue cent, not a blooming *tiekie*. But the Lord will provide, it's no use complaining. *He* will provide.

Shit, who'd believe it's been eight years since Hennie went missing. I can still see his face like when it was on TV. But I reckon he's alive. One of these good days he will return from his long trip to see Lelik. Ja, that dog is still here. Man, he barely leaves the yard. It's just a pity I don't speak dog language. I can't accept that he doesn't know or care where his friend is.

MAKING A WOMAN

Thabisani Ndlovu

Skhumba is trying to say to Aunt Mongi he can't sleep at night because he loves her. Grown-ups can say stupid things like that and their eyes tell you these are useless things. Look at Fana's eyes, they are naturally small as a porcupine's and always slide away like those of a thieving dog; and now they are small small slits. And people say women die for Skhumba and some even scratch and bite each other over him. A man with a bull-frog nose like his, and smelling like a billy goat! His hands move hesitantly as he tries again. He gets the signs wrong and it comes out as 'I love sleep.' With open palms facing the blue blue sky, Aunt Mongi is asking, 'So?'

'Tell her,' Skhumba says to me, 'that she has the most amazing fig-ure I have ever seen and that everyone in Janke District is saying that. Unlike some men who think she is cursed, I don't. And even if she is, I don't care. Tell her she is my honey from the *mbondo* tree. I can't eat when I think of her. My heart is burning and only she can cool it.'

Skhumba is asking for too much. I only spend time with Aunt Mongi during the school holidays. How does he expect me to say 'cursed'? And his 'burning heart'? This Skhumba thinks he is clever, speaking so much gibberish through his teeth that make him look as if he has been eating brown mud because he smokes newspaper-rolled cigarettes. When a man says these kinds of sweet-sweet things, closing his eyes like that and talking softly as if talking to a sick person lying on a hospital bed, he just wants to put his thing inside the woman's. I know that. So I point to Skhumba and Aunt Mongi, and show the thumb of my right hand sticking out between the cleavage of the fore-finger and second finger.

How the cooking stick finds Skhumba's head, I don't know. I just see its broken flat end rolling briefly in the sand, the white of cooking *isitshwala* barely visible through the overall brown of sand grains. Aunt Mongi is chasing Fana and whacking the back of his head. Many blows rain on him and he bawls like a boy. He should have known that Aunt Mongi used to herd cattle and is tough and fast. She is a woman now, Grandpa says, she must not do that anymore. Now she does a lot of cooking, especially for Grandpa who likes her cooking. When she kneels in front of him, offering him food, a smile is always twitching at the corners of her mouth. Later, when we are alone, she caresses her chin and points at her chest, repeatedly makes the sign for eating and getting fat, and laughs. Grandpa and I make a good match and she throws her head back till tears sparkle in her eyes. But she must start cooking for her own man, Grandpa says. What use will it be if she continues cooking just for him until her hair turns white?

But I don't know of any man who wants Aunt Mongi except this Skhumba who is liked by women so much in spite of his ugliness and terrible smell. Women are strange. So I laugh at him until I cry and when Aunt Mongi returns, I'm still laughing. She wags the stick at me and makes as if to beat me. I raise my hands in mock fear as if to protect my face. She points at me then makes circles with her index finger touching her head, *You're just as mad.* I nod my head. She makes as if to beat me again and shows her white buck teeth. Then she hugs me, and acts out how she beat Skhumba and how he ran with his heels almost touching the back of his head. I roll on the sand and when I'm nearly dead with laughter, mother comes out of the kitchen hut, and says, 'Hey, you two, leave some laughter for the rest of us.' Facing Aunt Mongi, mother does the both-palms skywards, *What is it?* Aunt Mongi just waves mother and her question away, looking aside, *Nothing and nothing you need to know.*

That Skhumba, serves him well. He will stop that nonsense talk of his. '*There* is a woman,' he always says of Aunt Mongi, 'she makes me soil all my trousers.' And some men laugh and say, 'You, Skhumba, that thing of yours is too greedy. Now you want *this* woman. She makes all our things stand but who are you to try her? Be careful what you ask for. You think the kind of body that can make some of us kill our mothers for, comes on its own? So you want to lift a *mamba* to see how many young she has hatched? Good luck.'

'Women,' Grandpa says and shakes his head, 'You know that underneath your grandmother's *doek* is white hair?' It is one of those questions he asks without asking. Look at how he is picking his teeth, looking away from me so that he does not even see me nod. He spits out whatever piece was trapped between the few teeth he still has, and continues, 'You would think she knows better, heh? Not at all. Here she is pretending she can't see that your aunt needs help.' Something is pricking me to ask, 'Help with what?' But before I decide whether he is still talking to himself, he says, 'Your Aunt Mongi needs to become a woman before it's too late. As God's own creature, she does.' People say that of Aunt Mongi, 'Agh . . . shame. She is God's own creature. What a body that woman has! How many women look like that? For sure, God can't give you everything.'

Grandpa looks at me with his cloudy eyes and I nod my head. He squints more and more these days and the whitish clouds in his eyes are spreading fast. It is good to sit on the stool that he carved for me three days ago. It is a smaller version of his. On the wood supporting the seat and the base are three snakes coiled around each other, their heads close together as if they are whispering. 'Son of my son,' he said when he gave me the stool, 'you are my first-born's son and I praise God and the ancestors that you are a boy. You will be the father of everyone here one day. Come sit and eat with me and learn to become a proper man. Now he is saying to me, 'Tomorrow . . . we will go looking for herbs. For now, can I drink this?'

He is like that - his talk jumping all over the place like a grasshopper. It is a dark-brown and slimy liquid that he gives me, not as bitter as the one he gave me yesterday. 'Makes your joints, sinews and bones strong, this one. And when it's time to father children.' He makes a sharp tek sound between thumb and middle finger, 'You must become strong son of my son. Very soon you will have a beard around your thing. Give me the bottle.' He gulps all of it and says 'Ahh' as if he has taken something nice, like those people who drink Coca-Cola on tv.

There at the bottom of the transparent cooking oil bottle are several little bulbs cut in half, on top of which is a green weed. He has many of these bottles and others with paws of animals and heads, tails and guts of little creatures in his hut, and people come from far away to get the medicines. Some come walking with their legs far apart. That's pain from the disease that eats their things, Grandpa says. That is why he has many cattle. Some people who would have come walking with their legs far apart come back walking properly and bring a beast or two. Some come to thank Grandpa for making them have children and some older men come back all smiles to say they are men again and may bring a goat or two. Grandpa makes people happy. He makes some of them young and strong.

Aunt Mongi is frying *vetkoeks* in a pan over the fire just in front of the kitchen hut. In a reed basket next to where she is kneeling are succulent brown ones. I point at them and cup both my hands. She looks at me, smiles and wags a finger. She points at the *vetkoeks*, rapidly thrusts the bunched fingers of one hand towards her mouth, puffs her cheeks, rolls her eyes and holds her arms out like wall brackets alongside her boy. 'Vetkoeks make you greedy and fat,' she is saying. But mother thinks it's the meat that Grandpa feeds me almost daily. I must learn to become umnamzana, he says. A *mnumzana* enjoys the fruit of his labour and sees to it that he, his children and grandchildren grow up to become proper people and not hollow things that are blown by the wind and laughed at by everyone, including poor and empty people. Above all, a *mnumzana* must make sure that in his homestead, the meat of the next beast is cooked in the gravy of the last. He says there are three Ndebele Kingdoms for a man to enjoy – meat, beer and women. He asks me to repeat the kingdoms. I get the order wrong and he tells me I would not have learnt the lesson if I get the order wrong. 'Women can leave you,' he says, 'but you're never too old for the other two. You can eat the meat of a calf and if that fails, you can grind the meat. Do you know that?' I say no.

Aunt Mongi points at the *vetkoeks* again and spits in quick succession, 'Ptuu! ptuu! ptuu!' The spitting goes with a flicking of both wrists and sideways glance. 'These things are rubbish.' Just like she says of people she doesn't like or things that don't agree with her, like cooking oil. She can cook *vetkoeks* for everyone but if she tries to eat one she vomits. Buses and cars don't agree with her as well. She can't travel on them because diesel or petrol makes her sick-sick. So she doesn't want to travel to town. This is how she says town: 'left-right' control of a steering wheel that is not there, and then pointing to the east, the direction of town. She went there once, before I was born, my mother says. Aunt Mongi vows she'll never travel there again; said by scooping a bit of sand on the ground, spitting into the small hollow and covering it up with the displaced sand. *Never.*

I know there are things she can say never to and mean it. Like she refused to inherit the family's *amadlozi* even though grandmother, who carries the spirits, said Aunt Mongi was chosen by the ancestors. They brewed the beer, beat the drums and danced but there was no Aunt Mongi. She returned home three days later and nobody knew from where. But she cannot say no to just giving me one *vetkoek*. I cup my hands, bend the head to one side and wave a forefinger. Just one please. She laughs showing her white buck teeth, throws her head back, flashing her black eyes. She points at the *vetkoeks* and slowly extends the 'arm-brackets'. *These things will make me fatter.* She reminds me of my classmates who call me *mafutha*. I make a sour face. In answer she becomes soft-soft, forks one *vetkoek* and gives it to me. The truth is that Aunt Mongi likes me too much to say no to things like this. When I was younger, she used to carry me on her back. Now she carries Uncle Talkmore's child, Sithembiso, on her back.

Lately Jamu has been here several times to talk to Aunt Mongi. He does not know how to talk to her well. He runs out of signs for what he wants to say. So I've been asked to relay his messages to her when he runs out of words . . . signs, actually. Is this really Jamu smiling like this? Like I said, when men want to put their things inside women's, they act strangely. Which herdboy does not know the sting of Jamu's cane if the unfortunate boy's cattle graze his crops? Which herdboy can outrun Jamu except Bafana? Jamu didn't catch Bafana because that one runs round trees and shrubs, twisting and turning like a hare. Even then, Jamu took his time. Just like you leave milk to stand overnight in a gourd so the cream can rise to the top for you to scrape off and enjoy. But for a while you forget or pretend the milk is not there and there won't be any cream. So Jamu stalked Bafana for many days after the boy's escape. Eventually he caught Bafana napping under a *gonde* tree and thrashed him so badly the boy peed on himself. Jamu . . . he doesn't play this one. And who can complain to him, tell him face-to-face what they think except my mother? So when Jamu beat me last rainy season and the cuts from his switch made mad patterns all over my body, one of them poking my left eye, mother got madder than the cuts and dragged me to Jamu's.

'You big-boned baboon. Do you want to kill my child . . . eh? Why don't you have children of your own that you can murder as you please? Three women and you couldn't make them pregnant. And why did they leave you if you're the tough man you think you are? It's not my fault you man-when-there-are-no-other-men-around. If you ever touch my child again, I'll make you see the buttocks of a snake!' Jamu just stood there, dwarfing my mother but looking as if he had been turned into a pillar of salt. Now I wonder if he ever tried any of Grandpa's medicines so he could have children. A few days later, my father was home from the city where he works for the weekend. When mother told him how Jamu had nearly killed me, asking me to remove my shirt so father could see the now not-so-mad cuts on my back, he cast one or two glances from the rim of his teacup, slurped and swallowed his tea, and said, 'He'll be all right. It won't kill him.

That's how some of us grew up as well.' Mother was angry. Was it *his* town women that were making him not care about his son? It was all right that he didn't care about her anymore. Now his son, too? Father gulped down his tea, stood up without looking at mother and went out in that Grandpa way that says, 'Women are mad.'

In getting mad at Jamu like that, maybe mother had forgotten that he has big fists and big boots. He used to work in a mine. Because there is no store that can provide his shoe size even his mining boots had to be specially made for his big feet. Now the boots are so scuffed in front they show metal caps that make them look like mother and father tortoise whose heads are about to completely retreat into their shells. Who doesn't know that Jamu's fists have broken a lot of noses and jaws at beer drinks and his boots have broken many men's ribs? They say he has *ngoromera*, the spirit of fighting, and the main ingredient of his *ngoromera* is a blind worm from a stubborn sheep's brain. People say if you are like that, you can carry on fighting even if your arms and legs break. You spray the person you are fighting with your bone marrow. Even if you lose both eyes, you keep fighting. That is why some people call him when they want to tame bullocks. I once saw him hold a bullock by the horn with one hand and with the other, put a yoke over its neck. Even stubborn ones end up kneeling on their front knees, people say. But now he is smiling and asking me to tell Aunt Mongi that she will have a good life with him, that he has many cattle and she will have all the food and clothes she wants. She laughs without laughing and says she has all the food and clothes she wants. It is true that he has many cattle. So many he has no idea how many he has. Some he has loaned to poor relatives and even there, they may number fifty or so per homestead. 'But he is so stingy,' my mother says, 'he only eats the meat of those that die suddenly or are weak from old age. God can't give you everything.'

Jamu does not know what to say anymore. He walks round Aunt Mongi as she washes the dishes at the *mopane* table close to the eastern edge of the homestead. He walks round her like a cock does before getting on top of a hen – spreading its wings, ruffling them against its body and hopping on one leg, making a gurgling sound that dies in the throat. His smile turns into a baring of teeth as he looks around to see if anyone is watching. He is behaving like my naughty dog Bazangenzani: quick look around before upsetting a pot on the fire

45

with his head then helping himself to the juiciest piece of meat before quickly slinking away to wait for the meat to cool a bit. Jamu tries to hold Aunt Mongi's hand. She quickly snatches it away and jabs a finger at him, making those noises of frustration that my friend Sipho said were goat noises. I gave him a bloody mouth and he hasn't said that rot again. Jamu walks away.

Jamu is talking to Grandpa again about Aunt Mongi. 'Yes, we should try,' Grandpa keeps saying and Jamu nods his head. 'Have you been taking what I gave you?' Grandpa asks Jamu and this time he nods his head very fast. 'Good,' Grandpa says, and looks at me, 'Son-of-my-son, bring us salt from the kitchen.' When I get out of the kitchen, I see Jamu sneaking into Aunt Mongi's hut, followed closely by Grandpa who ties the door from outside with a strong piece of wire. She is in there I know because when mother and others go to church every Saturday, she remains in her hut, mending clothes, cleaning her hut or just lying on her bed. Grandpa dashes back to his stool.

I hear her raised voice, the one that says she doesn't like what is happening and then the sound of something like a piece of clothing hitting a person or a wall. Then silence. She screams. Grandpa is just seated on his stool, taking bites of liver and chewing like someone whose mind is far away. I run to him and dump the salt shaker in front of him? 'What's Jamu doing to Aunt Mongi?' He looks at me the way blind people lift their heads in the direction of a speaker they are listening to. 'What did you say, son of my son?' I repeat the question. I can hear some groaning now and then several thuds against the wardrobe and then against the wall. Striding towards Auntie's hut, my idea is to rescue her. Grandpa yanks me by the hand and says, 'He is making her into a woman. Come sit with me it'll be over soon . . . ' Crash! Down goes the door to Aunt Mongi's hut. She and Jamu slide over the door like two overgrown children on a mountainside slide. She is only in her panties which are a bit torn on the side and Jamu's trousers hang round the ankles. His thing is as stiff as a goat's horn. Aunt Mongi runs to the barn and hides there. Jamu quickly raises his trousers to where they should be but his horn is still stiff in there. You can see it bulging in front. His left eye is swollen. He is spitting blood and shaking his front teeth to see if they are loose.

Grandpa does not know what to do. When Jamu starts walking towards the barn he says, 'Leave her for now.' Both men try to fix the door and give up. They will have to repair the frame as well. They make the door lean against the wall, leaving a yawning gap they stare into as if it has called them rude names. Inside her hut, clothes are strewn all over, as if a powerful whirlwind furiously swept through her room. The little cupboard in which she keeps her underwear is lying on its side with its door flung wide-open as if saying 'see.' A bottle of Vaseline lies on its side on top of a black petticoat. Some panties and petticoats are still in a neat pile. Grandfather picks up her yellow dress, hands it to me and says, 'Go in there and give her this dress. Tell her to come out. No one will harm her. It is for her own good.' He sighs and says, 'This curse of mine.'

It is dark inside the barn. It was re-thatched not so long ago and has the smell of new thatching grass and *shumba*, the green powder we add to grain so it can stay longer without being eaten by weevils. Grandma added the *shumba* a few days ago; after two or so weeks its smell will go away. Right at the end of the corridor I can make out the handle bars of an ox-drawn plough. On both sides of the corridor are small window-like openings that mark the number of compartments the barn has. I love going into the compartments to pour grain, to stand on rising piles that caress my bare feet until I reach the level of the opening. I stand still to listen. No sound. Peering through the first window is useless because it's too full of sorghum. Besides, Aunt Mongi would not have fitted in there. The other compartment, full of maize, is also not a possibility. The third, of *rapoko*, is half full. It is her smell that makes me peer harder into this one. When she sniffles as well, I see the outline of her body. She is curled, with her head resting on her raised knees like the unborn child in our science textbooks. Throwing the dress through the window will be rude. So I climb into the compartment. She accepts the dress and puts it next to her. When I try to hold her arm she pushes me so violently I find myself lying on my back on the sorghum. I quickly clamber out of the compartment and out of the barn. Jamu is gone and Grandma is shouting at Grandpa outside. 'So you have turned my child into a *tikoloshe* that lives in a barn? You must be happy with that.'

'Lower your voice,' Grandpa says.

'I'm saying get my child out of there, you greedy man.'

'What? You of all people calling me that? I love her, just like the rest of my children. But you, the mother, who is supposed to know better want her to die an empty person, just a shell of a woman. Look at all our children. The boys all have their wives and children and the girls too. All our children are married. Well, except for Sithabile who has just left her husband because of your poor teachings and her head that is full of wasps.'

Grandma is now standing arms akimbo, thrusting her neck forward and backwards to punctuate what she is saying. 'Were you the one who got your children their husbands and wives?'

'What kind of a stupid question is that?' Grandpa asks and carries on, 'They didn't need my help with that. They could hear and talk. How about this daughter of mine who has no mouth, no ears, God's own creature?'

'Didn't she say, right in front of us all that she doesn't want to be married, not to Jamu, not to any man?'

'What does she know?'

'I'm sure she knows, like I do, that all you want are Jamu's cattle.' And with that Grandma turns and her skirt swishes angrily past me. She is muttering something under her breath. 'Nozizwe,' Grandpa shakes a finger at her fast receding back, 'Watch your mouth. Don't shit with your mouth. If you have to, go to the bush.' She walks more furiously, waddling on her rickety legs.

'Women,' says Grandpa to me. 'You see how mad your Granny is? Come sit with me under the *gonde* tree. There's a bit of meat left in the plate.' I drag my feet there. The meat is catching in my throat and all the time I can't stop my eyes swinging to the barn door. Grandpa also looks in that direction but he looks out of the corners of his eyes.

The following day Aunt Mongi is out of the barn. Maybe she came out in the night, maybe just before dawn. Anyhow I see her in the morning sweeping the yard with furious strokes, a branch of the *umtshekisane* tree in her hand. Dust billows around her and her teeth flash through the cloud that gets thicker and thicker. She sees me. I wave hello. She stops sweeping and raises her hand to say a reluctant hello. I smile. She does not smile.

Jamu is here again and has been talking in low voices with Grandpa, my two uncles and our neighbour Timoti. This Jamu can lift a mother *mamba* to see how many little mambas have hatched from her clutch. Yes, he must try again, they all nod their heads. 'I'll be very grateful,' Grandpa says to Jamu and continues, 'The ancestors laughed at me and gave me a disabled daughter. But I don't think they can forgive me if she goes unfulfilled as a woman – if she is buried with a rat.'

'I know we will succeed *baba*,' Jamu says. '*Baba* Siwalu said it should be a woman that has not known a man before and there should be something strange about her. He also gave me some herbs and I'm sure the ones you gave me, together with Siwalu's, will make sure we succeed.' Siwalu is the only other healer constantly on people's lips like Grandpa. But people say he has both good and bad medicines.

The next day, just as one begins to make out the shapes of trees around the homestead and the huts in it, four men are speaking in low voices in front of Grandpa's hut. Like hunters scared that the buck or hare might escape before they strike it, they hurry to Aunt Mongi's hut. Jamu bounces the door in with his huge shoulder. I listen so intently not to miss any sound of Aunt Mongiwa being made into a woman by Jamu. There's a brief scuffle and what sounds like one of her cardboard suitcases getting knocked over, a scream that is soon muffled and what I think is Grandpa saying, 'Hold that leg.' Then silence. After a while, a man groans like a bull that has been stabbed by a spear through the heart. More silence.

The four men emerge from Aunt Mongi's hut. When they see me standing there, their eyes are slippery. They slide sideways like those of Bazangenzani caught stealing. 'Why are you up so early?' Grandpa asks. I don't answer him. There is no answer and I walk away, not wanting to have the slightest look at them.

This is the last school holiday this year. Mother says I should avoid going anywhere near Aunt Mongi. She has not been talking to anyone, not going to fetch water and not cooking for anyone. She talks to herself and throws objects at everyone when she is angry, even children. She keeps not only a sharp knife with her but a long sharp wire that was once one of the spokes to my father's Impala bicycle. She made a handle for the wire, mother says. 'What for?' 'To keep Jamu away,' mother says. 'Your aunt is now dangerous. Don't go anywhere near her.'

Jamu is here. He has brought more clothes for Aunt Mongi and most of them are the big balloon type that women wear when they are pregnant. 'For the moment, she is as mad as a rabid dog. She won't let me come anywhere close. What kind of a daughter points both a knife and sharp spoke at her father? But once the baby is born,' says Grandpa, 'she will come to her senses. Don't worry Jamu.' Jamu is smiling his honey-badger mouth. They say ever since he heard Aunt Mongi was pregnant, he has not fought anyone. He just drinks beer and laughs his big teeth. But Aunt Mongi does not look pregnant. Mother says she is pregnant because when it started she had all the signs, including vomiting.

It is a crazy thing to do, going into Aunt Mongi's hut. I walk in with trembling legs, eying the door for a quick bolt. From the pocket of her yellow and red apron, come out the knife and the long sharp wire. They shine wickedly and for a moment I'm ready to dash. But when she sees me, she smiles a faint smile and beckons to me that I should sit down next to her. For some reason I do. She caresses my head and smiles. I point at the pocket in which the two weapons are hiding and do the palm-up. 'What about those? Do you want to kill someone?'

She runs a finger across her throat and laughs but only with her mouth, and shakes her head. 'Are you scared of me?' she asks. I nod. She shoos my fears away and smiles.

Today I am happy. But I cannot tell mother that I was in Aunt Mongi's hut. I can't tell Grandpa either because he might want to give me messages to take to her. Someone left the dresses that Jamu bought in her room whilst she was out. She poured paraffin on them and burnt them in the middle of the compound. But now I think she is coming to her senses because here she comes with food on the big reed tray. It must be cold ox tongue and liver because that is what gets served Grandpa in the big wooden plate with a lid to it. But there is something wrong with the way Aunt Mongi is walking towards us. She walks with her legs apart like some of Grandpa's patients whose things are full of sores. Grandpa's smile grows bigger the closer Aunt Mongi approaches. Then Grandpa's smile starts vanishing like the sun behind clouds as his milky eyes also see what I see. Aunt Mongi's hands and arms are full of blood. Dark red blood covers her feet and some of it is still trickling down her left shin. She kneels in front of Grandpa and puts the tray in front of her, with traces of that smile of hers that says Grandpa likes eating too much. She gets up and leaves, walking like Grandfather's patients whose things are causing them too much pain.

When Grandpa opens the wooden plate, there is something that looks like a big rat in there. Except it has two legs and a big head. It is in some water that is mixed with blood. The thing squirms for a while and is still. Next to it on the one side is the long sharp wire with a bloody handle and on the other, the knife. I leave Grandpa like that, his mouth open as if he cannot see that flies have started settling on the big rat in his plate and might get into his mouth.

LIGHT PURPLE AND A BIT HAZY

Ricky Groenewald

Now

Cold . . . Wet . . . Hard . . . Discomforted.

He woke up on the bathroom floor next to the toilet, dazed. Then, as he became more conscious of his surroundings, he realized the bathroom was not yet completely painted.

'Shit! I hope she's not going to bitch again?' he thought, helping himself up from the mess on the floor.

The paint was everywhere except on the walls – it was even on the new denim jeans she had bought him two days ago, the one she had specifically told him not to wear (you know, because of the paint), which would have made perfect sense if she *did* freak out, but she didn't, instead she rushed in after the commotion and loud thud and looked more concerned with the deep red (already turning purple) bruising on his cheekbone rather than why the bathroom was not painted as planned.

Earlier that day . . . (much, much earlier)

His eyes opened up from a very vivid dream that proved to be yet another sign of what was to come. If he stays with her, they'll have a lot of work to do, and lots of compromising. Should he leave her, things would be easier to manage (without her breathing down his neck all the time) but would he find love like this again? After all, two years is a long time to get this close to someone and not have that someone be there anymore.

I lay watching her sleep from an inner depth she has not discovered yet and of course this is bothersome because she does not take the time either . . . *Twee jaar . . . twee jaar! Is daai' nie genoeg tyd om iemand te leer ken nie?* Maybe it's just me . . . I know she loves me . . . but is it enough? . . . I mean I know her better than she knows herself . . . Is this the kind of love that I want . . . *is ek rerig lief vir haar . . . is 'it wat sy hê?* All the shit we've been through . . . Is it worth it . . . for how long would I tolerate it? No! I told her already . . . Why do we always fight . . . Why do we always have to come back to things that we've already spoken about and agreed to leave there and move on . . . Yesterday's fight was just too much for both of us and this time I'm not apologizing . . . *ek was mossie verkeerd nie . . . voel ek skuldig? Nee!* Not gonna happen, not this time . . . I want to leave! . . . But she's so beautiful, what if she meets someone else? I can't even imagine her with another man so why can't things just work out long enough for us to find out the problem . . . Why doesn't she trust me enough to tell me what she's hiding? Her eyes are twitching . . . She's waking up . . . Do I tell her what my heart's been harbouring or do I let it blow over again? . . . *maa' ek is moeg* . . . Emotionally spent . . . In fact, *wat doen ek nog hie'?* Surely there must be a greater love out there . . . Or is this as good as it gets? All I want is happiness . . . Is that too much to ask?

She woke up and found him deep in thought, lying on his back, staring at the ceiling. Now this would have been fine if it was before month-end and there were no bills that needed to be paid . . . but the thing was that this wasn't the case, and besides, she had long suspected him of cheating on her with someone at work, though she had no proof of this and she had even met his female colleagues on a couple of occasions, and they hadn't seemed too close for comfort. This, however, only existed in her mind, while he, on the other hand, couldn't keep his eyes off her; this might sound sweet and loving, but not exactly in this context. It bordered on obsession to the extent that he'd occasionally take off from work just to make sure she was at her job and the flowers that accompanied him were just a front to keep his plans of checking up on her out of sight, which is why she suspects him of cheating on her but he just had an awkward way of loving that she didn't understand and that he couldn't explain. I mean, she was, after all, breathtaking. But as you know, beauty isn't ultimately what most men want. It's the whole package, and there were some optional extras that didn't come with this one.

'What are you thinking about so deeply?' comes her voice through his tunnel of space.
'Hmmm?'
'What are you thinking about?'
'Oh, er . . . nothing much. Have to get up for work soon.'
'You're awake rather early. Is everything ok?'

(Sigh) 'Ja, sure.'
'Are you sure?'
'I said yes, didn't I?'
'Well excuse me for caring.'
'Oh! How nice of you, I didn't think you did.'
'Ag! You know you're impossible sometimes.'
'Well, I learn from the best.'
'Oh shut up! You make me naar!'

Saved by the *fucking* bell . . . *ek gaan mossie met die kak opgeskeep sit'ie* . . . I'm sick and tired of it . . . It's not right...I don't deserve it . . . *is goed dat hy moet opstaan en werk toe neuk* . . . I'm not in the mood for his shit today . . . My mother doesn't even talk to me like that, *wie's hy?*

'I'm tired of this shit,' he mumbles under his breath.
'Ja! So am I! You have no right to talk to me like that!'

That's when he flies out of bed and heads for the shower but turns around and yells at her, 'You know what? Whatever! When you decide to change your fucking attitude, then maybe I'll treat you better. Things were so good between us until you started with your insecurities, and NO! I didn't give you any reason to start acting that way, I'm home early every day waiting for you to get back, and even when I cook I get no appreciation from you. What happened to you? I feel like I don't know you anymore.'

And with that he slams the door, leaves the room and leaves her gobsmacked. Even if she wanted to say something she had some things to think about. And with that she turns around and once again the tears start rolling down familiar paths. When soon afterwards she starts realizing, 'What am I doing? That's probably why he's so far away of late . . . I thought he's just depressed . . . I hope there's not someone else, oh my God! I hope there isn't anyone else . . . I'd be devastated . . . I still love him so much . . . I know we have our shit, but there's no one out there who will do for me what he does. Still, that's no way to talk to me. *Ek het 'ie 'n form ingevul om met hom te wees'ie, ek is mos my eie mens, waa' val hy uit?* I know he loves me, *hy bring dan elke week blomme, vi' wat meer kan 'n mens vra?* I can be a bitch sometimes, but that's to protect me. How am I supposed to know how he feels? Can I see into the future? *Magtig! Hy sal hom wat verbeël* . . .

One day earlier

'There's much work to be done in the bathroom,' he explained, 'so we'll leave 'til last!'

'Well, as long as we finish it soon so we can get done with painting the house,' she pauses, 'but, why last, why can't we just do it with the rest of the house?'

'Well! You can't just paint over it, and there's lots of moisture present and the type of paint we're using will start peeling in no time and I'll have to do it all over again, I'd rather do it the proper way.'

Emphatically she reassures him,'Maa' ek gaan ook mos help!'

'Ek weet! Dis hoekom ons dit laaste gaan doen, want dan help jy my rerig uit.'

An argument nearly ensued if he hadn't given precise details on what the hell he was talking about. In his man-brain everything looked clear as daylight, but in her mind, paint was paint, what's this nonsense about textures and blahblahblah.

If only she had listened.

Ek is seker hy praat wee' straunt oor'ie badkamer . . . kyk dan, daa's mos niks verkeerd nie, is mos net paint oppie mure sit dis ok . . . ek doen'it sommer, dan surprise ek hom . . . ooh los maa' ek moet nog na my ma toe gaan . . . is al laat . . .

The next day he got home tired, after working some overtime on Saturday (a really kak day to do something you don't like doing, much like a Monday) and headed straight to the bathroom. His bladder kept reminding him that at any moment the slightest movement could set it off, and he'd flood the whole car with the alcohol-enriched piss from the couple of 'malts' he and the boys had had after work when he was greeted by the traces of white paint 'tested' on the now obvious backdrop of light blue that the bathroom walls were originally painted. His disappointment was overcome with anger – lucky she wasn't there, and a good thing too.

The brush strokes felt incomplete as they ran randomly roughly on different parts of the bathroom wall. Reading deeper into the situation, he realized that it smacked of their relationship, which was going nowhere (not even slowly). The incomplete action on the wall was the same incomplete expression lying there in both their eyes –

unfulfilled dreams, half-baked emotions going vocal. There was no doubt that they loved each other, but their goals were not the same and the timing just not right. Neither could see what lay in the future. Still, he always tried saving the relationship, and why not show her yet again by finishing off the paint job in the bathroom. Bu then, just as he got lus to do the job, she walks in, her face reflecting just how her day was, and then there was the slight hint of – 'he didn't even do the *fucking* dishes' – written all over her face. Her mother probably told her about something her one sister had told her but the other one has no clue about, this just like her mother doesn't really have the full story, and it probably has her featured in some part she doesn't feel is true . . .

So there goes the whole evening. Pissed off, no hug, no kiss hello. All the day's stresses felt like dishes rattling to show how easy it is to break them, crack at any given time. Now he'd rather flee the scene, calm down somewhere safe, and wait till she de-stressed enough to talk, but not this time. So he headed straight for the bathroom that she so badly wanted painted.

'Maybe it will better her mood.'

But he didn't stand a chance.

There she stands saying, *'Ek wonder wat het hy heel dag wee gedoen? Seker wee gaan suip met sy chommies, wee niks in'ie badkamer gedoen nie...'*

One hour later

'Maybe she's calmed down,' he says to himself, 'maybe now we can talk!'

But when he turned to the mirror and saw in the eyes facing him no more hope for this relationship and when he realized he was looking at me, I stepped on the paint tray, slipped and fell, and knocked my head against the toilet bowl.

LOVE FROM COLOMBO

J.Kaval

John, the Office Manger of Ansaari Recruitments, opened the door. He put on the lights and the heater. He let Rajani, the Sri Lankan maid from Colombo, come in. Like a typical *Tamil* bride, she entered the living room right foot first. She had neither trepidation nor temerity.

'My dear, this is my *koodaaram*. Look into every nook and corner of it. Take your time,' he said and walked into his bedroom.

Rajani stood in the middle of his living room and surveyed it. It was spacious and cozy and beautifully decorated. It had everything the living room of a modern apartment needed and everything was in order and in its own place: carpeted floor, new sofa set and an elegant *divan*, teakwood table with book shelves filled with books and magazines. On the table there were two telephones; a color TV and VCR rested nearby; a mini fridge stood in a corner. There was also a showcase full of cute bric-a-brac.

She went into the kitchen. It, too, was roomy and airy, fitted with modern gadgets and filled with appliances and food packets. It had a double door fridge, medium size cooker, mixer, grinder, micro-wave oven and a toaster, fit for a married couple. There was no mess of things. It was neat and clean.

When she returned to the living room he was at the door of his bedroom.

'You saw the *koodaaram*. How's it?'

'Wow! Amazing! It's very nice indeed, tastefully done. I don't feel like going away. I hope soon I'll have a nice house!'

'Sure. You'll have a better one'

'This *koodaram* is really beautiful. I wonder how marvellous your inner *koodaaram* would be.'

'To my temple, no admission without permission'

'Why don't you let me in? Am I a pariah?'

'If you wish, I don't mind. Listen. Don't you want to go to your room in the office? I'll take you there now'

'No. After that wonderful outing in Salmania water garden and the sumptuous Iranian dinner all I want to do is to rest. Tonight I want to sleep here'

'I don't have any women's clothes here. I can offer you shirt and *lungi* if you like.'

'Anything is ok with me'

He thrust a silk shirt and a Keralite *lungi* into her hands.

'Sorry, no spare bed. You may sleep either on the divan or on the sofa – or anywhere you like.'

'Anywhere? Really?'

'Yes'

'Thank you. It's very kind of you'

'You can watch TV or see a movie on the VCR. Goodnight'

He retired to his bedroom to change, and she made her way to the bathroom.

Pin drop silence reigned while the lights burnt in the rooms. The heater began to warm up the air inside.

He lay on his back on the double cot. He looked at the ceiling. He blinked. He saw the Khajuraho temple. He saw the erotic sculpture – the mating figures of men, women and the animals. He found them vivid, lively and moving. Lyrics of *Kamasutra* of Valtsayana appeared on his mind's monitor. Unfortunately he had never watched a blue film nor leafed through a Playboy magazine. He never knew what was in store. He didn't care. Why should he? He was calm and composed. He closed his eyes. He listened to his heart's beating. He wondered at the evenness of his heart's pounding. He felt he was slipping into a sort of haze

Minutes ticked by.

'Please move a little.'

Without a word, opening his eyes, he moved away a little. She lay beside him. The smell and the warmth of a vibrant female body, fresh and fragrant, were irresistible to his senses.

'Goodness gracious! You're sweet-smelling. Are you a burning sandal stick? What did you do?'

'I used your razor, your soap, your sponge, your powder and your perfume. I shaved. I showered. I perfumed. I powdered. I'm neat and clean. That's it.'

They lay quiet. The ceiling saw every curve and curl of those two bodies. The walls felt their breathing, warm and vibrant. The wall-clock chimed. The bedroom lamps blinked. The curtains closed their eyes and remained dead. The warm air inside the room enviously waved at them.

'Did you lock the door?' he asked.

'Yes. Locked and bolted it.'

'The bedroom lights are on,' he murmured.

She turned towards him and whispered, 'I don't mind. Do you? Let them shine upon us. Don't you want to see me?'

She moved her hip and waist closer to him.

He put his right hand around her shoulder and pulled her towards him. Their eyes met. Their noses touched. Their chests closed in, their groins kissed each other. He saw two large ripe *alphonso* mangoes bulging out of her half open shirt.

'Aren't they alluring?'

'Breathtaking, indeed.'

'My husband never cared for my needs as a woman. He had no concern for the children. He would just screw me like an animal. There was no love between us, never any sort of affection. That was a marriage imposed on me. Thank God, he eloped with another woman to Jaffna. I pray he never comes back!'

'How do you know for sure? After a couple of years, one day, he turns up at your gate with a pack of bugs . . . '

'I will not chase the beggar out. He fathered my children. He could stay in our outhouse and die.'

'Rajani, you're a wonderful woman. I like you very much. The temper of your heart and the texture of your body are tempting.'

He planted a soft kiss on her tender lips and asked, 'Rajani, you have delivered twice. How's it then that your tummy is still flat and smooth without stretch marks?'

'The elderly woman who used to look after the deliveries around our locality used to massage my tummy with gingelly oil and wild herbs. She used to apply hand-made balms around my belly before bathing me. In those days no one knew of such medicines except the local midwives. I did a lot of exercise while I was working in the hotel. I controlled my diet.'

'Your marriage's already broken up. Why didn't you divorce him and marry a man of your liking? At the hotel no one bothered you?'

'Yes. A few. At night there were knocks at my door. I never opened it. I received discreet invitations to become a call girl. Even the pimps from the Red Light area in Colombo approached me. But I ignored them all.'

'Idiot! Why did you throw away those chances? Were you an angel?'

'No, I wasn't. And I'm not. I knew for sure that those affairs wouldn't do any lasting good to me and to my children. I didn't want to be an HIV patient. Divorce? That would not solve my problem.' She said gravely, 'I did not want to get into another trap.'

'Rajani, why did you bare yourself to me, a stranger? I am here looking for petrodollars, just as you are. I have an aged mother, two sisters and a brother to care for at home. '

She paused for a minute and said, 'I don't know. Your agent in Colombo spoke about you highly. His secretary painted you beautifully. Then I began to feel that there was something salutary about you. When I met you at the airport for the first time those feelings were reinforced. During the past few days of my stay in your office, I knew I was right about you. You enriched me with care and concern. I got respect, love and affection from all of you in the office. No strings. No obligations. I am very happy and content. I wish to work in Bahrain or in Saudi Arabia for some years and return home for good.'

She became silent, pensive. Then after a long while she spoke.

'I learnt a lot from books and experience. I am now informed and erudite. I did not get love and affection from my father and step-mother. Neither did I get any from my husband. I never knew that man but I never knew another man. It has been years now.' She turned to him and said, 'Do you believe what I have just told you?'

'Yes. I do.' He was honest.

'I think you have met many women. Haven't you?'

'Yes, I've met women from different countries.'

'Did you love them?'

'No.'

'Did they love you?'

'No. Frankly speaking, those were ephemeral encounters. I'm not a lewd and lusty man. Sex isn't my cup of tea. I have already passed the holy year of my life. During our solitary journey in the Arabian desert we sometimes needed a break, a sip of wine and once in a while a woman lest we break apart and die like a donkey.'

'Exactly, John. So I know I may not be the last drop in you cup. Never mind. I love you.' She paused for few seconds and again spoke quietly and coolly. 'John, make love to me, please. Make me sing the song of my life, make this night memorable, play your melody on me and rinse me well with all your notes.'

Her candid words stunned him. He could not utter a word. She had touched his heart. He began to burn with desire for her.

'How do you know for sure that you are the last drop in anyone's cup?'

'I know this because no sane and sensible man will marry me. I'm more a liability than an asset. My marital life has reached a dead end. But I wish to leave here happy and contented. Make this day memorable for me – for life!'

'Rajani, have confidence in yourself. You are thirty, handsome, industrious and daring. We will find a way for sure.'

Rajani sobbed in silence. He sat up and looked at her.

In the bright light in the room she lay on her back, bare and bold, brimming with vigor and vitality, beaming a profusely innocent smile, with gleeful eyes, rosy cheeks and lips. His eyes feasted on every contour of her body.

He began making love to her. Their shimmering bodies trembled against each other, nude, tingling, twisting and sweating. They panted. They breathed heavily. They sweated. Then they lay abandoned to each other in a tight lock and knot. Goddess Venus carried them into the land of blissful serenity. But Cupid soon brought them back to love and lust.

Before dawn they made love twice. They then had a ceremonial bath together before breakfast. And then as they kissed with devotion and mutual thanks, she smiled and asked him, 'Am I just another cup of tea?'

And he laughed and sipped her till she boiled over and over and . . . over.

SEX IS THE OPIUM OF THE PEOPLE

Monde iNxele

The point is the longer you go, the deeper you see into your own sexuality. It is like coming face to face with your shame of sex. Everyone has something to be ashamed of, and most of the time it has something to do with sex. That says something about the society we live in.

Tshepo *from K Sello Duiker's* **The Quiet Violence of Dreams**

That day, that fateful day in January, I'd woken up at exactly six o'clock. I straight away became disgusted at the prospect of what was usually to follow: I did not want to go to school; I wanted to be left alone to learn with my Imagination. I could read and write and knew the basics of arithmetic and I really had no need for them. But dropping out was unthinkable; it would have broken father's heart. If I'd done so, father would have asked for help from the church. They'd all have then ganged up on me declaring that it was Satan's fault.

The Sun had risen. I left the 'cabin' for the main house where father was still sleeping. There I lit a primus stove to boil some Water and, as I waited for that to happen, I couldn't help but gaze at the flames that issued from the stove. At length, I wondered at the Mystery which is Fire; I felt that it was more than just heat, it was more. I gazed at the Fire, meditating on the Myth of Prometheus.

When the Earth was in its infancy, Prometheus stole the Secrets of Fire from the gods and taught mankind the arts of cooking and boiling. He was isolated and hanged on a mountain rock where an Eagle would eat his liver, bit by bit, till such time that he recanted his subversive ways and repented of his misdeed. But Prometheus – half man and half god – refused to disown his benevolence; his liver grew whole again, and the Eagle had his feast. Indeed, Prometheus was one of the first Rebel-Outsiders, if you believe in Myth.

I stood gazing at the Fire, and meditated on the relationship between Science and Myth. Is Myth 'primitive' Science or is Science 'advanced' Myth? The water soon grew hot. I took it back to my 'cabin' so as to prepare for the first day of my matric year. As I washed, I wondered what type of Science they'd be feeding me at that level. I'd become nauseated by the dead textbook Science of formal education. I dreamt of a dynamic, living Science that is conscious of its indebtedness to Myth.

Now that first matric day was relatively uneventful – except for my encounter with the physics teacher. Ms Maneli was a quiet woman in her early thirties. I had seen her many times at assembly and in the female staff room, but up until she walked into our class-room, her existence had been on the margins of my conscious experience. However, meeting her face-to-face was a very disturbing experience: she frightened yet fascinated me. I did not want to look into her eyes, yet I hadn't the will to look away.

Strangely enough, her first lesson was uninspiring; simply more of the usual dogma of objectivity and verifiability. Halfway through the lesson I raised my hand, saying, 'Absolute objectivity is a false doctrine. In the quest for knowledge, the knower cannot be separated from the known. What the knower perceives is inescapably conditioned by his subjectivity'. I was breathless by the time I finished delivering this statement, surprised and frightened.

'If absolute objectivity is a 'false doctrine' then there would be no science in the world,' was her rebuttal.

My interjection had obviously been considered an insult or a challenge. So I answered her, beginning to tremble as I spoke.

'If we could overcome the illusion of objectivity and the 'scientific' tendency to disregard that which cannot be verified by the outward eye, then we'd develop a more wholesome way of knowing. Science would cease to be something that you do, or a state of mind that you adopt. It would be The Way you Exist.'

To my relief, the bell rang for lunch break; I trembled even more when Ms Maneli told me to see her at the staff room after break. There was no choice: I sneaked away from school and made my way through the streets without my books. I was overjoyed to get away; I felt released from her sterile influence. I decided to stop at a shop on the way for some apples.

As I got out of the shop, I saw Ms Maneli's blue Mazda 3 approaching from the distance. I panicked but took my chances and hurried away without looking back. When she pulled up beside me, I longed for the earth to open up and swallow me.

'Need a lift?' she wore a pleasant and reassuring smile.

I was absolutely dumbfounded. She opened the passenger door and signalled me in. It was comfortable and warm inside but the windows were tinted black. I felt undefended, vulnerable. Then I noticed for the first time how pretty she was.

'I will carry you to your destiny.'

She was surprisingly soft spoken, totally unlike earlier in class.

'My destiny?'

She laughed. 'Destination! I meant to say I will carry you to your destination.'

Owing to the dimmed interior, there was a strange air of secrecy, as if we were hatching a conspiracy.

'I don't know where I'm going really, I'm just drifting.'

'Drifting away?'

'I suppose so; but I don't know where I want to go.'

'I hope you're not drifting away from me.'

'I'm kinda drifting away from everything; you just made it worse by trying to confront me.'

'Who said I'm trying to confront you?'

'Because of what happened in class. I figured. . .'

'I just want to know more about you, I want to know what makes you different from the others.'

'Who says I'm different?'

'You have courage and wit, that's what it took to do what you did in class today; your courage and your passion make you different.'

'I was frightened.'

'But you spoke anyway.'

We'd been driving around for about ten minutes when she suddenly stopped the car and let go of the wheel, looking distant and thoughtful.

'Since you're just drifting, why not come have lunch at my place? I'm also taking the rest of the afternoon off'

Then she winked and laughed mischievously.

'I don't see why not; these apples aren't going to do me any good and I'm starving.'

'Excellent! I love nothing more than making food for a starving man.'

She considered me a man! Within the space of a few minutes, what she thought of me became momentous, and I more and more liked the way she laughed.

We got to her flat almost an hour after noon. It was a modest dwelling place; just a bedroom, bathroom, kitchen and lounge. Unlike most women, she didn't seem to be too obsessed with stuff; there were just the bare necessities. But it felt surprisingly warm and comfortable.

We said very little to each other, which unsettled me at that time because I was yet to learn to be comfortable with Silence. I thought her Silence meant that she regretted inviting me into her private space; that she wanted to withdraw from contact and have her Solitude again. But when I looked at her, I saw that her eyes were eager and expectant. It was as if she was saying, 'Action is the prerogative of Logos, I look to you to initiate the conversation.'

I began to tremble as I initiated a different kind of conversation; I put my hand on her thigh and started kissing her. She woke me up from my dream with a slap across my face, saying, 'Zifune sies! Can't you see that you're a child? I could be as old as your mother!'

I was a bit dizzy and confused and resolved to go home and hang myself. The shame of it! What was I thinking? I started making for the door with my 'tail between my legs' when she suddenly leaped for me and pulled me down to the floor with incredible strength.

She wasn't at school the following day. I was brutally disappointed after waiting what felt like a lifetime for that physics period. But the day after, there was a substitute teacher. We were told that Ms Maneli would be on leave for the next three weeks.

I became a divided individual during that time. No, I became a battleground between longing and self-restraint. I was dying to see her but I did not want go to her place. What if she refused to see me? Perhaps I made her feel ashamed of herself. The days and weeks went by. I got on badly the whole time though I was sustained by the possibility of seeing her again. I just wanted to fill my eyes with the sight of her and when she didn't appear in class on the day she was due to return, I was baffled because I had earlier seen a blue Mazda 3 in the parking lot.

During break that day the news went round: Ms Maneli had been in to submit her resignation letter and had immediately left.

I quietly slunk away from school and made my way to her place, determined to see her. However, when I got there I saw that it was locked, and there was no sign of anyone inside. I went round to the back of the building and broke a window. I desperately wanted to look at the spot where we had laid, and savour her presence one last time before I walked away from our extraordinary encounter. But when I finally got inside, I discovered that the flat was completely bare except for a half-empty rubbish bin behind the door. She had taken everything and disappeared. There wasn't even the smell of her left there.

I felt cheated; even if I'd just sat in her favourite chair that would have been enough for me. But it was increasingly clear that there wouldn't even be a memento of the brief spark we had shared. Then, in defiant desperation, I searched the rubbish bin behind the door. I discovered a used home pregnancy test kit; the result was positive.

I received a letter almost a year later. It read:

Dear Zifune,

I could have written to you sooner but didn't because I wanted you to focus on your studies. Knowing how intelligent you are, I'm sure you did well.

What really happened between us? I have been pondering this question ever since we were together, and I still fail to come up with a satisfactory answer. Whatever it was, it has changed my life forever.

I like to believe that it was love – if it is possible for a teacher to fall in love with her pupil. The seed you planted has grown inside me, and I have become a mother of new possibilities. You must believe me when I declare that our love was meaningful. But on the other hand, it is forbidden contact. Besides the legal consequences for me, society would punish us both with an open or implicit ostracism once our union came to be known.

Society teaches us shame about sex. I will never forget the incident of mob justice that I witnessed in my childhood.

We were skipping rope in our neighbor's yard, and two dogs were getting intimate in the middle of the street. Of course, at the time I had no idea what was really happening. Nonetheless, it was fascinating to watch. This fascination had nothing to do with the conscious idea of sex; it was more akin to the fascination that children get from watching a fire.

The commotion started when a few teenagers laughed and cheered at the dogs. One of them offered that the male dog was 'bonking' its own mother.

When I think about it now, I remember your love for Myth, and the story you told me about a wise King Oedipus from the West.

'A bitch!' one of the female teenagers said with conspicuous disgust.

Then some church-goers came by in their Sunday best. An old man who seemed like the leader of the congregation was the first to spot the abomination. He quickly began talking about a chapter in the book of Leviticus and they all passed along without appearing to notice anything. However, in a short space of time, the gathering round the dogs grew significantly. There were teenagers who were fascinated by the show as well as their parents who were anxious that the children not start asking difficult questions. And so the dogs kept mating while the crowd grew and grew. But after a while we saw that the dogs were stuck together; they could not separate and began to bark in pain.

It was a sober and respectable man who threw the first stone. 'Incest!' he shouted. When his stone hit one of the dogs, he gritted his teeth and clenched his fists to keep himself from shaking. He was not married and lived with his mother. And it was a tipsy Sis' Julia who defended the dogs and their right to be animals with the words, 'Let them be, this is what animals do! And let me remind you, in case you've forgotten, you are also animals!' But her words were lost in the uproar as other members of the mob followed suit with stones until the dogs became a bloody mess. I had to look away.

My point is that the consequences would be tragic if they found out about us; and so I had to get away. I know it was unfair of me to decide on my own; it's just that I love you too much to see you live through this scandal.

I conclude by asking you to not try and find me; if we are destined to be one again, then it will happen without any contrivance on our part:

> It is the way of Heaven not to Strive,
> and yet it skilfully overcomes;
> not to speak, and yet it is skilful
> in obtaining a reply;
> does not call, and yet
> men come to it of themselves.
> Its demonstrations are quiet,
> and yet its plans are skilful and effective.
> The meshes of Heaven are large,
> far apart, but let nothing escape.

Lao Tzu

With blessings,

Nolubabalo Maneli

There was no return address.

BAZIANA

Jean Francois Couvadio

François Gavana, leader of the opposition socialist party, and his press attaché decided to meet Yassa. They found the president of the Apostolic Church and political party, reverend-pastor, God anointed delegate to the Ivory Coast, Charles Yassa and his disciples in the middle of a politico-biblical study. As soon as the Reverend President Pastor saw Gavana, he stood up from his delicately soft sofa and shouted, 'Alleluia! God bless you son of Israel, son of Abraham!'

'Amen!' Replied the dozen Yassa followers; mainly members of the *Spiritual Commando for the Apocalypse and the Final Assault against Satan* who were sitting by.

'Thanks reverend, for such a hearty welcome. God bless you,' Gavana replied.

The two leaders and Gavana's attachés sat down.

'My dear Gavana, I heard about the satanic arrogance of the security minister regarding your peaceful public protest.'

Gavana, a Roman Catholic, was a little moderate. But he knew that at crucial times such as these, one should bury one's own convictions and use a likewise aggressive tone to content the pastor and make him his calculated ally.

'Alleluia! The cancellation of my meeting was a satanic decision indeed.'

'Amen! But my dear Gavana, how can the man of God help you today?'

'Well, on Monday I would like all sons and daughters of this country to invade the streets of the CBD to ask President Baziana, the dictator and thief and the . . . ' Gavana paused, looking for the right words to touch Yassa and his fanatical lieutenants who were attentively following his every word. 'How can I say . . . that thief and . . . '

'Satanist!' Shouted one of Yassa's disciples.

'Yes, the Satanist . . . to leave the presidential palace at once!' re-echoed Gavana.

'You know my dear Gavana, Satan holds this country at ransom. We must kick him out of here. Satan and his agent Baziana must get out! Ha! This Baziana!' Yassa was really disgusted.

'But reverend, I believe that in order to create a more massive movement, we must invite our brothers from the *Revolutionary Rally of the Northeners* as well.'

'Keep off Satan! Keep OFF!' roared Yassa as he suddenly stood up. 'Never! Ne-ver! The Bible declares that all have sinned and have fallen short of the glory of the Lord. The curate of the Lord, mixing with northerners? Muslims? This is a joke my dear Gavana, isn't it?'

Yassa then started to speak the language believed to be that of angels to exorcise the 'satanic words' Gavana had just pronounced: rococo-rocaca-rocaba-chidada.

After noting that his last proposal was disturbing the 'tactical alliance', Gavana decided to redeem himself.

'My humble apologies, reverend. But can I count on your support this Monday?'

Yassa stood up once again and turned towards his lieutenants. Smiling broadly, he said, 'The Lord has just spoken to him. Alleluia!'

'Amen!' The disciples droaned.

Yassa slowly sat down and murmured to Gavana, 'Forget about the northerners, the Muslims and their master Satan, and I will be with you on Monday.'

Light shone from Gavana's face – he had the support of the President Reverend Pastor Charles Yassa!

'My dear Gavana,' the reverend added as a conclusion, 'You should think of giving your life to Jesus. He told me that he loves you. Without him in your life, you won't achieve much.'

Gavana, fearing that any maladjusted answer might change Yassa's mind, kept quiet.

'Do you hear me?' Yassa insisted. 'I have to deliver you from Satan's claws.'

After a few moments, praying that he was on the right track, Gavana said: 'I am already a Christian, reverend. I am a Roman Catholic.'

'Jesus Christ!' Shouted back Yassa. 'Rather be a pagan than a Roman Catholic! Anyway, I will deliver you later. At least for now you accept Jesus in your life.'

After these words he stood up. The exchanges were over. Taking his leave, Gavana said, 'May God bless you. Of course I will give my life to Jesus.'

The following day, the opposition newspaper *The Direct* ran a tactical story on Gavana. Fearing that the information might not be taken seriously if the headline quote was provided by Yassa (who was generally seen as intolerant and crazy), the journalists wrote, 'An anointed man of God pronounces, 'Gavana, God loves you!'

Abidjan held the world record for rumour-mongering. No one knew how supporters of the *Revolutionary Rally of the Northerners*, not invited by Gavana, got the information. They were feverishly getting ready. It was now or never for them to sort out their own cause. How long could they stand to be persecuted for carrying bushy beards and dressing in robes? Baziana's police systematically and carefully checked the papers of any individual sporting a beard – especially one dressed in a long robe; all this while the non-Muslim population went around freely. It was also true that Muslims in the Ivory Coast were not easily distinguishable from citizens of neighboring Burkina Faso and Mali who were predominantly Muslims. However, the extreme zeal shown by some tribalistic police officers who would systematically ask any man with a beard or dressed in a robe to show his visa or visit permit, had grossly upset the Muslims of the Ivory Coast. When a group of people were walking along the street, the police would let those who did not have a beard pass through while the bearded ones were stopped and questioned for hours. A Muslim could not easily get a certificate of nationality. He needed to provide more than his identification documents. He needed to attach to his application the I.D. book of his parents and grand-parents and prove that he was not from Burkina Faso or Mali. Was it a secret order from the president Baziana? Were the police officers, mostly southerners, over-doing their job?

On this other Monday of December, at 7am, the CBD of Abidjan was experiencing an exceptional atmosphere. There were strident whistles and noisy horns as two thousand marchers headed by François Gavana and the famous reverend and president of the Apostolic Party for the National Redemption, Charles Yassa, stomped the streets of Abidjan. The two leaders held each other's hand. But they looked surprised after failing to see any police ready to disperse the procession as the minister of public security had promised.

In the streets of the business centre, other crowds were busy with their daily worries. On a sidewalk some tourists were standing, cameras dangling from their necks. At least they took note – and filmed the impressive movement of the marching crowd. Nearby another bunch of strollers went about preoccupied with their usual exchanges. Meanwhile the marchers started singing some local songs and headed towards Republic Square where Gavana and Yassa would shortly address the crowd. Still there were no police forces around.

Soon Republic Square was fully packed. Around the large plank-made platform, where Gavana and Yassa were standing hand in hand, were some large and vivid banners.

Where is press freedom? Baziana must resign. Gavana for president. Boss Baziana's whore gets fucked in a bar. Baziana = billionaire. No more Misery for Ivorians! No to the Hegemony of Baziana's tribe!

Gavana, to whom someone handed a loudspeaker, opened the show.

'My hearty greetings to the brothers and sisters of the Apostolic Party.'

A thunder-like applause erupted from the crowd.

'Alleluia! Amen!'

'I greet the tireless freedom fighters of the Socialist Party!'

'Viva! Viva!'

'Comrades, we are sick and tired!'

'Sick and tired! Sick and tired!! Sick and tired!'

The crowd turned the expression of his anger into a chorus. They were fully behind him! He lifted up his right hand, waiting for the euphoria to cool off before carrying on.

'Comrades, we are here at this very place where just a few years ago our hero, Andrew Mane, was murdered!'

'Baziana murderer! Baziana murderer!!'

'Are we ready to face his guns?'

'Baziana must resign! Baziana must resign!!'

'Comrades, once we are done here, we will pay a visit to Baziana. He should give us the keys of the presidential palace. He should hand them over . . . today!'

'Baziana, dictator! Baziana, dictator!! '

'Can you allow thieves to rule you?'

'No thief, no! Baziana burglar!'

'Can you accept bitches to rule you?'

'Arleta, Baziana prostitute! Arleta prostitute!!'

After several more venomous invectives against Baziana and his spouse Arleta, Gavana passed the microphone to Christ's delegate in

Ivory Coast. When President Reverend Pastor Yassa took the relay, excitement was at fever pitch.

'Alleluia!! Glory to the God of Abraham!! God of Israel!!'

'Amen!! Alleluia!!'

'Brothers and sisters, the time has come for our Lord's glory!'

'Amen! Alleluia!!'

'The Devil is cornered like a rat. No escape is possible at this stage!

'Alleluia!!'

'Satan, and his disciple, Baziana, will be defeated!'

Then Yassa and his devotees started singing a combat chorus.

'Higher, higher, higher!'

'Jesus is higher!'

'Lower, lower, lower!'

'Satan is lower!'

'Higher . . . higher . . . '

Finally Yassa yelled, 'Brothers and sisters, let us pray for the immediate downfall of the Devil and his agent Baziana. Let us all close our eyes and pray.'

The whole crowd, pagans in the ranks of Gavana included, took a praying position. At such moments it is not a bad idea to compromise. Anything likely to facilitate the collapse of Baziana could not be neglected – one never knows where the divine grace that could make him bite the dust could come from. Now Baziana was a son of the Baule ethnic group who thought themselves superior; they were the richest farmers in the land. Did this make them the only group whose members qualified to become president? Enough was enough! The demonstrators bowed down their heads to pray for the immediate end to this injustice.

'Brothers and sisters, I said close your eyes. I know some of you still have your eyes open.'

Yassa was really anointed. How else could he tell some eyes were still open when his own were already closed?

'Lord,' he started, 'Your children are here. They are asking you to remember the promise you made. Give them the political power to enable your Mighty Name to be glorified. You promised to floor Satan and his agent Baziana. Talk to your people now! Talk to them – abata-cococorida-cocoshiba-rabatacacasha! Alleluia?!'

The prayer was accompanied by powerful applause. It seemed to François Gavana, who stood behind Yassa, that the pastor imagined he was in his temple. The crowd saw him whispering something into the pastor's ears.

Yassa suddenly turned to the crowd and screamed, 'To the presidential palace! All of us! Now!'

And he marched down from the podium and began walking towards the palace which was only five hundred metres away. As one person, the huge crowd started to follow him.

Unlike the Republic Square where everyone could casually take a walk and kill time, the security round the presidential palace was formal and tight. The republican guards, armed with automatic assault guns, ringed the massive building. In front of them, the wire mesh beyond the gate made a significant barricade. The front entrance was heavily guarded but the presence of the soldiers did not seem to intimidate Gavana, Yassa and their militants.

Soon those in front pushed their way towards the colossal gate. They were promptly challenged as one of the guards commanded them to HALT! Gavana cleared a way through the dense crowd. In a few moments he was at the gate. He was sweating copiously. He drew a face towel from a pocket, wiped his sweaty forehead and bushy armpits. And after he had blown his nose into the face towel, he delicately put it back into his pocket and said to the standing guard, 'We are here to see Baziana.'

'Who the hell is Baziana?'

Gavana could see the soldier laugh and touch his gun handle.

'You don't know Baziana? Dieudonné Baziana – the so called president of Ivory Coast.'

'And what makes you think I should?'

Meanwhile the crowd had flooded all over Republic Square and now started to chant.

'Here to meet Baziana! Here to meet Baziana!'

'You don't know Baziana? You don't know the fool you're guarding?'

The soldier was now silent as the opposition leader became more vocal.

'If you don't know the criminal you're guarding, then I can guess what's inside your skull.'

'And what is inside my skull?'

'Cotton, pure cotton; not a single piece of brain. Open this gate right now. We must speak to Baziana at once!'

Two meters separated Gavana and the soldier standing behind the massive wire mesh gate. The soldier pretended not to have heard Gavana's sarcastic words and came closer to the gate. He looked amused and used a pleasant tone full of those diversions known only to an expert republican soldier.

'I beg your pardon, sir.'

Gavana literally screamed at the soldier.

'Listen carefully this time! I said if you don't know Dieudonné Baziana, the thief, then you are not . . . '

He was not allowed to complete his insult. A violent and burning gun butt struck his jaws sending him meters away from the gate. He did not collapse immediately thanks to the militants massed behind him. But streams of blood flowed down his mouth. His four front incisors crushed by the butt fell out of his mouth. His chest was red with blood. Who can handle such pain? He collapsed. Two militants quickly dragged the leader of the Socialist Party along the rough asphalt away from the scene.

The soldier at the other side of the gate walked back cautiously.

Someone shouted from the crowd, 'Gavana has been killed! Gavana is dead! Ambulance, ambulance!'

Gavana seemed to have completely lost consciousness when he was carted away. But the Reverend Yassa rose to the occasion. Lifting up his right hand, he called on the crowd to retreat. Then the militants picked up some sizeable stones from the side-street and, as they retreated, pelted them at the windows of the downtown skyscrapers and luxury fashion shops. Their fury was unquenchable. Hawkers, tourists and passersby scampered in all directions. Drivers hooted chaotically. Interminable traffic jams quickly formed along several streets as cars sped out of the business centre.

Then the police arrived. Strident sirens aggravated the panic as well as their throwing tear gas canisters in all directions. The street sellers packed up whatever they could and fled amid the general confusion. Alerted, all cab and bus drivers abruptly modified their schedules, and in less than fifteen minutes there was no public transport at the militants' disposable. Taunted and surrounded by the police, they capitulated en masse. But the police were merciless and the disorder was indescribable. Those severely injured and unable to run or escape the force's fury lay on the ground as a sign of surrender. The only happy people about were the looters whose task was eased by the general confusion. The police arrested dozens of protesters among whom was the Honorable Reverend President Pastor Charles Yassa.

Two police officers held the reverend by the collar of his shirt and dragged him off. Then they sat him on the ground, and grouped in a semi-circle, pitilessly thrashed the man of God. Their captive bled abundantly from the mouth, his left eye closed up. Yassa lost consciousness. One of the officers, turning towards the captives packed in the back of a police van, shouted:

'You'll get your share, sons of dickless!'

An officer jumped into the van, struck out with his bludgeon, breaking a couple of ribs and heads while pushing back the already crammed militants to create space for the pastor. Then he grabbed Yassa and brutally threw him inside.

The vans, full of captives drove off towards the central police station.

The following day, the 'title readers' of Abidjan or titologists (those who never read further than the newspapers' titles) gathered in front of the city's newsstands to get a general picture of what had transpired. Front page headlines read: *Gavana in coma: Gavana almost dead; Gavana is dead; Yassa: the Man of God is with his Maker; Baziana challenges the Almighty.*

It was three o'clock. The whole of Abidjan had moved to the city center where the justice court was under unusual surveillance. Since dawn the police had encircled the entire CBD to prevent Gavana and Yassa's sympathisers from protesting what they suspected would be a parody of a trial.

The severity of the fifty years old, bald judge, Samuel Nogo, was a well-established fact. 'The Opposition Crusher', as they called him, entered the justice courtroom an hour later than scheduled. He spent an additional thirty minutes murmuring an inaudible speech to the public prosecutor sitting at his right. He threw a bemused glance at the defendants, numbering about a hundred, massed in front of him. A throng of Yassa's comrades had turned up to attend the session. But from the gallery where they sat, they could not even see their leader, whose left eye was covered by a leaking yellowish plaster.

In most politically motivated crimes of vandalism, very few magistrates in Ivory Coast followed the official procedures; the outcome of the trial being known to all in advance. The judge seemed ready to ensure that the current one was no exception.

'So that's it,' he said, addressing himself to the defendants gathered in front of him. The contemptuous look in his eyes betrayed his eagerness to mete expeditious justice. 'The snake,' he carried on, 'is biting its own tail.'

'Boss,' said a perfectly illiterate accused from the *Revolutionary Rally of the Northerners* before being invited to speak. 'Boss, I am done no crime ever.'

'Is that right?' the judge replied. 'You did not commit any crime, you say? Please tell me, sir, who broke into the shops? Who burned down the car dealerships? Who attacked the police forces?'

'Boss, we was peaceful. I don't know nothing about breaking shops and burning what-what. I know nothing.'

'That is so true, you really know nothing at all.' In a more serious tone the judge carried on. 'Did you know your public protest was illegal, not authorized?'

'Not knowing.'

'You did not? Why were you marching anyway?'

'I am march from Ottala.'

'Oh, yes, of course, for Dr Ottala. And what is your name, dear sir?'

'My calling is Musa Sula.'

'Please bear with me while I consult your file'. The judge then began to flip through the files slowly. 'Sula, you said?'

'Yes boss.'

'Here we go. *Musa Sula, country of origin: Burkina Faso. Born 1967; Unmarried, father of three kids.* Is that correct?'

'Yes boss.'

The judge who was reading the file turned back to his interlocutor and proceeded.

'And what was our friendly Burkinabe citizen doing in a protest march intended for the citizens of this country?'

'I born in Ivory Coast.'

'I know, it is clearly mentioned in your file. You were indeed born in Ivory Coast.'

'I am work for Ivory Coast. My dad, my mom is work for Ivory Coast always long before.'

The judge slowly pulled his spectacles down to the tip of his nose.

'So?'

'So my kids is born to Ivory Coast.'

'What is your point?'

The defendant smiled. '

'So I march. The protest bring good to Ivory Coast.'

'Do you know that foreigners are not allowed to practice politics in this country?'

'I not be a foreigner. I born, all my kids born, to Ivory Coast.'

The judge took a deep breath so as to suppress the urge to laugh at the supreme ignorance of his interlocutor.

'So, since the gentleman is born and has been working in Ivory Coast, he is a citizen of this country. Is that correct? And he has full rights to do politics in this country?'

'Yes, boss,' the accused said with assurance.

The judge held his chin, looked at the accused and shook his head once more. He knew that most foreigners sympathised with the *Revolutionary Rally of the Northerners* because they believed it was only a matter of time before Baziana's administration would deport them to their country of origin. Indeed, did Baziana not suspect all northerners of being foreigners?

He sighed before continuing, 'That's so strange.'

'I say to you Mr. Judge, sir, I am not stranger,' shot back the accused, Musa Sula.

The judge was not surprised. It was well known that the foreigners born in Ivory Coast were numerous and generally ignored the fact that they could be issued citizenship on simple request once they clocked sixteen years of residence. He also knew that most foreigners were illiterate and believed that Dr Hassan Ottala, the *Northerners* leader, would immediately grant them citizenship upon assuming the presidency.

The judge then proceeded, 'Who else is innocent?' While waiting for an answer, he saw someone in the crowd murmuring to himself as if praying.

'My goodness, who do I see there – the son of God himself? Pastor Yassa! What do you have to say for yourself? I was told you refused any attorney's assistance. Pastor, what do you have to say for yourself?'

All the accused turned to the Pastor who was still deep in prayer.

'Please say something,' someone in the crowd begged.

79

Then suddenly President Reverend Pastor Yassa shouted through clenched jaws, 'O Lord, all have sinned and shall be deprived of Your glory! 'I punish fathers' iniquity till the last generation! The revenge is mine! Vanity of vanity, all is vanity! Nations fooled me, but the stone that the builder refused turned out to be the cornerstone! No one is righteous on earth!' Rabata-chococo Ripaparipopotipotipatipo . . . Alleluia!'

'Amen!' Answered the militants standing next to him.

The judge looked at the public prosecutor who did not seem to understand the pastor's plea. In a low voice he asked the prosecutor whether he thought the pastor was mentally ill.

'I doubt that,' the public prosecutor said.

'Is that all, reverend?'

Yassa remained silent, his head bowed as he was still deep in prayer.

'Pastor?' The judge tried once more.

The Pastor then, pointing his finger at the judge, shouted, 'You are the Devil, I recognise you! Out of here! Get out of there! Your fate is sealed, Satan! Shut your big mouth, Beelzebub! Show me your hands! Put them up! Up, up! If not, I'll send you back to the desert where you belong. Surrender now, Satan! Rococo richadadatipaTipatipotipo.'

A deep cathedral silence descended over the Palace of Justice. Did the judge think this was a dream? He only knew Yassa through the press; this was his first face-to-face encounter.

A few minutes later the public prosecutor, bored with Yassa's gibberish, read out the incriminating charges and, without giving the accused the opportunity to defend themselves individually, Judge Noko promptly confirmed their collective guilt with respect to vandalism, making a public nuisance and aggression towards the state police. He then handed down a blanket sentence which affected each one of them: three years imprisonment and a fine of 500 000 CFA.

Pleased with his day's work, the prosecutor sat down smiling.

'Thank you, Your Honour. This most important matter is now closed.'

François Gavana, his wife and children at his bedside, was still in hospital recovering from his injuries. At first his gums were swollen and his lips sewn up so that during the first week of hospitalization, he had not been able to utter a single word. But now, two weeks later, he began to regain his usual spirits for he still felt determined to knock down Baziana. His political advisers, who came to comfort him, had several excellent propositions. One of them, Séverin Kolo, suggested it would be wise to attract the attention of the international community.

'Alone,' he said, 'we won't achieve much against Baziana.'

'That's true,' Gavana replied. 'But weren't we supposed to use our next weapon . . . the strike at the University?'

'Yes, but that can wait for a while.'

'Till when?'

'I beg you not to worry about that. Think of those who finance Baziana, think of those who give him the money that keeps him in power.'

'I don't follow you. Be more precise.'

'Think of France, of America, of England. Think of messing up his collaboration with the superpowers. Believe me, once they disavow Baziana, the people of Ivory Coast will turn to us.'

Gavana, still doubtful, asked, 'What if they don't disavow him? Baziana and his Baule brothers have been looting this country for so long and it suits your French, English and American friends. That's why they say nothing.'

'That's true.'

'So why should they react now?'

'Because we will ask them to.'

Gavana laughed bitterly. 'Because we ask them . . . '

'Look, we are here with a photographer. He will . . . '

'Take a picture of me in bed? Come now, that won't work. Beside I am almost fine'

The head of the Socialist Party was expecting something more shocking, something more likely to compromise or humiliate Baziana. Was he not dreaming of an 'historical' revenge after what the republican guard of Baziana had done to him?

But the advisor was bent on pushing on with his plan. He knew that if Gavana would let him speak further, he would be able to convince him.

'Gavana,' he said. 'Please listen, you might just find yourself interested.'

'Well, I am listening.'

The counsellor made a sign with his finger. The photographer sitting next to the entrance stood up. From his bag, he pulled out a camera and a big chain. The chain was made of some heavy steel links like those fastened around the necks of Negroes during the slave trade.

81

The photographer also took out an official uniform of the presidential guard, with a truncheon.

Gavana still did not understand.

'And then?' he asked impatiently. 'What is this?'

The counsellor simply smiled before offering an explanation.

'Great!' he said. 'So, here we are. We put these chains around your neck, your armpits and your ankles . . . a voluminous bandage on your mouth, stained with a few drops of red ink, that will do for the missing blood . . . Someone wears the uniform, stands by your bedside displaying a terrible mood, and plays the watching guard with a hanging from his belt. And click! The camera flashes. The picture tours America, France, the U.K. The impact will simply be unstoppable! How's that?'

Gavana almost fell from the bed where he was lying as he shouted, 'That's marvellous! You are a genius, Séverin! That's exactly what we need. You are right. But something is still missing in this picture.'

'What can that be?' the counsellor asked.

'There is no gun for the one who plays the republican guard. All Baziana's guards carry weapons; their absence will make people doubt the photos's credibility.'

'I thought about it. But remember the opposition is currently under strict surveillance. It's too risky to drive around with a gun at this time. We can clone a gun to the picture using the computer.'

Gavana was visibly joyful.

'Séverin, you are my lifetime brother! Let's do it now.'

It was almost 10 a.m. The curious crowd, as always, had gathered round the busiest newsstand in 'Soweto', the most miserable shantytown of Abidjan, to peruse the headlines on the dailies. These avid readers of headlines had that morning gathered in a greater number than usual for all opposition newspapers had published on their front page the disturbing picture of François Gavana, with such sensational titles as *Baziana the new slave driver; Gavana caged by Baziana; Baziana resurrects slavery; Gavana in a neo-Nazi concentration camp.*

'No, I can't believe this,' one bystander said. 'Do you guys see how Baziana treats the opposition?'

'Worse than farm animals,' said another.

'This is totally unacceptable,' the first bystander said. 'Look at this picture. Is this the way to treat a human being?'

'I think the people should show Baziana and his friends that they are not indispensable to this country. On the contrary, they are the very obstacles to true democracy in Ivory Coast.'

'I don't agree,' another person in the crowd cut in.

'Why not?' Someone else said.

'Because anyone who plays the bad sheep needs a tough shepherd to lead him! Human rights are for humans only! No animal needs human right! What democracy can Baziana install amid a bunch of animals and vandals?'

'Who is a vandal? The vandals are the police and the members of Baziana's party who infiltrated our march.'

'Liar!'

'Yes, I may be a liar but surely not a slave driver!'

'The wages of vandalism is jail! Well done Baziana!'

'My brother, I can see you are a Baule from the president's village and surely a member of the Democratic Party . . . '

'Of course. So what?'

'So I say only thieves mingle with thieves. You are certainly a thief!'

'How about you? Your twisted western accent marinated with some stupid socialism stinks like shit!'

'Yes, I'm from the west, and I support Gavana who is a son of our region, but I am not a thief!'

'I tell you what, you and your loony Gavana, you are not good enough to wipe the ass of Baziana! Gavana is dirty! He blows his nose at every street corner. He'll never be president as long as we are in this country!'

This last insult was greeted with laughter from the sympathizers of Baziana and the Democratic Party while enraging the socialist who shouted out, 'I advise you to talk about Gavana using another tone, you donkey! I never take too long to crush the big mouths of idiots like yourself!'

'Who's an idiot? Your fucken mother or your stupid father?'

The mockers found this funny and laughed their heads off at the expense of Gavana's loyalist.

'Be careful. I warned you. Do you hear me?''Please go home, take a shower and there, fuck yourself!'

Before anyone had time to react, the socialist jumped into the crowd and punched him hard in the face. Baziana's supporter collapsed to the ground, his lips dripping with blood. The crowd of onlookers became more agitated. Upon realising what was happening, more sympathisers of the Democratic Party gathered around. More socialists came to give a hand. The wrangle between the parties escalated. Stones were thrown and the wooden newsstand was broken up and turned into weapons. The papers were torn into shreds and scattered all over. Suddenly a siren announced the arrival of the police and the crowd fled in every direction through the alley's of the labyrinth that was the shantytown. That day, neither Baziana, who was surely relaxing at home while sipping some divine nectar, nor Gavana who was still recovering in hospital, knew that a fanatical crowd in this squatter camp was fighting for them.

The following day, the opposition papers headlined: *Baziana Militia Pitiless with Opposition Paper Readers; Press Freedom Abuse: Police Tear Up Opposition Newspapers; Baziana Hates the Poor of Shantytowns.*

'I thought you said Gavana is a free man,' President Dieudonné Baziana asked his security minister.

'Yes, of course, Your Excellency,' the minister, Gaston Akassu, assured him.

'And this . . . what is this?'

Dieudonné Baziana, ensconced on his favourite couch, grabbed the magazine on the pedestal table close to where he was. On the front page of this famous international paper, which specialised in political scandals, was the disturbing picture of François Gavana wrapped in chains like a Negro in the belly of a slave ship crossing the Atlantic.

'Your Excellency, I am also surprised to see this picture. He's at the Saint Theresa Polyclinic.'

Baziana slowly sank even deeper into the comfortable couch and before continuing.

'That's true. The paper confirms it. But why is he chained up in this clinic? Why?'

'Your Excellency, I did not instruct my men to guard him in this hospital, much less ill-treat him.'

The minister was completely taken aback by the information. He took a close look at the picture. He was convinced that this was the work of an over-zealous policeman.

The president shook his head some more before posing the one question that had been burning inside him of late.

'Tell me,' he said, 'have you finally found out who authorised Gavana's protest march? Have you discovered who imitated your voice? You promised to give me the culprit.'

'Your Excellency, we are still investiga . . . '

'You have made two mistakes that only begin to make sense in light of the malfunctioning of your team. Would you admit that?'

The minister equated the president's remark with an accusation of serious deception and he knew what the implication was.

'Your Excellency, I request additional time to finalise these two cases; I will shortly be able to solve both.'

Baziana, who had all along been talking to his minister without looking at him, now faced him – his expression considerably softer.

'You know what I've been trying to figure out lately, Akassu?' He paused and dropped his voice. 'Could there be a spy in our party . . . a spy working for the opposition?'

The minister's face suddenly radiated with life. He had never thought that the extreme vigilance of his team (that had guaranteed his position in several governments) could allow for such mistakes. If he had never doubted the efficiency of his team, he had always suspected a spy in the ranks of the Party. He was even happier that the suggestion had come from the president himself.

'Your Excellency, I must confess I have always suspected that much.'

Well, then,' the president said. 'Why don't you take a good look around and see? I'm sure it will lead to something. And relax, for God's sake. Take some whiskey, some rum?'

'I'll have a few drops of *whiskey*, Your Excellency.'

'Help yourself.' The president took a sip of the refined Scotch he was drinking. 'I hear that Ottala has decided to use the foreigners against us.'

'Absolutely, Your Excellency. Quite a number were arrested during the march.'

'I thought as much. Very sad how these foreigners are ungrateful.'

The relaxed atmosphere and the liquor seemed to inspire the minister. He began to talk more freely – though only in acquiescence to everything the president said.

'I've always known these foreigners to be very ungrateful. Still, I can't believe that they, who were born to sell cereals at street corners and keep cattle in the deepest regions of the desert, can do this to Ivory Coast, a country that feeds them. They're nothing but a bunch of simple fishermen and kola nut retailers who take peanuts and tea for dinner in dusty tents. How can they be so unthankful and become politicians! My goodness! And why? Because their stomachs are quite full! And now, we are said to be xenophobic! How more wicked and unappreciative can you get?'

The minister spoke with increasing passion which President Dieudonné Baziana quietly put down to the magic effects of the Scotch.

'Your Excellency, we need to contain the foreigners as soon as possible. We should . . . '

'Akassu,' the President, who was starting to feel bored and tired, called out, 'Of course we should. Why do you think we are having this discussion? Please investigate those two cases thoroughly and stay alert to every plot in and around the party. I have to rest now. Good night.'

And with that, Dieudonné Baziana gulped down the last drop in his glass and slowly closed his eyes.

BLACK BOY FLY

Thabiso Tshowa

Black boy fly is a story or maybe it's a game about the human race – about how we can be loving and hurtful at the same time but if you play your cards right you can actually act a poes and still get the girl of your dreams, but it goes deeper than that. It's about using hurtful words to express our deepest thoughts, about how we feel about our loved ones without actually being negative to the point where we hurt their feelings or say something out of spite.

Black boy fly came about the experiences I had growing up in Geluksdal, a coloured neighbourhood where people can be loving and hurtful at the same time or maybe they expressed their love in an unusual manner. Geluksdal was a place where you'd find some of the most unstable minds and the most beautiful mix breed people you could ever possibly find on earth. I stayed in extension 2 with my mom and baby sister, Zet (though she's 7 years older than me), later known as 'sister boza' because she was so gangster, taking after her mom, of course. Violence has never been an issue. Everybody in my family was exposed to gruesome violence from an early age from parents to their offspring thus cycling back to grandparents. I've witnessed some of the most terrible assaults in my family but mostly against other families and neighbours.

Man, it was like gang wars growing up in the streets of extension 2. I was no angel either. I have hurt many people in my childhood and throughout my youth but luckily my mind wasn't right either so whenever I committed an unspeakable act, I would fall into a deep sleep afterwards and wake up with no recollection of the ordeal ever taking place. I think that's what set me apart from the rest of my sick minded, mixed up fellow people. Not remembering the bad things I do, meant waking up the next morning a happy camper. They (my loved ones) would allow me to stay in that state of bliss and ignorance of what had occurred because whenever I acted out in an aggressive manner it was mainly the product of me being pushed into a corner. Even now as a 24 year old man trying to find his way in the world, I still relapse and act out aggressively but not to the point of seriously hurting people. I manage to bring myself back to a calm state of mind but I guess the remnants of Geluksdal are still within me.

Black boy fly was born when I first heard Lucky's older brother, Bobo call his girlfriend, Sharice, a fat ass and then expressing how he likes her in that manner. His exact words were 'Jy het 'n dik esel but I like you like that'. She never got mad at him for saying that, she was actually excited by the phrase because every time he knocked her down he would follow up with 'But I like you like that' so my friend (Lucky) and I figured we would use it on the local girls from Tsakani at 'Faranani multi-purpose centre', a local swimming hole. We figured it would work wonders because we were at an advantage from any competition from the mean, older Tsakani boys because kids from Tsakani were not too familiar with English and/or Afrikaans; they spoke mostly Zulu and/or Sotho.

Lucky would sometimes go visit his Coloured relatives on his mother's side of the family in the deep dark section of Geluksdal and I would be left to play with Rokney, my best friend, so we ended up using black boy fly on the beautiful neighbourhood mix breeds and I specifically used it on Shanice, the younger girl from my neighbour's house but I guess it was too dumb or too intricate for her liking because she got offended and almost gave me a hot clap but she didn't, because she liked me just as much as I liked her. *Black boy fly* successfully worked on her mom though I guess she was matured enough to grasp the full scope of the game and I think she fell for me because she figured I was too matured or nonetheless too wise for girls my age. Talk about a beautiful, sick, twisted fate but it was cool.

GOODBYE, SOKHULU

Andile Cele

When everyone gathered to say their last words, I was the last in line – I had to make sure he was really dead. His body was squeezed into a brown shimmering coffin; his face looked rather puffy as though he was wearing cheap foundation. An old lady burst into song as his coffin went down, a Zulu hymn that made everyone cry. A young woman, who seemed to be in terrible pain, asked me for a tissue. I immediately recognized her as the girl who was my brother's friend. I hadn't seen her for a long time. I was perplexed by the degree of pain she was in.

'Are you okay?'

She looked at me and began crying, and then later, started wailing. From my side the events that had led to this particular funeral did not give me any reason to cry. But she couldn't contain herself and gave me a desperate hug; it didn't help that my expensive designer dress was now covered in tears but she held on to me as if she had known me for most of her life.

'What relationship did you have with the deceased?'

She remained silent and couldn't say anything. She even stopped crying as if I had said something so shocking that even tears were out of place. Then she calmly let go of me and took a step back, wiping her face.

'I have known him for quite some time now and he was very kind to me and I just cannot believe that he is gone.'

When she started crying again, I became worried that a stranger had known my father more than I did. Who was she? I asked myself.

'How did you know him?'

The young woman could well have felt this was an interrogation, but I really wanted to know what gave her the right to cry for a man such as my father. My mother, dressed in black, looked as beautiful as ever, and here was this skinny young woman seeming to be in more pain than anyone else.

I heard my aunt screaming my name, 'Londi!' Her crude voice always annoyed me. As she came close, the strange young woman decided to walk away from me. I was immediately curious. Had she done this because she saw I was part of the family? My nosy aunt wanted to know about her, about this girl I was standing with. I wanted to shrug her off but she was on me like a leech.

'*Aunti nami ngifana nawe*, I don't know who she is or where she comes from, or why she's here. She was crying and I helped her, that's all'.

My aunt was disappointed at my lack of persuasion. If it were her, she would have known who she was by now.

'You can be so slow sometimes! I mean, I have seen that girl from somewhere, with your brother Sakhi, and you are telling me you don't know who she is'

My aunt could have passed for a demon at this point; I couldn't understand her lack of thinking and her brute outlook on life. I had to walk away from her to keep myself sane. My father's funeral was proving to be the dramatic fiasco I had always imagined it would be. I was still surprised that he had no wives coming from Nongoma to bury him. I mean, we couldn't possibly be the only ones. My father, a staunch Zulu man, with just two children!

In the midst of all the cries, songs and chaos, my brother was having a conversation with the strange girl. I went up to them. At last, I would be introduced to her. But as I approached, I sensed discomfort from my brother. Did I stop? No, I had to know who she was and what she stood for.

He looked at me carefully for some time, then said, 'Londi . . . why aren't you helping aunt Zoleka with things?'

'What things, Sakhi? No, I am not helping anyone with things.'

'You know, all the things for the funeral . . . all the things a woman needs to do . . .'

I stared at my brother. Why was he asking such senseless questions? Then I then realized the strange girl had probably told him about our meeting and so he felt the need to hiss me off. But I stood my ground. I was not about to leave without an explanation, I mean why was she crying so much? Who is she? And why was my brother caught up with her?

'Londi, this is Zanele from Tongaat. She knows dad and that's why she's here.'

So that's who she was! But this didn't answer the question as to how and where she knew my father. I was not going to give up.

'Where does she know dad from?'

A long pause from my brother and a distraught Zanele showed

91

me the young woman had a story to tell. But why was my handsome brother so silent? I just wanted to understand why she was crying more than me. There had to be a reason.

So we stood there. Sakhi, lost for words, began to turn pink in the face; his very light skin (which he inherited from my father) always turned that colour when he was nervous; his hands played with his ugly, pin-striped tie.

And then he said, 'Londi, Zanele is kinda related to us.'

'How related and how come you know about her and I don't? Why do people hide things from me? Who exactly are you, Zanele?'

I felt a heat rush all over my body. Not only was my dad a liar, he was also a freak. He had a daughter named Zanele, who looked at least four years older than me, which meant she was my brother's age. What I didn't understand was Sakhi's pinkness all over the face. And why was he suddenly so meek? I would have loved to shake it off of him with a clenched fist.

'Sakhi, why are you looking like the world has failed you? We should all be celebrating a life. Yes, our father is dead, but come on, man, no need to sulk. He was old and he lived a happy life.'

Our newly found sister Zanele started crying again. This really frustrated me. Once again she was seeking too much attention. She then told me that she had been dating my brother for a year now and had met my dad on many occasions but didn't know who he was until she got a call from her mother from Nongoma telling her that she had a funeral to attend, her father's funeral. And then she realized that she shared a father with her boyfriend. I personally knew that my family was a mess but this was icing on a damned cake.

I felt sorry for Zanele, for being tricked by nature and for being in love with her half-brother but this just showed how much of a coward my father was, he had children whom he never visited and this proved that there were more Zaneles out there. While I was trying to wrap my head round the fact that my father was such a foul being, aunt Zoleka screamed for me again, this time she knew I had the full story.

Ever since I was a child my aunt always milked me for stories about my mother and father; she has always had this peculiar interest in my parents relationship. As a 23-year-old I felt the need to stand up for myself and stop my aunt for being such a pain in my life. She screamed for me again and I had no choice but to free her from her misery.

'So tell me Londi who is that young lady and what does she want from Sakhi?' I wanted to tell my aunt where to get off or rather to tell her to jump off a cliff but she was my mother's sister, so I had to respect her.

'Auntie, why are you so interested in knowing the identity of a young lady who might be Sakhi's girlfriend, or maybe a stranger crying because she loves to cry, who knows? Why do you want to know her so badly?'

I then realized that aunt Zoleka knew more than me but she was just testing the waters on my side. She stormed off without saying a word. Come to think of it, why was she walking around like a headless chicken instead of being with her sister under the black cloths? It occurred to me that aunt Zoleka could have had an affair with my father; it would explain her interest in my parents' relationship.

When the pastor announced that everyone should come to my house for the after tears, I knew that even those who failed to be present at the funeral would come and feast at my house. My aunt Zoleka became the CEO in the kitchen, it didn't help that we had a catering company doing everything but she felt the need and took charge. Ever since our conversation at the graveyard, she couldn't look at me in the eye which didn't bother me because I really didn't care about her and her melodrama. Sometimes it felt like my aunt was still in high school; she picked the weirdest times for her tantrums.

I saw my brother holding Zanele by the hand, taking her to the house; the poor girl couldn't even walk, and my brother was still pink in the face. Was he about to tell my mother about Zanele? I found it very important that I should be there to listen – or maybe even help my brother.

When my mother greeted Sakhi and Zanele, my brother suddenly fell onto my mother's lap crying like a part of him had died with our father. My mother knew that Sakhi was not exactly close with dad, so she was greatly surprised by his sudden emotional display. Yes, there he was, failing to speak and choking on his tears.

I had to step in. As polite as I could be with respect for the dead, I addressed my mother.

'Ma, Sakhi is going through a very tough time.'

My brother was looking at me, ordering me to stop speaking with his aggressive look. But I was not about to back down, I was not going to let him ruin his reputation by crying throughout the speech, I was going to bail him out of this one.

My mother trying to be as respectful as ever in her black funeral clothes, looked at me as if I had lost my mind but she was about to see that I was the only one who was sane.

'Sakhi and this young lady named Zanele were dating and they have both just found out that they share the same father, our father, Sokhulu, which is why they are both so emotional.'

My brother started crying even louder; as if he was going through excruciating pain. To cover his loud aggressive cry, one lady started singing a song called 'Siyabonga Jesu', my mother ordered the woman to keep quiet, her eyes filled with enormous rage, you could tell that if it were not a funeral, it was clear that the poor woman would have suffered a great bruise.

My mother told me to leave the room; I dragged my feet towards the kitchen only to find that aunt Zoleka had been listening. She stared at me with a big grin on her face; I wondered what could have made her so happy.

'You see, I knew your parents were not as good as everyone thought they were. I mean look at this mess your father made, and what if this Zanele girl is pregnant?'

At that very moment I wanted to hit my aunt so badly my hands started trembling, my eyes were heavy and I knew I was about to cry. From the other room I heard my mother asking Zanele how she knew that Sokhulu had died. It then became clear that aunt Zoleka was a real demon walking around in human form. She had called Zanele's mother and told her about my father's passing – meaning she had known about her for quite some time but kept this from my mother and I and Sakhi.

Suddenly, with great force, she pushed me aside and demanded to speak to my mother outside. The elders tried to speak to her, that she would 'dlula', and that being so disrespectful at a funeral would bring bad luck upon her. Hell, no, aunt Zoleka couldn't care a foot what the elders had said – she wanted to see my mother outside.

I saw that she wanted to a make a spectacle out of our family and feared for the worst but my mother stepped outside looking as beautiful as a swan, and calmly asked her, 'What do you want Zoe?'

My aunt was so taken aback that she started speaking riddles and no one understood what she was getting at.

'Yes, sisi, you think your husband belonged to you. I have seen you walking around as if you were better that me. Just because you have a bigger house and nice furniture, you think you are better than me?'

My mother was confused and didn't understand what was happening; however I automatically knew from that moment that my aunt Zoleka had had an affair with my father and I saw the need to step in and fix her.

From the crowd, I called out her name. But she ignored me, still mix-matching things and throwing my mother off.

'Aunti Zoleka!' I called out to her again. She suddenly saw me and rolled her eyes, placing her hands neatly on her figure, fixing her floral dress with the other.

'Aunti Zoleka, why don't you tell us? What makes you think you can come here and ruin my father's funeral?'

Whe she started laughing so much that she started crying, I knew that my aunt was demented.

'Your father, Londi, loved me better. I was more of a woman for him and I knew him more than most of you here.' My aunt suddenly fell on her knees, crying like she was in labour, catching her breath as she continued her story. 'I loved him more than all the other women. I loved him more than you, sis. He shared stories with me, he told me his dreams and you knew he was going to leave you so you killed him.'

I felt sorry for my aunt. The spectators stopped laughing and others started to weep; my mother went back to the house and embraced my brother. I was the only one who was sane and I went to my room and I started to weep for my dead father. Then I realized that I never knew him and I was weeping because he had died so long ago in my heart.

Sokhulu was gone and I never knew him.

MEMORIES OF HER

Elizabeth Joss

A walk along the frothing beachfront: waves pounding the shore, the beach scattered with hard blue-black shells which crunch as I walk over their delicate surface. They were once mussels, once alive. Now blue-black bruises, which scatter the skin-white beach. They are traces of the inexplicable. And they lie so close to the vibrant, crashing ocean; their surfaces cracked open.

From the shore I see many white, graceful seagulls like spots on rigid rocks that outline the beach. They squawk and signal to each other the first signs of fish, playfully emerging near the surface of the water. I imagine myself, a small girl of six playing with our old Alsatian, Marilyn, near the man-made pool. I am a chubby little thing, with an ugly bob haircut and skin golden from the sun. My aunt is with me; she staggers across the sand helping me collect seashells. We observe a homeless man making images on the sand with the blue-black mussel shells. She converses with him, and they laugh jokingly. People stand above on the promenade and look down to where he works on the shore. He is most artistic, creating a sunny landscape using the beach as his canvas. I remember his later works, of children and their parents holding hands. I grip my aunt's unsteady hand and walk with her and Marilyn back up to the promenade, across the grass stretch and over the road outlined with palm trees. Tranquility at our fingertips . . .

But there is something you should know about this scene from my memory. Something that has permeated all my thoughts up till now: this was the age when the void started; when the black and blue knot inside my chest first emerged.

Images, little things: my aunt's room and the objects she kept in perfect order. Her love for organising porcelain dolls on her bookshelf and her China tea set which sat on a floral plastic tea tray. She often confided with me when I helped her organise these little items she so cherished. I remember her showing me how to stand photo frames on a slant on the shelf instead of placing them in a linear fashion, one next to the other. She no doubt disrupted the implicit rules in my head to do with order and logic. And from these little items she kept and her delicate manner towards them, I began to think of my aunt as strangely eccentric.

96

At roadsides we would talk about life. The two of us . . . and Marilyn. The intimacy we shared. Our family sitting in my mother's small, half-loaf blue car. My grandmother and mother in the front and my aunt and I in the rear. The car comes to a halt. We arrive at our destination, the block of flats where my aunt and my grandmother live. I feel a tightening sensation in my chest as I emerge from the car, my blood pressure rising. I'm devastated. I shout something at my aunt, something about her ruining the family. My aunt's faltering response; her hazel eyes saddened and heavy with guilt, which she quickly tries to hide. She walks through the gate in a daze, a pattern I became so accustomed to witnessing. I will not see her until morning. My mother holds me tightly in her arms and that evening we pray for something exceptional. We wait and wait. That something arrives, years later. And finally we notice a change – her face fuller and healthier but her drinking increased. A trade-off I guess. But we are happy for a while. And so is she. She holds down a job as a manageress at a restaurant. She makes good money. It is spent on me, spoilt little thing.

She once gives me hundreds of butterfly clips when they are in fashion. They break years later when I put them all into my hair and go on a roller coaster. The colourful pieces fall everywhere as I emerge from the dizzy ride. I manage to save only three. And still I try to recreate her image in my mind, to put the pieces together and bring her back into the film of my mind. Bits resurface . . . slowly. The doctors we used to see so often. Her and I. How I came to know each and every one of those doctors. Chemists, too. The pills they would dispense for her. The haze of walking from one doc to another. The trip I became so accustomed to after schools and during the holidays. The trip I knew ended the next morning when she would sleep the world away. Awake grouchy and then read a novel as if nothing on earth had happened the previous day. In rages, stricken with frustration, I would flush those pills down the toilet. The pills we fought to obtain. She never forgave me for such a thing. Ever. Those pills were her escape. Her everything. The irony of their name: Seconals. Ticking away every second.

I had just started high school. My mother gave me three orange pills she had found in my aunt's room and told me to throw them down the dirt shoot. I didn't listen. Instead I put them in my green school blazer pocket with the intention of taking them. I wanted to feel what she felt. Why they were so amazing that she kept on taking

97

them? Our school went to Maynardville that evening to watch Romeo and Juliet. I didn't watch the play. I sat making a hole in the ground with the black heel of my school shoe, contemplating what to do with those pills. Contemplating. At the show end, when the lights went off, I threw the pills into the hole I had been making and quickly covered them up with soil. I knew it was right to bury them. But they were not buried deep for the soil was coarse and it was difficult to make such a deep hole without attracting attention. So they were buried just below surface level under my chair. Memories I tried to bury in the darkness from the stage glare. If someone had to walk over the soil where those pills lay, they would surely expose themselves. Lie there in the open for everyone to see and wonder.

And who knows what happened to them – perhaps they have disintegrated into the soil since then, running like memories through the porous ground. Or perhaps they are still surfacing, the ground too hard and coarse for any permeation to take place.

Memories surfacing my skin; me, hardened.

THE PREGNANCY

Monde Mdodana

We are having an argument again. From where I stand, the situation looks hopeless. I try to speak with a full heart but the deepest part of me knows that she will never understand me. I find it impossible to fashion my Intuitions into a reasonable explanation for the way I act. These very Intuitions tell me that it's Madness to attempt to be logical and reasonable about them for by their very nature, Intuitions defy reason and logic. I can't make her understand me. I have to suffer alone.

She compares me to a dog that is chasing it own tail and accuses me of fancying that mine's the way to God . . .

'Mine is the way to the Outsider. But, since we'll never know what or where God is, it could be that my way is one of the ways to God.'

'Are you this Outsider? Do you fancy yourself to be God?'

'The Outsider is – The Man of Solitude. If God is The Man of Solitude, then the Outsider is God.'

'Come out from behind your riddles and say something substantial.'

'What I have to share is insubstantial, so much so that I myself struggle to grasp it.'

My answers are not very impressive. They won't move her. The deepest part of me knows that she is too impressed by her own answers. But no objectivity lies beyond them. She accuses me of vanity . . .

'Get over yourself. Excusing yourself from reality with these fantasies is childish, fish yourself out of this vanity!'

'What is vanity, what is reality, what is subjectivity? The sea of Existence is too deep. I am too deep in it, not even death can fish me out!'

'Listen to me Siya, if you lose your sanity now, you will be condemned to seek it without end.'

'Seeking is not sinful; I was not born to be constant!'

This is futility. I stop arguing and look away. There are people around me; I think they love me but I'm absolutely alone. We mainly communicate through speech, which I feel is inadequate. My deepest self would rather communicate through dance. I must suffer my Intuitions alone.

I want to forget these dreadful insights so I let myself be carried away by the thought of Pretty. Sometimes her efforts to break my isolation gain considerable success. But most of the time the orgasm is just not enough. I have to find some Higher Way to redemption. The orgasm is like speech; it only half releases me. But I keep going back to it, just like I keep going back to speech.

She interrupted and half released me this morning while I was reading *Thus Spoke Zarathustra*. I would have preferred it to be *Thus Danced Zarathustra* . . .

'Babes, I want our relationship to deepen. I'd like to cultivate an interest in the things that make you happy. That t book you're reading for instance, you've probably gone through it more than a hundred times. I'd like to know what it's about.'

I let myself be carried away by the enthusiasm . . .

'It is the tale of the ancient prophet Zarathustra who descends from his Solitude in the mountains to tell the world that God as we understand 'him' is dead, and that the Superman or the Free Spirit or the Outsider – the human embodiment of divinity – is his successor.'

'This Zarathustra person must have been very shy. To live by himself in the mountains . . . was he running away from people?'

'No! He wasn't running away, he was running *towards*. He was running towards the Superman! He was running *towards* the Free Spirit. He was running *towards* the Outsider! He was running *towards* Himself!'

'But isn't this vanity, what makes him think that he is different from other people?'

'It's not vanity, it's *Individuality*. What makes him different from others or what makes him more like the Outsider is that he unreservedly accepts the risk of being himself, an individual human being, this specific human being alone before Existence, alone in this enormous accountability!'

'He reminds me of my cousin Phikelela. Phikelela always wanted to go 'the other way'.'

'Was he a Swimmer against the Tide, was he a Dreamer?'

'A Swimmer against the Tide, a Dreamer, Phikelela went the other way because he didn't like to take a taxi to town. He preferred walking alone and having a conversation with Himself. Taxi conversations disgusted him.'

'That makes him a Swimmer against the Tide and more than a Swimmer against the Tide!'

'You use big words to describe him but he was no big shot, nothing like the people you read about. He was shy; he never kissed a girl; he quit school to work in a grape farm so that he could support his grandparents. The truck that he and his co-workers took to work ran him over one sunny afternoon and he died, silently, obscurely.'

'We must not underestimate the intensity with which he lived. I know that the wonders that occupy The Man of Solitude are infinitely more rewarding than fame and fortune. The Outsider revels in the wonder of Existence; he revels in the wonder of Consciousness itself. Men like Phikelela live with a full heart . . .'

My enthusiasm sags and I sink into a mild depression. Speech is useless noise! Yet I must speak. The people don't have a spiritual eye; I can't make them see otherwise. I want to forget these dreadful insights so I let myself be carried away by the thought of Unathi. She is the one girl who has the power to make me doubt myself. Oftentimes it feels like my very sanity is dependent on her approval.

I was listening to Beethoven's *Egmont* in a sort of half-trance so I didn't hear her come in. She'd been in my room for a while before I returned to the Common State of Consciousness. She'd been 'glossing' over the titles in my bookshelf. And she didn't approve.

'Your sickness comes from that cursed bookshelf; *The Will to Die, Ways of Dying, The Sickness Unto Death.* These books are the cause of your obsession with the darker side of life.'

'Perhaps my – as you put it – obsession, with the darkest manifes-tations of Existence is the cause of my reading those titles. You can never be too sure about these things.'

'Stop making riddles Siya. This is not a problem of Philosophy, this is your life!'

I look away hopelessly. It's not that I can't sustain the argument. I have Sartre's Doctrine of Commitment to put forward. I'm hopeless because we are talking about problems of Existing, answers for which she has to exist herself into finding. If we were merely talking about a problem of Philosophy, I would explain myself to her and she would think that she understands. She needs to pay attention to her Intui-tions. In her statement, 'This is not a problem of Philosophy, this is your life,' she makes a distinction between Philosophising and Ex-isting. But her distinction is for the worst; she wants me to be more practical about the problems of Existing than I am about the problems of Philosophy. She lacks commitment despite the commonly held illusion that women have a keener sense of commitment.

She preaches sanity . . .

'The risk taking of this Outsider madness is childish. It smacks of a morbid obsession with the irrational.'

'There's risk taking even in the obsession with safety and reason. The death of a man who lived in one room of his Spiritual Mansion – fearing that the other rooms might be haunted by spirits and demons – is a tragedy. The rational evolves from the irrational; every Madness has enough sense to follow characteristic patterns. There are not opposites in Existence, only relativities.'

'But your Madness is absolute – to believe that these damned books will give you the answers to everything. Books are not an alternative to living. They will only teach you to ask the Unanswerable Questions ever more frantically.'

'That you cannot answer them does not make them Unanswerable.'

'Do you fancy that you know everything?'

'No, I only wish to draw your attention to the fact that *my* Unanswerable Questions may not be the same questions that *you* consider Unanswerable. I'm apathetic to all forms of tyranny and everything vaguely or otherwise dogmatic.'

We are quiet for a while, I resume . . .

'Every artist should know, intuitively!'

'Know what?'

'That the infinite growth of everything in existence is indeterminate and chaotic. Every artist should understand that there are external limits to what our minds can know and the fruitfulness to which our Spirits can ripen. The only limitations that exist are those that we impose on ourselves and, even more dreadful, those that we impose on each other.'

'But there are questions that will always remain Unanswerable – like what is God?'

'Or what is Existence? Long ago I decided to paint the greyer pieces of Existence with my own understanding and my own ignorance. I do not wish to take someone else's as much as I do not wish to impose mine, knowing that it is an experiment, a chance taking, a gamble. My reply to the greyer shades of Existence is not an answer, it's a question . . .'

I want to kiss her but I feel that I'd be embarrassing myself. Besides, kisses are absolutely unnecessary. We are focussed completely on each other. There exists a Mystical Magnetism between us.

I shoot the question straight at her.

'Are you Faithful?' A confused look takes over her face. 'Do you believe in the worthiness of our unborn child, do you consider this pregnancy a miracle?'

'I do but we have to be realistic about these things. Publishing a book is not something you decide to do under the influence of that thing you smoke. Think about the money that will have to be spent in printing. Once we have the printed copies, we'll have to put up even more money to market the book.'

I work in a movie theatre. I don't earn much but, if necessary, I vow to sacrifice my whole wage for the book.

'I have Faith in the Providence of Pregnancy.'

'You have to keep in mind the possibility of a stillbirth.'

'The future is one of the greyer shades of Existence; let's reply to it with this question. Let's affirm our Faith through this definite act.'

'I'm faithful now. I'll start typing my poems, we 're going to have a baby.'

Now I wait. I nurse with Faith the miraculous work that is growing inside me. I don't get the morning sickness, but I suffer from a constant Nausea. It is mild most of the time, only intensifying when my Faith slackens.

We're having an argument again. I don't have the energy for it so I tell her to go away and not come back for a while. She takes her toothbrush from a container and – pretending not to be troubled – makes her way to the door. She doesn't go out, she doesn't look back, she says . . .

'I'm going to need some money.'

'Money, my Money?'

'Yes, I 'm going to have an abortion. I'm going to abort your baby.'

'No, you're not pregnant.'

'I am pregnant.'

'You don't know that.'

'I took a test, three times . . .'

She's pregnant. The air is infected with disgust. The Nausea radiates from us both. I look away. Twins? A purposeful act of Faith and an unexpected Tester of the Strength of Faith? What is the nature of Faith? Is faith something you have less trouble with when you *choose* the experience on which you must nail it? What if Chance doesn't allow you to choose, as it often doesn't'?

I'm pregnant with the Outsider. The very Blood of me has Faith in his worthiness and his ultimate Triumph. Pretty is pregnant with my child. The more susceptible the temperament is to Faith, the more susceptible it is to Despair. Thus teaches Existence.

KEEP THE SHIP MOVING!

(An extract from an autobiography)

Mpumelelo Cilibe

I arrived at Ford dressed in khaki clothes. I had just washed off my face the red ochre daubing of post–circumcision, initiation ritual for I was an *ikrwala* and only nineteen. I needed the job in order to raise money to return to college and buy new clothes to replace those I'd had to discard as required by tradition. Had mother not dared me about going into circumcision with my elder brother, I wouldn't have been there. Traps are easy to get into and hard to extricate oneself out of: just check every caged animal.

Actually, this was my second job. I'd just escaped slavery at Dulux Paints down this same road. They had lured me into that place with a juicy lie about a white clerk who had supposedly resigned and that I'd be filling his position. Now, whites don't do much at work; so to be told you're replacing one of them and you're pitch black like me, is no small matter. On my first day they had me loitering around in the factory warehouse, weighing bits of paint mixing samples and doing some other house-keeping shit. Then at three o'clock I heard this goods train whistle shrilly at the back of the factory and the guys started whistling and going wild, shouting, 'E sidin! To the siding!' I was a bit flustered and lost. And then this series of long sliding steel doors opened up and revealed an overloaded train with about half-a-dozen carriages of 210 litre drums of oil and 100kg bags of some powder. Someone called me to follow the rest of the fellows to the train which I did. With hindsight, I always marvel at my stupidity not to quit then and there. They packed my back like a long dicked mule! I could be wrong, but I think I saw something in their eyes, some sort of strange, knowing glint. Those bastards must have been laughing all the time behind my bent back. I've never slaved like that in my life and I never bothered to go back – not even to collect my wages for that day. I now know for sure that a man's back doesn't break that easily, it's far too supple, just like a donkey's. At home I just went straight to bed without once opening my mouth, to rest my hurting back. It was morning the next day when I woke up, in my khaki clothes, right on the same spot where I was resting when I returned from work the previous afternoon. I just played with Bobbie, our mongrel, that day.

Patric Tarr was the personnel officer, reporting to Mr Munroe, the human resources manager at the Ford Struandale assembly plant; a big guy with a slightly bent back – a froggy looking guy who wore glasses. He looked over the large, green, cursed paper that the labour bureau had blessed me with, and freaked out.

'We can't take you! I know this thing, it's a clock card; it means you don't keep jobs!'

Of course he knew what a clock card was – he was the one who gave them to guys like me at the labour bureau where he'd worked before his current job here at Ford. This was how it worked: I quit a lousy job as I'd done at Dulux, go report at the labour bureau, they stamp my *dompas,* issue me a most humiliating A3 size green paper with blocks to present to every employer I approach for work; the employer then signs that indeed I came to him to look for a job, and that he didn't have one, and stamps it with his company stamp; only when it's all filled up with sorry signatures can I take it back to the bureau as proof that I'm serious about work-seeking. Failure to follow this process would earn me a free train ticket to the state potato farms in Bethal, Eastern Transvaal, for forced labour at harvesting time. And that's finish and *klaar.* How do I know? My eldest brother, Thobile, was a graduate of the system. So of course I was horrified when the same white guy offered to send Emerson Tsotsobe, the guy in front of me, there. Emerson was the lead vocalist of the popular 'Black Slave' band but the white man didn't give a damn about that.

'Why are you not working?' he had barked.

'I'm a musician,' Emerson had responded.

'Are you mad? I'll send you to the *foken* potato farms if you're so stupid!'

And Emerson, flushed pink with fright, took his green card and left.

What could I say? Risk the truth?

'*Baas,* please, they made me offload a goods train by myself at Dulux!'

I don't know where I got the courage to say those words but Tarr seemed surprised, and asked for my *dompas* before taking my documents into his office. I realized afterwards that in that moment of panic I'd called him *baas,* forgetting Black Consciousness and bra Steve Biko and Barney Pityana and Moki Cekisani. These guys were always telling us never to call whites *baas;* but I just figured it was okay when they weren't around, and circumstances demanded it – compromise, compromise, comrades. When the other guys weren't around you'd be a fool when you didn't have your *dompas* with you not to say baas to a furious white cop jangling his chrome handcuffs between your eyes while holding a baton in the other hand. Okay? So Tarr dispatched me and my friends and some strangers to the Neave plant for medical examination.

A Ford station wagon, called a company bus, disgorged us outside the medical offices at the Neave plant. Two of the guys and I were fresh from the Lovedale teacher training institute in Alice. The fourth guy, Richman, had been suspended in the final year of his BA degree studies at Fort Hare. Soon I was next to Richman, Totoma, Sdima and Dopla, all standing naked before two well-built white guys in white doctor coats – we were as *kaalgat* as a bunch of peeled bananas. The two orderlies circled us slowly, examining with their eyes, looking too uncomfortably closely at our penises as though they detected some strangeness. One of them suddenly came to a stop just behind Richman and pointed at an old wound on his shoulder:

'What happened here?' he barked, opening his mouth for the first time.

'I got stabbed by my father,' Richman answered straight faced.

I turned to look at him, stunned by his spectacular lie. And then, beside myself, I just fell on my knees with laughter. The white guy was far from amused:

'You laugh like that again you'll be out of here very fast!' The man was scowling and flushed red with irritation.

I got back on my feet, almost hating myself for losing control like that. I mean, can you imagine Richman's father actually stabbing him? Look, the old guy was a knobkierie type. Hard as I tried, I couldn't form a mental picture of the old man chasing my friend with a knife in his hand. I suddenly remembered the ancient knobkierie wound on the back of my head – a present from Bhele, the girls' hostel nightwatchman at Lovedale. But I'm not discussing that now.

'What happened?' insisted the medico, apparently enjoying the taste of that lie, and full of fatherly sympathy for the suddenly teary-eyed, foxy one standing next to me. MaRichie then expanded his story to include his having beaten up his sister which led to the stabbing. Man, it was so creative I genuinely envied him.

Luckily we all passed the medical test and the technical induction and then moved on to the personnel department. One of the officers, a Coloured guy, I think by the name of Heilbron, when he learnt of my teaching qualification, told me he also had one. He conferred with his colleague and decided to assign me to the *Material Handling, Unboxing* section at Struandale where the Cortina sedan and pickup truck were built. He started me at fifty-nine cents per hour, three cents more than the other guys.

I reported to Deon Vermaak, the foreman, who engaged me as a line-feeder.

'Silly-bee," he said (that's how most whites pronounce my surname), 'you'll be feeding Trim 1, paint-shop and the body-shop.'

'Yes sir.'

I could feel my heart do little somersaults of joy on account of the difference between pulling the kind of trolley standing before me, and off-loading a bloody goods train. Hell, I didn't even have to pull the trolley all the way to body-shop and the paint-shop. I parked it in Trim 1 and carried a couple of small boxes of grease caps to paint-shop and plugs and floor sound-deadeners to the body-shop. And on top of it I got to wear a blue dustcoat instead of greasy overalls like those of assembly line operators!

Now sound-deadeners were part of standard Luxury Décor Options for the most expensive model – LDO's. The assembly line was marked with station numbers. Car-body shells were hoisted over from the paint-shop to Trim 1 where they were fitted with door handles, window winders, channels, heater boxes etc. I learnt quickly; I got to know every nook and every part that went into it, every station and every part number, my mind working like a camera. But a negative consequence was that I soon sensed the envy and resentment of some of the assembly line operators; one guy even sneered and called me a pretty boy with a soft job. I simply disregarded them and did my job. When they complained of a stock shortage I took note and informed the line store-man or went myself to check at *Unboxing* for the part. I could understand the envy of the operator – he was lower than me in the value chain, only the janitor was less than him; I was placed between the store-man and the foreman, who was lower than the general foreman, who in turn was lower than the superintendent, who reported to the manager. It goes without saying that all positions above mine, with the exception of foreman, were reserved for whites.

A soft job? I slaved and sweated though perhaps less than the body-shop men in their safety goggles, leather aprons and filthy overalls, or the paint-shop men in grey space-suits and masks, or the helmeted guys at the Cross-feed-line area underneath car bodies, with hammers and air drills. My friend Totoma was one of the Cross-feed-line men; he sighed wearily and heavily each time I checked on him. Richman worked as an operator in the front suspension section and complained about a heavy bar he had to lift continually to place over the parts he had to drill holes into.

I pulled trolleys behind me, tottering like a cursed mule, fully laden with auto parts to be fitted onto those body shells by the same assembly line operators, some of whom hated me. I had to move fast, pulling and emptying those trolleys, and rush back to fetch yet another, then another filled to the hilt from the *Unboxing* station. The trips to the assembly line became slower and slower as the heaviness seemed to increase. Another result was that, as I pulled it behind me, the trolley often hit and hurt my heels. Added to that, I had to make way for the faster forklifts and tow-motors as we all hurried past the *Engine Stockade* with the daily stock of two hundred car engines, past *Hardware* where all the bolts, rivets, screws and nuts were kept, past *Receiving* where all local content landed before delivery to the lines, past *Clothing* where overalls were kept and exchanged – and finally passed *Quality,* where whites-only, often broke, quality control inspectors bent and pored over every suspect part.

The trip back was faster. The *Unboxing* guys were waiting for emptied trolleys. The foreman shouted at us line feeders 'Roer!' – move our backsides. 'Keep the ship moving!' Tarr, who was now a production general foreman, was wont to shout.

The atmosphere was ablaze with activity and sounds: air drills sang their own melody, forklifts, men, tow-motors forever droning, moving on the ground, hoists overhead. Bang, bang, hisses. Bang! Vigilance and caution were key necessities. There were dipping pits with black steel galvanizing chemicals and grey spray paints and the acrid reek of paint fumes in the paint-shop. Vigilance and caution: red skull and cross-bone emblems spelt DANGER. There were Drysys ovens resembling Nazi gas chambers, swallowing car body shells. You slipped and fell at your own risk: IOD; INJURED ON DUTY. All that for fifty-six cents per hour; take it or leave it. There were more men waiting at the gates to take the job from you.

South-west of the plant was the body-shop where it all began, where mallets banged on metal panels, steel frames and chassis, where air hoses spat hisses, and air guns puked blue-orange sparks into early morning factory air. Heavy green canvas and yellowish split-double plastic curtains cordoned off the spark-vomiting welding guns: a place of darkness corralled in mystery. The guns hung like fat alloy AK47's off a maze of tubes like hang-man ropes from above. I didn't look too closely. Just rushed in to deposit the sound-deadeners into their bin and swung around to dash out of that hell faster than a swallow in summer. The guys were un recognizable because of their outta-space outfits, like sci-fi movie characters, the sort one saw in Star Wars, or Batman: scary, unsmiling guys who looked so alike they were their own a nation. Legend had it that one *tjanjarag* overbearing boss got violently slapped across the face as he walked past the area one morning and failed to identify his assailant.

The body-shop men were the only ones in the entire plant who had the liberty to smoke their dagga openly without fear of reprisal from the bosses; no one dared enter their work space without safety gear, and they knew it. What boss would want to go find safety goggles and oily overalls and an odorous leather apron to don before going to challenge a crowd of red-eyed dagga-puffing labourers? And these were the most dedicated and fearless of men; like soldiers. They called that pungent odour of their narcotic, 'Chicken braai smell'.

Drunkenness, drug-taking, theft and fighting were all high up the list of offences one could be dismissed for. They didn't even get into an offender's record card – a guy got fired on the spot, and case closed. A record card was where they parked every other offence, such as late-coming, exchanging insults, or any other minor transgression. When it got full, it worked against any holder during retrenchments. Were we all scared of that damned card! The personnel office was built on a mezzanine floor over a section of Trim 2. We regularly watched offending employees being taken up by the relevant foreman to have their supposed offences recorded. The only other office on the mezzanine was for the Time Study guys, almost all African mathematics and statistics whiz kids.

The *Body shop* was known as a high staff turnover area, and so it helped to keep those guys happy and not unsettle the balance of things. So, one could imagine the sort of commotion and pandemonium that ensued when this new Jan Smuts look-alike white foreman took offence and grabbed a guy by the throat, calling him a kaffir – for some reason known to only the two of them.

Welding guns seldom ceased firing; when they did the entire plant went silent and everyone wanted to know the cause. Amazingly Jan Smuts got fired on the spot. And the plant restarted and rumbled on incessantly as usual. To me this was a first in the land of apartheid: firing a white guy and leaving a black one behind! It was almost the first wild-cat strike in the car industry, and thank God it was averted quickly. Steel mallets resumed their percussion on ISCOR metal frames and chassis and body panels. Each bang and every spark, every hiss behind every pop rivet fashioned a car body shell out of bits and lengths of ISCOR steel. Those units were to be spray painted in colours pre-ordered by moneyed owners waiting eagerly to take possession and ride. All that pride began here beyond yellow lines painted on the cement floor, demarcating safe and unsafe areas, smoking and non-smoking areas, green squares and red squares. Sweat, sweat, sweat, turned into cars, turning into profits for bosses and unknown shareholders smoking cigars and quaffing whisky in America: *America, America the Beautiful*, at home I listened to Ray Charles singing that song, and then Billy Preston sang: '*My country 'tis of thee*' and I so wished to see such a bountiful country.

And true to that image, Ford was the best paying company in town – an American firm with Medical Aid and pension fund. Workers qualified for false teeth within a couple of weeks, shiny Amariva safety shoes, and received a company ID with a photograph the same day. A job with a name: Line feeder, or janitor. Job names or descriptions were unheard of in most other local factories. And there was a canteen, too, offering subsidized hot meals displayed on a menu. From Monday to Friday, a different meal was served each day – and I'm not talking mageu and magwinya, and chicken walky-talkies here, no. I mean spaghetti bolognaise on Monday, grilled steak or mutton on Tuesday and Wednesday with yellow rice and two veggies, roast chicken quarter leg – or the upper part with breast and wing, my favourite, rice and roast potato on Thursday, and fried or pickled fish or grilled pork chops on Friday, all prepared by a qualified chef and cooks in starched white hoods, jackets and aprons.

Early Thursday mornings some guys quacked loudly and shouted, 'Ingaba-ngaba!' – sea-gull. Others laughed out loud in response, know-

112

ing it was roast chicken day. I was even prepared to work weekends just for the meals which were always followed up with dessert of either vanilla ice-cream, chocolate mousse, pudding or custard and jelly. Restaurant stuff – even though I'd never been inside one; restaurants were for whites only. There was no apartheid in the food but there was apartheid in the canteen seating. All that canteen fare had to be enjoyed separately from the white employees who wanted no goddamn view of kaffirs while having their meals. Africans were partitioned off out of sight in their own section. And, of course, even the toilets and the locker rooms were separated according to skin colour. But needless to say, this was the case everywhere so it shouldn't surprise that guys were begging to come to Ford and be exploited; real happy to be in and exploited. And it goes without saying that it was very hard to leave once one was in – as hard as leaving a beautiful, sexy woman.

Now Friday was pay day. Shebeen queens scrubbed and dusted their hovels and chased the *tsararas* (won't-works) out of their joints in anticipation of our visits: we were real men with false teeth and company ID's with photographs and job titles: janitors, forklift drivers, material handlers. Those were big names in the townships; men with pay-slips. One easily got laid by telling a girl: I'm a janitor, baby. Payslips were mostly unheard of in places outside our company. Some guys were still known to be paid out of their bosses' wallets or back pockets; the very lucky few got paid in envelopes with pay details written by hand in pencil. And their bosses *moered* them and called them kaffirs and *bobbejane,* or even black bastards. Not at Ford: at least, not after that Jan Smuts look-alike incident.

Strike? Oh no, that line could not be crossed. To go on strike was to risk going to prison. It was illegal. The bosses had committees with their workers called Liason Committees, chaired by the boss himself, see? If one had something nasty to say about the company, one had to say it directly to the boss.

'You black bastard, I'll kick you out of that fucking door right now!' A very irate boss might say if you offended him. It usually just often ended there.

I got to hear that threat quite often, and often not knowing for what reason, from important looking white men who weren't even my own bosses. I got to be called 'Engelse man' because of my sin of speaking English far better than Afrikaans. There was this line store-man, Els, on Trim 1 who wouldn't have me work overtime with him because of the constant transgression of my English speech. Of course, he had no idea how fluent I was in that home language of his: I'd just completed five years of learning Beginsels van Onderwys, Skool Organisasie, Metode vir die Onderrig van die Amptelike Tale, Taalkunde, Aardrykskunde, and a whole lot of other shit he'd never even heard of with his own Afrikaner ears. When the kids burnt down schools in '76 rejecting that nonsense, I'd already grown fat from imbibing it all.

'Nee, Engelsman, geen overtime vir jou nie – gat huis toe!'

Fok hom; I went home.

He could give that overtime to his garden-boy/kitchen maid Afrikaans-speaking bastards for all I cared. Els was new in that job, having just replaced a nicer white guy called Nel, who left to study further and become a marine biologist in Cape Town. Els himself was later replaced by a black guy, Zim Duna, when he, just like Joy Lolly, couldn't cope.

The money was good anyway, even without Els' overtime. The factory was like a vicious vixen with an acid tongue; beautiful with a great body and melon titties and super-duper sex to offer, you know, the tough type it's best to turn your back on and leave. You knew there were many other guys eyeing her, waiting for you to let her slip out of your grasp before they waded in unannounced. Ford was that kind of bitch. Good food I didn't get to eat at home I only ate there. What, with medical aid, pension fund, leave, holiday pay, and outside in the shebeens, with jazz and Soul music blaring, the groupies tossing themselves at us.

I listened to Stanley Turrentine and Shirley Scott, Jimmy Smith, David "Fathead" Newman, Gene Ammons, Miles Davis and John Coltrane, and many others. Avant-garde jazz had landed with a giant bang in New Brighton in the form of the Jazz Crusaders, Bob James, Chick Corea, Stanley Clarke. I wore clothes labelled "Made in America". The shoes too came from the States: canvas shoes, Keds, PF's, BF Goodridges, and shiny moccasins and brogues or semi-brogues, Florsheims, Nunn Bushes, my favourites – Edwin Clapps, and much more. Only moegoes didn't dress that way. Arrow shirts and Monatic Viyellas were the only shirts to wear. Underwear was either BVD or Fruit-of-the-loom. Even headgear was American, Stetsons or Borsalino hats or ten gallon berets, Kangols, or one or eight piece Ayres and Smith caps.

If I didn't find that stuff in the local stores I ordered directly from Joburg stores: Kays, Kotzen, Skipper Bar, PAMO, and others. Mail order was fast, efficient and prompt; no one in the post office stole my mail. The kit was called 'mngca Jewish' because only Jewish store owners knew how to dress us; they got style, man. In Port Elizabeth I bought from Rubins, Trouser House, Romens and Schultz's. Dan Watson came late into the picture with the Watson brothers choosing to defy apartheid and play rugby with our guys in Zwide. I met Moki Cekisani when he worked for Hot Spur Clothing; he was a fearless Black Consciousness man who boldly displayed political posters on the doors of his Volvo. He later lost his hearing to Special Branch cops' punches.

We were too dumb to see all that American Ford money flowing back to America. We were competing with clothes and winning over girls from one another: The Arrow Gents, Bostonians, and Crusaders. There were no fisticuffs or stabbings; it was all fair and peaceful.

I gave my weekly wages to my mother, Sissy, every second week. She encouraged me to save for further studies and buy new clothes for changing out of my *ikrwala* outfit as planned. I opened a savings account with Standard Bank at Berry's Corner: got a bank book, bank cards had not been invented yet.

"Sissy, I spoke to bra Mandlomzi to come fit bedroom doors," I told her.

Mandlomzi was a carpenter who lived in Connacher Street, two streets away from us. Our City council-rented house never had bedroom doors. I bought a new meranti-wood front door to get rid of the green-painted council one. Mandlomzi fitted it and the bedroom ones, and additional wall panelling, changing the way our dining-room looked. That old picture of Jesus and his disciples at a long dining table, with arches behind them exposing blue skies, had to go. It'd been there since I was a bungling toddler. I bought a new three piece brown, buttoned leatherette lounge suit. Sissy was ecstatic with happiness.

"Dogs I raised, and never abandoned, give me fuckall,"complained Dad bitterly. I paid him no attention.

My elder brother Dee, looked at him in amazement and then back at me, shaking his head from side to side:

"Did you hear what he's just said? So he did actually think about deserting us, would you believe it?"

On weekends I toured the shebeens nightly, getting home around 2am Sunday and Monday mornings, pissed, and often with a girl I danced with in one of the joints. I slept in the outside tool-shed when I brought a girl with me. I hijacked the shed from my three younger brothers who hated me for it in silent protest.

Before the end of that first year at Ford, I was driving my own car, a VW Beetle. Now, look, some guys, my own father included (may his soul rest in peace), had toiled for ages for peanuts without a glimmer of hope of ever owning even a bumper of a push-push skorokoro, or donkey cart. And here I was, a fresh faced *ikrwala* coming home smiling behind the wheel of my own *voongoo* as we called cars in New Brighton.

Father came outside on hearing the hullabaloo, circled the white bug slowly with a serious frown on his face, and came to a final stop outside the driver's door. Then, stooping lower, checking the dashboard through the open window, he placed his left hand on the roof, tapping his fingers, before declaring a verdict: '*Ngumnqund'wemoto lo!*' – 'This is an arsehole of a car'. I didn't mind. It tempted me to ask: '*Iphi eyakho?*' – 'where's yours?' I remembered that he had a dream since the time we were toddlers – my brother, my sister and I – when he would bring home a brochure with a bevy of shiny, well-fed horses draped with colourful sashes. This was around June each year. We kids each had to indicate which horse we each fancied to win the Durban July race. His dream was to win what he called 'eighty pounds to start my own home café business'. It failed to materialize.

The fact was none of us could ever hope to afford the Ford cars we built: '*Neenyosi zibenza zibutya*' – 'Even bees get to eat some of the honey they produce!' moaned the workers. It was a constant complaint that fell on deaf boss ears; I don't think it ever even reached their ears. I sweated for my fifty-nine cents each hour and bought clothes and LP's from America. The cars we built must have been heading for the rich provinces and cities of the Transvaal, Western Cape, Free State and Natal because I seldom saw them on local roads.

One morning I was returning from off-loading a trolley when I found Vermaak next to his desk, talking to a process engineer, Lombard, about a part which Vermaak appeared to have no knowledge of. I reeled off the part number and Trim 1 location of that grommet as I passed them. They rushed after me, wanting me to repeat what I'd just said. I did, and offered to lead them to the part located at station 27, Trim 1. That little episode earned me promotion to the position of Unboxing checker and an extra five cents per hour. All I did then was open and check the pack-slip of every crate shipped to the plant from Dagenham, UK, tick every part my packers picked and told them which trolley to load it on. Some parts were headed for Trim 1, others for Trim 2, or Mainline. I was now released from pulling trolleys behind me like a befucked donkey. I worked with a pen and a clip-board and earned better.

One of the trolley loaders named Bobbie had this sickening habit of disappearing for a while, leaving the other three sweating alone under tremendous pressure. I suggested that the matter be reported to Vermaak in the presence of the fellow so that he may defend himself.

'You see, Bobbie, you can't accuse us of selling you out; we are reporting you because we are not happy with how you treat us; there's a big difference,' said Veza, one of the guys. So we approached Vermaak and told on Bobbie in his presence.

Selling out was a no-no those days of Black Consciousness; we were schooled never ever to sell a brother.

'Bobbie? Why? Why?' asked Vermaak, visibly angry.

'Hulle's maal; hulle like nie vir my nie!' – 'They are mad; they don't like me.'

Then he opened and closed his small bird-like mouth. He was lean, tall and non-aggressive.

I was shocked by the lie, but the other guys thought it was funny as they laughed and shook their heads sideways and moved away from him and the foreman. How could he say we didn't like him when he was our friend?

That afternoon Bob invited us to help him build a 'coffin'. He was always at his happiest when he built those miniature coffins for smuggling car jacks and batteries out of the plant. He was the quiet type, kept to himself, whistling under his breath like somebody with lots on his mind.

At five in the afternoon, after work, I passed security at the gate with Bob and Veza, carrying the coffin sandwiched and cocooned within a bundle of scrap wood; I was in front with the gate pass, the white security guy checked and stamped it. This was how I got the overtime dough Els was stingy with, thanks to Bobbie. '*Siyazibhatala*' – 'We are reimbursing ourselves' – was how we justified the thefts. Apartheid economy was dual: African economy redistributing from the white economy. But then who had made the wealth in the first place?

Mr Mothlalogo

Itumeleng Molefi

You know class.

The surging waves of energy subsided as he calmed down.
The other day my beautiful wife and I were doing some shopping at the supermarket.

Suddenly that glow swept over his face. His eyes flicked with a reassured, all-knowing flame; his smile broadening, his entire face alight. He could not see it, but he knew it was there. He could feel it.

There I was, with my beautiful wife walking next to me, you know, pushing the trolley, with the shopping list and all. Then, I saw this man looking at me and I immediately became concerned.

He quickly got into character, a tendency of his when he told one of his stories, and a look of deep concern fell upon his face

Not only was this man more handsome than me –

There were the usual giggles.

– but you could see in his eyes that he was sharper, more intelligent.

More giggles.

Now, I was very concerned. After all, I've always known that I am the best. The best there is, was and ever will be! So after I saw this man, I was . . . I was really, really down. And you know, my wife noticed and asked me what was wrong. Of course, I didn't tell her because she might just leave me for this brilliant man. And, you know, when we left the supermarket –

The concern was wiped away by a sense of reform.

I came to a decision. I wanted to shake this man's hand and let him know that he really was the best! So I went back into the supermarket to look for him; back to the spot where I had seen him. And there he was, standing there, more handsome, more brilliant than ever.

Disapproving, questioning laughter.

And then as I walked towards him and noticed that he was walking towards me as well.

A disorientated look.

In fact, I actually noticed that he was wearing the same pants as me and the same shirt. And I just stood there for a while, looking at him, and he looking back at me. Then, as I blinked, he blinked; when I raised my shoulders, he raised his as well. And when I smiled, he smiled back. And I asked myself: 'Why is this man imitating me?' And you know what, I realised I was actually looking into a mirror.

The look on his face grew from an incredulous one to one of stupidity, to one of sheer glee. He flashed his reassured, confident smile as everyone, including himself, laughed at his anecdote. Just as he had known they would. A magnificent performance.

So now I know that there is no one like me; the undisputed, the best of the best! The results show it. Only A's and B's come from this class, A's and B's. And I expect no different tomorrow. You know why? Because I am the best there is! The most handsome man you'll ever come across –

The incredulous laughter.

– the most brilliant, most intelligent there is! Don't look at me like that my girl – To one of his victims. He calmed down for a short while. An old joke, but still effective.

– I'm a married man.

Everyone was in a fit of laughter and he looked at them with his confident smile, a bold smile; a cockiness almost. But his was warranted. He knew that he was the best mathematics teacher, in fact, the best teacher, any of them would ever have.

He looked around: everyone was filled with energy and enthusiasm, despite the tiring, summer heat. The same energy that he always exuded for all his students to absorb – something all his colleagues failed to do.

Now, listen to me, grade twelves.

The laughter died down.

I've decided not to include derivatives in tomorrow's calculus test. So there is no need to stress about it.

A loud siren rang in the distance; the end of the school day. Noise erupted as everyone hastily packed away their stationary. Not so in Motlalogo's class. They all awaited his signal. He always made them wait in anticipation.

Good afternoon class.

He smiled.

Good afternoon, sir!

You may leave.

A deafening noise of tables and chairs being shuffled filled the classroom as everyone packed up and had their fill of chatter as they left the classroom.

Walsh.

He looked up from his textbook. It was Michael.

Did you finish going through those scripts I gave you yesterday?

He sat down next to him.

Yes, actually I did.

Scratched his head.

But they're in my classroom and I've already locked up. Can I give them to you tomorrow?

Sure, that's fine.

Great. Here's the test for tomorrow. I'll need at least forty copies by first period.

Okay, no problem.

Thanks. Shall we get going?

No . . . um . . . actually somebody's picking me up today.

Alright, see you tomorrow then.

He got up and headed for the parking lot. He should have asked Michael who was picking him up. Probably another girlfriend. Honestly, even at his age he was still dating. He and Michael had been friends since college, half their lives. Michael envied him for his energy and unique teaching style but he thought Michael was being ridiculous. There was nothing to be envious of. He could be just as good; he was just teaching a very dreary subject – biology. Plus he had so many other administrative responsibilities – making photocopies, recycling textbooks, organizing first aid, amongst others. He couldn't just focus on his students. Hell, he lacked focus in many other areas of his life. That was what had caused his divorce. Michael could have saved his marriage but it would have cost him what he loved most—teaching. Of course, he, Motlalogo, had had no choice when it had come to the end of his marriage.

Bye, Mrs Clarke.

He drove through the main gate. He didn't like that woman much. She was the reason why everyone, including his students, knew about what had happened.

Keitumetse, his wife, had also been a teacher. The best English teacher there was. She could take anyone who had never been acquainted with the language and within a few months have them reading the likes of Shakespeare and Faulkner. However, she had had an illicit affair with one of her students; then given up the profession after she'd confessed to Motlalogo. This had happened after she'd found out she was pregnant with the boy, Keith's child.

It had been a hard blow to take, but he had taken it and lived through it. That was how strong he was. They had had a perfect marriage; one of friendship, companionship and deep, affectionate love. But one thing had always been missing, something they could never resolve. They had tried for many years to have children but later found out that he was infertile. And then to have someone else, a mere boy, give his

123

wife the one thing she wanted most; that had been almost too much to bear.

They had divorced, of course, and she had raised the child (in shame) with the help of the boy's parents. But he'd found that he could not live without her; no matter what she had done to him. And so, they had reconciled and were now living together again. He had had no idea that he was capable of such forgiveness.

Almost home. He drove into the street and was met by the most peculiar sight.

Was that . . . was that Keith he saw closing the gate behind him? The gate to his yard!

He couldn't believe it.

How could she?

How dare she! How dare she do this to him -- again! He pulled the car over in front of the garage in a fit of rage.

Sn*iff* . . . He breathed in deeply. Another deep breathe and he left the car.

He found her in the kitchen, cooking. Perfectly fine, except, she never did cook, he usually did. Just like the last time.

Hello Keitu.

He remained at the door leading to the lounge.

Hello, sweetheart.

How was your day?

It was okay. She did not look at him.

Keitu, I just saw someone leaving here; who was it?

Oh nobody. Just Mrs Thibedi's grandson.

Really? And what did he want?

Well . . . um . . .

Hesitation. Just as before.

Keitu.

A deep breathe.

Look at me.

She turned round with her warm brown eyes and shoulder-length, dreadlocked hair. She looked as young as ever.

Yes, dear.

Don't lie to me!

Walsh, what's going on?

That person I saw . . . it was Keith, wasn't it?

He rounded the table, moving to her side.

No.

She frantically shook her head.

It wasn't him.

Are you sleeping with him again?

He was on the verge of tears.

Are you sleeping with him again?

No, Walsh, I swear.

Don't lie . . . to me . . .

He raised his hand . . .

Walsh, no, please !

He couldn't . . . He still loved her . . . couldn't do it . . .

Sleeping with him again . . .

Her face was bleeding.

She was . . . he loved her . . . *in my bed* . . . everything . . . but how could she! . . . he loved her . . . she was doing this to him . . . she lied . . . again.

You know class.

He was calm once more.

I can't remember when exactly, but my beautiful wife and I were travelling to Bloemfontein by train once and we ended up in this compartment with these two ladies sitting alone on each of the two benches. So my wife sat next to one and I sat next to the other. As soon as she saw me, the one sitting next to my wife left the compartment and came back after a few minutes and sat down on my other side. So now, I was in the middle of these two ladies.

A baffled look crossed his face. There were sceptical giggles, just as he had expected.

So now we arrive in Bloem and when we get off the train, one of these ladies walks up to my wife and says: 'You know, you are such a lucky woman to have this man.'

Roars of laughter as he smiled confidently.

And the other lady comes up to me and tells me: 'I am never going to wash my left side that touched you today.'

Even more laughter, as he shook his head, playing the innocent victim of his good looks.

Anyway, class.

He was overwhelmed with energy as the laughter slowly died.

Now I want you to close your eyes and visualise what you are going to get today. I want you to see it!

Absolute silence as everyone closed their eyes.

Do you see it?!

Yes, sir!

I can't hear you. Do you see that A?!

Yes, sir!!!

Their roaring voices sounded as if they had the ability – like little children usually do – to do anything. A feeling he always gave them.

Good, now let's begin.

He started handing out the question papers.

Motlalogo could not believe this was happening to him again. All emotional strength had forsaken him. How could Keitumetse do this to him – again!

He sat behind his desk, trying to mark that morning's tests. But he just sat there, twiddling the red pen between his fingers. Then, the unthinkable happened. There he stood, in the middle of the door, looking at him.

What the hell are you doing here?

I'm here to tell you that I'm taking her away.

Keith slowly walked into the classroom.

No, you can't do that. She won't leave me for you!

Do you really think she loves you?

Yo! What do you know about love?

Enough to know that she doesn't love you anymore. There might have been a time, very long ago, when she did, but she doesn't now.

Get out!

Not before I say what I came here to say. You know what I think? I think she never really did love you. I think she would have left you even if I had never come into the picture. You could never please her the way I did –

Shut up!

You couldn't give her a child! I did! You're not a real man! You couldn't conceive children and you expect your wife to love you?

Shut up!

Motlalogo moved quickly. In no time he had moved from the back of his desk towards Keith. He threw punch after punch at him, but he ducked each time. As he threw blow after blow at Keith without hitting him, the boy continued to taunt him.

You're pathetic! Look at you, you can't even hit me! You're like a little child.

You're pathetic Walsh Motlalogo! You've always been pathetic.

GET OUT! NOW!

He buried his face in his hands and cried out loud. He could not believe the guts of that little kid! How could he come here? And how could he just break down in front of him like that? He despised himself for it.

Maybe his wife really was leaving him. Maybe she never had loved him. Maybe his marriage . . . maybe his whole life . . . was one big lie. Maybe he really was pathetic.

Walsh.

It was Michael.

Walsh, are you okay?

No, Michael.

He looked up at his friend. He probably did look pathetic.

What's wrong?

Remember Keith Richards?

The boy that Keitu . . .

He was here just a minute ago.

Michael looked shocked.

No! The nerve of that boy . . .

And . . . and he says he's taking Keit' away.

Where to?

I don't know, Michael. I mean he was at the house yesterday . . . and Keitu says he wasn't . . . She lied, Michael, she lied.

Michael looked even more confused.

Whoa! What house?

Our house. I went home yesterday and saw him leaving the house.

Keitu lives with you?

Yes, Michael . . . And I don't know what to do . . . I can't live without her, Michael . . . Then I hit her Michael . . . I don't know what came over me . . . Now she probably does want to leave me.

Walsh, what are you talking about? You and Keitu have been divorced for three years now.

We've been back together for six months now.

Six months! You never –

Michael gave him an incredulous look. Everything started to make sense.

– you never told me that . . . look . . . I have to go to the office quickly. It's urgent. I'll bring you back some water or something.

Michael, I just don't know what to do.

I'll be back.

Michael got up and closed the door behind him.

Is this what his life was going to be like now? Is this what he was to amount to? Nothing was certain anymore. He felt, for the first time, like he was going nowhere. Absolutely nowhere. It left him calm and serene almost, but he knew it wasn't what it would feel like in the end.

Michael returned with a tall glass of water.

Walsh.

He looked uncertain.

I just checked the visitors' register. And . . . and Keith's name wasn't on it.

That's impossible!

I even checked with Mrs. Clarke, Walsh. She said that there was only one visitor today; for Tebogo.

No, no, no. That's impossible. Unless . . . unless security is falling apart at this place.

He got up, determined to check for himself.

There it was; in black and white. As plain as plain could be. Only one visitor. 'Andrea for Tebogo on personal business.'

Mrs. Clarke, are you sure that there wasn't anyone else?

Yes, Mr. Motlalogo, I told Mr. Green the same thing.

No, that's impossible, Mrs. Clarke. A boy came to see me not more than ten minutes ago and you're telling me that he got in without signing the register.

Mr. Motlalogo, I'm telling you again, sir, there was no boy.

So what, I was seeing things?

Mrs. Clarke looked at him silently. 'Yes, you were,' her eyes were saying.

Walsh!

He turned around. There was the principal, Lesedi Phiri, with Michael just behind her.

Can I see you in my office for a moment, please?

He followed her pass Mrs. Clarke's desk into the office and closed the door behind him.

Please have a seat.

They sat down. She had this strange look on her face; deep concern.

Walsh –

She took a deep breathe.

– have you been taking your medication?

FACE THE NATION

Africa Boso

The day Reggie Fortuin joined the chocolate factory, his overzealous radicalism and showmanship was very pronounced. He outrightly rejected the standard, factory-issue uniform that was forced on all new recruits and then deducted from their meagre weekly wages over a period of six months. The major fault with the outfit, Reggie protested to all who cared to listen to his shrill voice, was that it was of Chinese origin. His vociferous solo protest against the Asian-produced livery had nothing to do with the fact that it was supposed to be freely dished out to all new recruits – as the labour laws of his beloved republic explicitly stated. Moreover, his stern rejection of the creasy, off-white overalls and matching rubber boots had nothing to do with the Umbrella Union's economic call for all sectors to create and save jobs for locals by buying and consuming local products. *No imports, buy local,* the union leadership had demanded during their recent three-day strike – a prolonged, no-work-no-pay mass action aimed at saving jobs.

Reggie's only gripe was that these working clothes were 'cheap imitations that lack class' and hence unsuitable for the health and status of fashion-conscious workers like him. *Fong kongs,* he labelled them. To work productively, he would need to wear his designer Guess jeans, Levi's T-shirt and Converse takkies. Yes, would you believe it, this is what he unblinkingly told the baffled Chinese factory proprietors. Man, they were caught off-guard – they had never experienced such open revolt. Up until this moment they had enjoyed such a docile workforce – men and women worked to the bone for long hours while locked inside the chocolate sweatshop.

Reggie was our new messiah and we rejoiced but only inwardly because showing open solidarity meant summary dismissal. And so we let our fat-clogged hearts jump a few steps in *toyi-toyi* to celebrate our militant hero. Viva comrade Reggie! But alas, this was the first and last time we saw our fashion-minded revolutionary in the oriental business hub. The fiery objector was declared *posin* (read poison) by our Chinese employers and immediately whisked off the premises by baton-wielding guards with oversized uniforms.

The next time we saw zealous Reggie was on prime time national television and on none other a programme than *Face the Nation,* the flagship current affairs programme of our cash-strapped public broadcaster.

An in-studio guest of the award-winning, tough-grilling, Margaret Thatcher-look-alike interviewer with a fake American accent dragged over a heavy Afrikaans voice, Reggie still had the fighting flames of defiance that scorched our chocolate factory bosses five years back. And the impeccable dress sense was still there. He looked deft in an expensive black striped Italian suit with a designer label still intact in the breast pocket of his jacket. The Armani suit was matched with a tomato-red shirt-and-tie combo. His pointy Black Economic Empowerment ostrich leather shoes protruded under the space-age designer interview glass table. The tiny square-shaped academic spectacles completed the intended intellectual look.

Our long-lost, one-minute, fashion unionist was looking straight at (or through) Ms Journalist of the Year's bulbous and sagging face while she rambled through a lengthy introduction. Baggy eyes fixed on the autocue, the Griller rattled.

'Our guest tonight, dear viewers, is the famous or infamous (to some) General Secretary of the Neglected Workers' Union, Mr Reggie Fortuin. In recent weeks Mr Fortuin has made national headlines but not for his union activities – he has been accused of fathering illegitimate twins with his married office administrator. Union members have also laid corruption charges against him for allegedly using their hard-earned pension money to maintain this tryst. The lady in question has confessed to her husband that Mr Fortuin is, indeed, the father of her month-old twins. Mr Fortuin has kept quiet throughout this controversy. But as your number one news breakers, we are pleased to be the first to bring him to 'Face the Nation', so to speak. Good evening to you, Mr Fortuin. Sir, you have been in the news for all the wrong reasons. Please give us your side of this sordid story.'

The fiery one adjusted his spectacles and cleared his throat before spewing flames.

'Firstly, I must categorically restate our Movement's dissatisfaction with the bias of this broadcaster in general and your programme in particular. For a while now, we have carefully watched you and your cohorts wage a concerted war against our leadership by indirectly branding us a bunch of corrupt, power-hungry and selfish leaders. While using our people's taxes, you have continued on your counter-revolutionary path of vilification and slander. We know whose dirty agenda you are pushing. Our people know who their legitimate leaders are and will never be confused by . . .'

Now heating up but unfazed by what she saw as a misdirected tirade, the Griller interjected.

'With due respect Mr Fortuin, stop looking for scapegoats and answer the questions honestly. Is it the national broadcaster which is calling for your immediate resignation for alleged misappropriation of union funds? Is it me who is alleging an extra marital affair which has produced the twins you are now denying?'

Our fashionista unionist shifted forward and nervously adjusted himself on the chair which seemed to be laden with burning coals. Nearly spilling his uncapped bottle of mineral water, he pummelled the table to drive his point across.

'Even if you were the last woman on earth, I would never dream of alleging an affair with you. You are way, way out of my league. Look at your . . .'

'So your secretary was in your league then? Is that why you stole union money to fly her first class and book her in five-star exotic hotels? Are you prepared to pay maintenance for the infants you have...'

'For starters, let me educate you – and free of charge. The few disgruntled workers you have been harping on, are paid agent provocateurs like you, faceless rats who are used as pawns to derail and reverse the political gains that this country has attained through the blood of our fallen heroes. May their brave souls rest in peace! But how can these braves rest when imbeciles like you are constantly spitting reactionary bile on the fruits of their hard-earned toil? Now I must warn you and others of your ilk, we will not be derailed from our set revolutionary agenda to improve the lot of our people. Those who think they will drag us back to the bondage of the past are delusional and they will never succeed. Our people know who their legitimate leaders are and . . .'

'And the woman?'

'What . . . what woman?'

'The alleged mother of your illegitimate twins, your married

134

roll-on, your concubine Mr Fortuin. Is she part of a plot to derail your revolutionary agenda? Is she also a plant sent to tarnish your impeccable struggle credentials?'

'As you say, these are *allegations,* unfounded allegations. Basically a figment of your small imagination, and I am not prepared to sit here and entertain rumour-mongering. There are important developmental issues that need my attention. If you have forgotten, many of us sacrificed their lives for a free country that guarantees every citizen the right to be presumed innocent until proven . . .'

'Mr Fortuin, are you telling the nation that these two innocent and starving children are not yours? If so, are you prepared to commit before these watching millions that you are prepared to undergo a DNA test to prove once and for all who is the father of these innocent babies? We are prepared to pay for such tests and any other related costs.'

The Griller was now smelling the sweet blood of her cornered prey. In response, with a forced grin patched on his now dry lips, our worker leader let loose his remaining kick.

'Take your dirty money to your favourite charity! I am sure your guilty liberal conscience will feel better after that. I am where I am because I have always paid my way. I have never lived on handouts!'

The jugular was now wide open for taking and the Griller could not wait to pounce.

'Mr Fortuin, are you a man enough to accept and pay maintenance for your children, your own blood? Are you prepared to look their mother in the eye and tell her you are sorry for breaking her 15 year-old marriage? Can you face your aggrieved union members and tell them their pension money is still safely banked, and that those who say otherwise are a bunch of commissioned liars who are bent on tarnishing your good reputation? After the break, we will talk to Ms Sesi Madumetja, the mother of the disputed twins. She will help us get answers to all these and other sticky questions. Stay tuned, there is more dirt, sorry, more juice, to come.'

The Griller faced the camera and winked at the glued nation. Fortuin fidgeted with the half-empty water bottle while writing copious notes. The studio cameras *froze* to give space to a low-budget advertisement selling the latest brand of disposable infant nappies.

After a minute, the rainbow-coloured *Face the Nation* logo appeared

accompanied by the unoriginal signature tune to summon the programme's faithful back to their armchairs.

'Welcome back, dear viewers. It is with great regret that we cannot
continue with tonight's lively programme. Mr Fortuin has bolted out
of our studios threatening a lawsuit against the national broadcaster
for defaming his character. In short, our honourable guest could not
Face the Nation any longer. We sincerely regret the inconvenience but
your Chuck Norris movie repeat will start shortly as a filler. Good
viewing. Join us again tomorrow night. Thanks for your continued
support. And don't forget – only local is lekker . . .'

THE EYE OF THE STORM

(Edited excerpt from a fictionalised diary-memoir 'Composer at Large')

John Simon

Johannesburg: Thursday, 23 October 2008

Obsessed by a mad desire to find out how my music stands in relation to the musical world, particularly the one in South Africa, I find myself once more in Johannesburg.

Little did I realise when I visited the Music Rights Organisation in Braamfontein a few days ago that a physical storm would unleash itself upon me with consequences that would recall the ones my minx's metaphorical storm had caused years earlier.

As I sailed into my bureaucrat's office, with the kind of swaggering confidence I hadn't known for a long while, he looked up from his desk in bewilderment.

'Whatever's happened to you,' he cried mockingly, adding that he was stunned to find me turning up 'like a bad penny' (Hadn't Rodney Blackthorn used the same simile while I was in Durban?)

'You seem so much better than when you were here last time. Whatever's happened to you?' he mocked cruelly.

I couldn't help recalling how excited he'd become at the drag queen contest at the Skyline Bar in Hillbrow in 1994. The purple rings around his eyes were, of course, far less deep-set then than they are now. 'They're like tiny blue moons,' I mumbled to myself. My unexpected arrival caused him to suddenly become agitated and the whites of those oh-so-self-satisfied eyes started to roll about like nine pin balls. Out of the blue he mentioned that he would be retiring next week.

Chastened by the thought of losing him for good, I made my way back to Kensington, where I'm staying, through a cloud-laden Braamfontein, where the familiar street names awakened memories of far-off happier days. Shortly after a bus I'd boarded turned into Eloff Street, claps of thunder and flashes of lightning announced the arrival of a torrential downpour. As the sky turned black and the temperature inside the bus dropped dramatically, the windows misted over. As the rain pelted down, a ten minute walk from my onward connection, dozens of homeward-bound schoolchildren piled on board. They clambered upstairs, some standing on the staircase, others filling the downstairs aisle to bursting point. Their number grew until it had reached a hundred or so when I decided it would be best to alight from the bus, since I felt certain fate had ordained this to be my last day.

A terrible fear of being smothered, of being squashed to a pulp, overwhelmed me, as I pushed, squeezed and elbowed my way from the back of the bus's lower deck to the front, tripping over rucksacks and cases lying inconsiderately in the aisle. As I reached the exit, opposite to where the insouciant driver sat, I announced to the scholars my intention to alight and with a shove of my elbows bounced onto the street, getting thoroughly soaked as I passed familiar street names and buildings. As I hastened towards my onward connection, I could sense the inner city seething with rage: a fury was about to unleash itself at any moment in the guise of a demented monster's anger. It was only three o'clock, yet it seemed as if night had fallen on Johannesburg -the benighted city- as enormous drops of rain continued plummeting through air that now had an Arctic feel.

When I reached a set of traffic lights that weren't working I realised a power outage was in progress and could sense that pedestrians and drivers alike had been gripped by a storm-induced panic to leave the city as soon as possible. For no obvious reason, yet as if a pre-arranged signal had been given, the agony of long-suffering Johannesburg exploded into a cacophony of hooting revving cars, which seemed to want to coalesce as they jolted and jerked along, bumper to bumper, before some of them became gridlocked, while people jumped hither and thither and snaked their way between the lanes of vehicles in a desperate attempt to cross the street.

With a titanic effort I reached Pritchard Street, and, about to cross it, heard the frantic wailing of police sirens. I looked to my left, towards Doornfontein, and saw five gargantuan police vehicles, manned from first to last by immense intense policemen, attempting to carve a path between the chaotic jigsaw of cars.

Was I imagining all of this? I wanted to scream. My life seemed to be mirrored in the chaos that surrounded me on all sides. With a resolve amounting to insanity I stepped off the pavement and tried to squeeze between moving cars as I made my way across Pritchard Street. The moments lengthened and it seemed as if all the trauma I'd suffered in recent times was being relived amidst a multitude of demented drivers who were hell-bent on taking off into the night. For interminable seconds I knew I stood alone in the world: the eternal outsider, exhorting the traffic to stop. But the cars ignored me as I battled on.

Near Ghandi Square I found a number thirty-two bus waiting for me. Almost all of the faces on board seemed harassed, despondent ones; a bus bereft of joy. A schoolboy offered his seat to a dismal woman. I smiled at the youth and he smiled back -a warm, radiant, seductive smile. It seemed as if the sun had suddenly come out. Surely it was our *Capeness* that was connecting us? Did he go through this every day? I asked. Quite frequently, he replied resignedly. Did any child deserve to be subjected to such madness? I fretted.

The following day I learnt that the driver of a lorry had panicked when lightning struck the electric cables above him. He and his passenger had jumped out of the vehicle, leaving it to slither across the road before it hit an electricity sub-station. This had caused the blackout. The ever-resourceful criminal community had seized the opportunity to smash the windows of as many gridlocked vehicles as possible, making off with whatever they could grab.

The next morning my taxi driver suggested that the only way to overcome the problem would be to send in the army to 'clean up matters' in the centre of town.

STONE WALLS

Muthal Naidoo

It was early in the morning and Mynah Bird, standing in the tree position, felt her left foot begin to wobble; she couldn't keep her balance and began hopping around until forced to put her right foot down. She tried again but every time she got her right foot to her left knee, her left foot began to wobble and she had to give up.

And the little bird, knitting away on her shoulder, wouldn't shut up. I know why you can't do it today. Mynah wanted to throttle the bird. Instead she shoved the sole of her left foot over her right knee – balance on her right foot was always better – drew her hands, palms together, straight up over her head and into the tree position. She grinned. But then she fell right over.

The little bird, who had taken off just in time, shrieked with laughter. Break a leg. Break a leg.

Mynah gave up on the tree asana and bent over into the triangle. The little bird perched on her hip. You know what you must do.

What do you mean 'must'? I have a choice. Mynah baulked at the thought of any kind of coercion.

Oh yeah? At this rate you're going to need a good orthopaedic surgeon.

Mynah rubbing her hip was forced to agree. Okay, okay, okay.

You have to put your money where your mouth is.

Mynah was cursing. My foot, more likely. Why can't I just keep my damned eyes shut when I drive past all those guys on the corner looking up hopefully, asking for jobs? Damn them. They're the ones pushing me into this situation. I can't save the world. I'm a pensioner.

Back on her shoulder perch, the little bird was looking for a new ball of wool to attach to her knitting, Excuses. Excuses.

Mynah snapped back. Mind your own damn business.

That's what I'm doing. I wish you wouldn't swear so much.

And that prompted more swearing. You're just a bloody convention from the Middle Ages.

That's nonsense. In those days, both shoulders were occupied; there was a good guy, the one with wings, that's me, and a bad guy, the one with horns. We've done away with him. There never was need for a bad guy. In this case, you're it.

Mynah wasn't interested in this pseudo-religious mumbo-jumbo. She had lived alone for forty years and couldn't stand the constant nattering coming from the bird. So someone else in her house would drive her crazy and turn her into more of a boor than she already was.

And the bird was going on. You're selfish; that's your trouble. You never wanted a relationship because you can't compromise.

Oh, shut up. You sound like those TV programmes. Mynah was always irritated with the way conventional notions of women interfered with choices that professional women in TV dramas made.

You're such a hypocrite. Always pretending you care about the guys on street corners, but you always look away. You don't really want to know about their suffering. And all your guff about prisons! The little bird screeched with laughter. What extraordinary rubbish!

Mynah was a Senior Citizen but she prided herself on not being one who sat around waiting for others to organise her fun and cheer. Only old people wanted that. She was still full of beans and had chosen a project for herself; she was going to tear down prisons. They were quite useless institutions. They didn't eliminate crime; they only increased it. And she, Jeanne d' Arc of the twenty-first century, was going to get rid of them. The only problem was – she didn't have a plan. So, hoping to find an angle, she took to visiting a couple of women in the prison in town. Now one of them, Gansie, was out on parole. And Gansie was like the men on the street corners, only worse off; she'd lost her home, her family, her children and her community; they wanted nothing to do with her. When she came out, she was accommodated at a church-run women's shelter. That's where she remained for about a month until she found a job and could move out. She changed jobs a few times and eventually landed a job with the IRO (Institute for the Reintegration of Offenders) not far from where Mynah lived.

The bird stopped knitting to yell in her ear. You could help this unfortunate woman but you don't! Jeanne d' Arc indeed!

When Mynah visited Gansie at work, she complained about her situation. She lived in the northeast, had to take four buses a day to and from work in Mynah's area in the west, and still had long distances to walk. And she was scared; a tall, disreputable-looking man was stalking her. The week before, she had been so busy looking out for danger from behind, she didn't see it coming smack in front. A couple of men hanging out on the corner suddenly made a grab for her. She screamed, lashed out wildly, charged off, missed her footing where the pavement ended and fell into the street. Luckily, there were many people about; someone helped her up and others turned to deal with the miscreants but they had fled. Since then, she has walked to and from bus stops in a permanent state of fear.

The bird on Mynah's shoulder began squawking long and loud into her ear about Gansie's dreadful situation and when Mynah tried to grab her and twist her ethereal neck, she went into hysterical fits of laughter. *You can't get rid of me and until you do the right thing, you'll never be rid of me.*

But Mynah had lived alone for so long, she had become completely anti-social. *Would it be fair to offer Gansie my spare room? Living here would be torture for her.*

The bird, who always took her stand on the moral high ground, just sniffed. *Excuses! Excuses! It's time you lived like a normal person. Who gave you the right to so much freedom?*

Oh, shut up. Shut up. Okay, I'll do it. Anything to keep you quiet! But the step she was contemplating, terrified Mynah.

The bird knew it only too well. *Are you really going to let Gansie have your spare room?*

Drat the bird. Mynah tried to pull her off her shoulder but her fingers could never find anything substantial there. *I said I'd do it, didn't I? So I'll do it. I'll do it. And heaven help us all!*

You shouldn't expect help from upstairs. You don't believe. A perplexed frown suddenly appeared over Birdie's eyes, *So what am I doing here?* But she dismissed the thought.

A few days later, when Mynah broached the subject, she could see that Gansie was only too glad to accept her offer of accommodation. Mynah had seen the digs Gansie had moved into after she had found work. Completely makeshift; a tarted-up garage divided into a tiny bedroom leading into a space in which the toilet-shower was curtained off from the kitchen-dining room. *I can't believe that white people would offer such awful lodgings to anyone, but to another white person! And at a R1000 a month! Half her salary.*

The little bird looked up annoyed. She was working on a complicated cable pattern and Mynah's shock had made her drop a stitch. You think only Indians exploit people? Everybody does it. You should take a look at what goes on in all the townships.

Gansie moved in at the beginning of December. On her first night, a desperate banging on the front door woke Mynah up. She looked at her clock. It was one in the morning. She went to the front room and found Gansie struggling to unlock the door.

'What's wrong?'

'I can't breathe. I have to get out. I suffer from claustrophobia.'

'The key is in the door; just open it.' But Gansie turned helpless hazel eyes on her so Mynah opened the door and the security gate and Gansie flew out. Claustrophobia? After seven years in prison?

The little bird was adjusting her nightcap, which had fallen off in the rush. That's probably where she developed it.

So why have a panic attack here where the keys are always in the doors? This is not a prison.

Birdie yawned. Really? With security gates all over the place?

That should make her feel at home. Birdie didn't think that was funny. I don't care what you think; I say this is nostalgia for the real thing.

The next afternoon, Gansie was attacking the door again. 'I have to get out. I can't sit in here. Can I go and sit outside?'

Why is she asking my permission? I have already shown her around the house so she knows she has free run of it.

Birdie snapped impatiently. But it's not her house, is it?

Gansie took her book and sat on the patio. When it began to get dark, Mynah switched on the outside light. But then all the insects came out – this was their exercise yard – and in their exuberance, they zoomed and dive-bombed Gansie and soon chased her in. As she pulled the sliding door closed, she pointed to the bushes along the fence. 'Those bushes are full of spider webs. You should see them.'

'I know.'

'I hate spiders.'

After supper and TV, Gansie locked herself in her room.

Okay, so what's happened to the claustrophobia?

The bird was casting off stitches for a wing hole. Give the woman a break. She's only been out a couple of months.

Gansie worked for IRO, a newly established Institute for the Reintegration of Offenders, which had created a position in the office especially for parolees to help them get back on their feet. She was on a six-month contract. One afternoon, she came back from work and collapsed on the couch in front of the TV. And she cried and cried and cried.

'What am I going to do? In five months I'll be out of work.'

Mynah brought her a toilet roll. She wiped her eyes and blew her nose long and loud and was soon hidden behind a mound of toilet tissue. Mynah waited for the sobbing to stop so they could talk. But when it ended, Gansie reached for the remote and turned to 'The Bold and the Beautiful'. So Mynah went off to her room with the little bird protesting loudly. 'If you're going to try to stand on your head again, I'll go on boycott.' Mynah, who had been trying to master the headstand for years, smiled sweetly, knelt down, put her forehead on the mat and clasped her hands over her head. The little bird was livid.

'I hope you break your neck.'

The next day, Gansie came home and cried her heart out again. 'How will I ever become independent, with my own home, my own car?'

Mynah waited and again was pre-empted by Ridge and the gang so she went off to her room and had birdie hanging on for dear life as she lifted her feet in the air and then came down with a crash. This went on for a week. Gansie cried about getting a job, a job in the office, a job overseas and lots of money so she could get back her children, her car, her house, the book she wanted to write and many other things that Mynah couldn't remember.

Saturday, no episodes of The Bold and the Beautiful and other soap operas but Gansie's TV viewing began early so Mynah had to get in before.

'The thing to do is to start applying for jobs.'

'Yes, I'll get my CV together and start sending it around.'

After that Gansie came home and cried about the fact that there were no responses to her faxes. When she got responses and went for interviews, she cried about unfairness – she was too old, had a record, no car. The world was against her. Mynah, who had given up crying after the age of ten, wasn't at all sympathetic. Snot and trane all over the place. The little bird tossed her head. A lot better than farting.

Luckily I don't have a great sense of smell. 'What would you do if you didn't have your pension, eh? You'd be just as desperate.' Not really. Mynah prided herself on her independence. 'I've always had to fend for myself.' But really she never had to. She went from her father's care, to her husband's care, to the State's care.

Birdie harrumphed. So it's worse for her. She's forty and has to learn to take care of herself for the first time.

Then one day the crying stopped.

When Gansie came home from work, Mynah saw her walking around the house examining all the keys. 'Is something wrong?'

'Some of these keys don't work right. I can't open that security gate.' She pointed to the sliding gate that protected the patio doors.

'I guess the lock needs oiling.' So Mynah got out her little can, oiled the lock then tried the key. 'Okay, it works fine now.'

'The front door, that's a problem too.'

'But you lock it every day! Are you having a problem with it even when you pull it up and turn the key? You know it's not properly aligned.'

When Gansie had first arrived three months ago, Mynah had demonstrated and thought that she had gotten the hang of it.

'Hmm! I wonder how big a key ring is needed for all the keys in the house.'

Mynah raised her eyebrows then laughed. 'Why? The keys are fine where they are.' But Gansie gave her an odd look. 'Don't you feel safe with the keys in the doors?'

'Isn't it better to have them on a ring? That's the way it always is.'

'Well, not in this house. I like the keys in the doors. What's this obsession with keys?'

The little bird was giggling. She set her knitting down on the end of Mynah's shoulder. She's like the thieving magpie, obsessed with bright and shiny things. 'It's a good thing you don't wear jewellery.'

Gansie was walking from keyhole to keyhole, examining each key. Mynah raised her eyebrows. What is she doing now? Does she think I'm going to lock her in . . . or out?

The little bird flew to Gansie, perched on her head and informed Mynah, 'She's making a note of the numbers of all the keys.'

'Why do you need the numbers of the keys?'

Gansie was writing down the number of Mynah's bedroom door

key. 'You know how hard it is when you lose a key.'

'Well, I have spare keys. So I don't really worry about it.'

Gansie spun around, quite shocked. 'Spare keys!'

Mynah laughed. 'Yes. Everybody keeps spare keys.'

'Where? Where are they?'

'In a drawer in the kitchen.'

Gansie marched back into the kitchen and pulled open the drawers until she located the keys.

The little bird was hopping around on Mynah's shoulder. 'This is hilarious! Life has become much more interesting now that she's here. You're such a bore!'

Gansie turned sternly to Mynah. 'You've just muddled all the keys in here. How will you know which is which? The keys need to be labelled and on a ring.'

'Ha! Ha! Ha! You've been caught out! Such a careless, untidy, disorganised old witch!'

'Oh, shut up!' Mynah turned to Gansie. 'I really don't care. If you want to make the keys your project, go ahead.' And she went off to her room to try the headstand again.

'Oh, no! Don't go to your room. Stay here and let's see what Gansie gets up to.' The little bird was squawking and jumping from shoulder to shoulder. Give up on the headstand! You'll never get it right!

A week or so later, Mynah found all the keys clearly labelled and on a large ring. 'Now you should get her to work on your files. You have papers lying all over the place. Instead of trying all these ridiculous asanas, get your papers in order.'

As the weeks went by, Mynah began to notice that she was missing keys. First, when the key to her bedroom disappeared, she didn't think much of it. She looked about on the floor thinking it may have fallen out but she didn't really bother about it because the door to her room always stayed wide open – she had only begun closing it for her exercises after Gansie arrived.

Then one morning, after several attempts at the headstand and as many tumbles, she gave up to go and have a cup of tea but found her door locked.

'My door's locked. I didn't lock the door, did I?'

The little bird shrugged. 'It's all that standing on your head. Your brain's becoming addled. You don't know what you're doing.'

'But I lost the key some weeks ago.'

'You don't keep this place ship-shape. You never know where anything is.'

Mynah knew she had several spares on her bookshelf. She got them the last time she thought she had lost the key. She opened her door and went into the kitchen. Gansie, at the counter drinking coffee, looked up with a start, 'What are you doing out of your room?'

'I beg your pardon.'

Gansie let out a sudden burst of laughter. 'I thought you were sleeping.'

'Oh, no, I was exercising.'

'Exercising!' The little bird shrieked with laughter.

'You thought I was sleeping because my door was locked. I am just as surprised as you. I actually locked myself in my room. You know I never lock my door. I don't know what made me do it; I don't even remember doing it.' Mynah laughed. 'Maybe I should go for an Alzheimer's test.'

Gansie laughed. 'Oh, I don't think so. We all do funny things now and again.'

Then Mynah lost the key again.

'Tsss! Tsss! Tsss! Well, you have to admit it now. You've got to give up all that standing on your head.'

Birdie was only thinking of herself; life on Mynah's shoulders was extremely turbulent.

On another occasion, Mynah wanted to water the garden but couldn't find the key to the sliding gate. I wonder where I put it. She looked but couldn't find it. She couldn't open the front door either because the key wasn't in it so she went out the back and after speaking sternly to her petunias, which were not growing, and scolding the marigolds, which were resurfacing even after she had pulled them out, she went back in. She wrote on her kitchen notice board, 'Keys – security gate and front door,' to remind her to look for them later and then went into her room.

Oh no, I've just preened my feathers. The little bird was dreading the next half-hour.

Mynah was not a fastidious housekeeper and when she couldn't find keys, she just said to herself, They'll turn up. As long as Gansie's not upset, not having panic attacks and feeling claustrophobic, it's fine.

She knew Gansie was preoccupied with trying to find a job. Her contract with IRO would end soon.

And, of course, you don't see how distraught she is because you won't allow her to show any sign of weakness. The bird was moving stitches from the back to the front with her cable needle.

But Mynah was adamant. She's got to learn to be patient. She's like a child – wants everything to happen straight away. It's hard to get jobs these days.

One afternoon the little bird, trying to pull her feathers into place after tumbling about, the headstand again, heard the key in the kitchen security gate and saw Gansie entering with a few parcels.

Mynah was sipping tea. 'Oh, you've been shopping.'

'Yes, I bought some boots and a leather belt.' She took her purchases into her room and then came back into the kitchen to make a cup of coffee. 'You know my contract at IRO ends in a couple of weeks and I have to get another job.'

'So how's the job hunting going?'

'I've sent my CV out everyday. I've had a few responses. But no offers as yet.'

'You've been trying so very hard. I'm sure you'll find something.'

Suddenly the coffee cup flew into the air and came crashing to the ground and Gansie was dancing around the kitchen, stamping her feet. 'Everybody keeps saying that. But when I go for interviews, 'I'm too old,' or 'I don't have a car', or they want me to work from dawn to midnight for a pittance. How will I ever get on my feet again? How will I ever get my own place, my own car and a life? Will I ever get my children back?' She stomped off to her room and locked the door.

Birdie turned on Mynah. 'You see! The poor woman is really suffering and you're not helping her. All you do is stand on your head or try to wrap your feet around it. You don't listen and you're not helping. You give her a room in your house and you think you've done something great. You are the biggest hypocrite in the universe!'

'Shut up! Shut up! Shut up!'

'She needs someone who will show her some sympathy and affection. But you can't do that, can you? You dried up old spinster.'

Then as the bird gathered the wool that had fallen during her tirade and began to untangle it, she saw Gansie coming back into the kitchen. Mynah, who was cleaning up the mess with the coffee, stopped, 'I'm sorry. I didn't realise you were so upset about your job.'

Gansie smiled expansively. 'Oh, don't worry. I've got a plan. I know exactly what I am going to do when my contract ends.'

'You do? I am so glad. What are you going to do?'

'You'll see.' Gansie smiled again, made another cup of coffee, went back to her room and locked the door.

Mynah felt vindicated. Now what do you have to say, eh? You see. She's developed backbone. I didn't let her sit around crying and feeling sorry for herself. Now she's found a way out.

But birdie was jumping up and down on her shoulder. She let you off the hook! She let you off the hook! You can't take credit for anything she does. You cold, desiccated excuse for a human being!

Mynah sniffed. You don't understand tough love. And you're just mad because she's making something of herself.

The bird let out loud cynical screeches. Tough love! Love! Don't make me laugh!

On the day Gansie's contract ended, Mynah was expecting her to come home full of tears and self-pity. But she didn't. She came home with big parcels. For a moment Mynah thought that they had given her huge presents at work.

The little bird was irate. 'You really are obtuse. Haven't you been listening? Didn't she tell you how those people at the office exploited her – got her to provide tea and coffee without reimbursing her, to shop and cook for their office parties without lending a hand? One even expected her to cook his breakfast and lunch every day and made her vacuum his office and buff the plastic mat under his desk. They secretly despised her because she's an ex-con. Are they the kind to give presents?'

'But they are supposed to be helping parolees reintegrate into society?'

The little bird sneered. 'They gave her a six-month job and thought they had done enough. Just like you; you gave her a room and you think that is enough.'

Mynah turned to Gansie, 'I know you feel terrible now that you are out of work but . . .'

'Out of work? No, I'm not out of work. I told you I had a plan.'

'You have a job?'

'Of course.'

'And you begin tomorrow?' Gansie's smile filled Mynah with relief. 'Well, that's wonderful. I am so glad for you. So what are the parcels?'

'Oh, the uniform for my new job.'

'A uniform?'

'Yes, let me show you.' She pulled out khaki trousers and shirt.

Mynah looked confused. 'Are you joining Correctional Services?' Gansie burst out laughing.

The little bird stared in disgust. Correctional Services! Really!

Well, that's what they wear. And she got the boots and belt as well some time ago. Don't you remember? Some time ago? Mynah was confused 'So how long have you known about this job?'

'Oh, I've been planning it for quite some time.'

'But you were so upset when they didn't renew your contract. You cried for two days!'

'I was frightened and depressed. You know how it is.'

'This new job . . . when do you start?'

'Right away.'

'That's wonderful. What time will you be off in the morning?'

'Morning? No, I start right way. Right now.' Gansie went off to her room and when she came out was dressed in her uniform. She was wearing a police cap, swinging a club and on her belt was a huge key ring with all the house keys.

'You look very smart.'

Gansie just glowered. 'Shut up.' Mynah was confused. 'Move!' Gansie shoved Mynah in the direction of her room. 'Lock up time.'

This must be a joke. Mynah looked into Gansie's eyes. It wasn't.

'But Gansie . . .'

'Shut up. Get in there.' She shoved Mynah into her room and locked the door.

Mynah banged on the door, 'Gansie, what's going on? Unlock the door.' There was no answer. 'What's wrong with you? Come on now, unlock the door.'

'Shut up! If you don't stop that racket, I'll come in there and deal with you.'

'Gansie, I don't understand.'

'No, you don't, do you? You're inside now. And don't let me hear you snivelling. No feeling sorry for yourself. You deserve everything you get.' Gansie stopped then laughed. 'I don't know why I was so worried. It was quite easy really. I thought it would be hard. But I have it all now – a job, a home, a car. And you're bloody lucky you're inside; you don't need a job and your meals and accommodation are provided. Lights out now! I'll bring you breakfast in the morning. I'm going to watch The Bold and Beautiful.'

Mynah Bird stood staring at the door. Good Heavens! She's turned my house into a prison. She shook her head. Trying to get back into the cocoon.

'Didn't I tell you . . . ?'

Mynah looked around for the little bird but she was gone.

PSYCHODELIC

Allan Kolski Horwitz

Trevor trembled in front of the safe. He had to move fast. The Old Man was almost dead and once he was gone, the bitch would immediately sift through everything with a fine toothcomb.

He dropped to his knees and clumsily punched in the numbers. His father had always kept the combination from him, made no bones about it being his secret, but a few weeks back had tottered over to the safe unaware that Trevor had a view of the dial as he had reset the pin. And now there was still no click, still no open door and it was probably a question of hours, not days, before that shrunken body finally surrendered to the virus. Hell, there was no choice but to keep trying.

He altered a number, a series of numbers. But the safe remained closed. He tried to visualize his father's trembling fingers as they had entered the combination.

One, then *seven,* then *nine,* then *one* again, then *five,* then *six,* then *eight.*

No, that was not it. If only he had immediately written down the sequence as he had watched!

Wait, wait . . . *Zero*! Yes! Big fat *zero* at the end! What else but zero . . .?

He made the change. The safe door swung open.

'Oh, my God.' Trevor closed his eyes. 'Here it is.'

A perfectly still summer night on the patio of his father's mansion. The funeral has gone off smoothly, well supported and amiable as if his father had had no enemies.

Trevor raises his glass.

'Here's to the old bugger. You must be very happy. Today's a fitting climax to your campaign. You're a pro, Crystal – I gotta give you that. So why you looking sad? Why aren't you clapping in triumph?'

The haggard woman sitting opposite him looks away. He takes another sip of wine. She adjusts her hair.

'Trevor, it's been a terrible few months. How can you be so insensitive? It's been . . .' For a moment it seems that she will cry. 'I so hated to see him in pain.'

He laughs. 'Oh, you did, did you? Poor, heart-sore Crystal. But don't you worry, I've got something to cheer you up.' He raises a DVD into the air. 'And guess where I found it?' He pauses, savouring her shock. 'Come on, guess! And what could this movie be about? Any ideas? And who are the stars?'

He pauses, picks out and sucks the last olive in his bourbon. Who wouldn't snigger? What a sight she was! So unlike the sleek, elegantly dressed beauty she imagined herself to be.

'Come now, it's one of the blockbuster's you and daddy made. A National Geographic special: 'The Human Animal in All its Glory'. Yes, *mommy* . . . an intimate exploration of both your private parts.'

The woman named Crystal covers her face with her hands.

'Wait, I mustn't forget the scenes featuring your good friend, what's her name . . . that red head who came for a little holiday before the old bastard really started to fall apart. She's right there between the two of you. And she looks stunning. I mean you *all* look stunning – one on top of her and one underneath. Gotta give it to the old bastard, he wasn't selfish.'

Trevor drains the glass.

'And this isn't the only one. You were all very productive and, I may say, inventive. What should I call the series? 'Madame Crystal's Guide to Deviant Mating Habits'?'

Her lined, weary face whitens to the point of ghostliness. Will he ever stop? What is she to do as he waves the DVD around? He is high as usual, and as overbearing, but today he is surpassing his normal limits.

'You think I'm bluffing? Well, we'll soon see about that, my beauty. You thought you could walk in here with your sexy swagger and take over. You thought the old bastard would do as you liked . . . do anything to keep you on hand to please him. You thought you could replace my mother and drive me out. You thought that one day this would all be yours!'

She has had to listen to this ranting for years; and on each occasion his dilated eyeballs swallowed her and any reply she tried to offer: now who could match the total commitment with which she has cursed his tenacious haranguing?

'You thought you could make him disinherit me, forget me, cut off my allowance, ignore me. You thought you could make me disappear, didn't you, sweetie? Slut! You want to take everything. The whole fucking lot! You don't want to leave me the tiniest crumb!'

This time she starts to cry – the pain in her head and her stomach are too much to bear. She gets up, turns to leave but Trevor bars her way. She tries to move past him, she must relieve herself, but he grabs her arms.

'Don't move, bitch! You came here with smiles. You took advantage of a stupid man who inherited a fortune and didn't know what to do with his life, the stupid cunt.'

Her arms are going numb. She feels her head explode.

'Killer *goddess* playing with a fat daddy who took my grandfather's money, shamed my mother's memory and brought you in with your curvy-curvy, little wiggle. What a fool! Didn't do a decent thing his whole damn life. May he rot in hell!'

She cannot stop crying.

She shifts the files to one side of the safe then the bags with gold coins, the inlaid mother-of–pearl boxes containing jewellery, the crisp bundles of dollars. For there is only one thing she wants. And there pressed flat against the back, she sees the brown manila envelope. How many times had she watched the old man shuffle round the bedroom (for so long really a sick room), this same grubby envelope stuck into one of his dressing gown pockets? How many times had she watched him take out the few pages that were housed there and with a cheap black ballpoint erase and amend, erase and fill in new instructions? Well, it was now about to slip into her pocket – the long sexy one that ran down her thigh.

She fishes the envelope out, carefully folds it then locks the safe and walks unhurriedly back to her room – the room she has always kept for herself despite the dead man's entreaties that they share one bed. With quiet satisfaction she slits the envelope open with her long purple tinted nails and triumphantly takes out the two page document.

The official stamp on the second page is slightly raised and slightly smudged as only an original can be – as are the three crisp signatures in black ink at the bottom. Sitting on the side of her bed, she begins reading. And thank God it is what he had promised. At least this part of their relationship had remained true and consistent; at least in death he had kept his word. For the bequests were final proof of his love – to have withstood his ex-wife's relentless, hysterical pressure and his son's drug-induced outbursts was an achievement that took more than a little stamina and courage. How they had trashed him, mocked him, called him names even as they implored him to dump her!

She pictures Trevor's shocked face when he sees the will nestling in her hands. She jumps ahead to his hysteria days later when the family lawyer tells him there is no chance to contest it. And lastly she visualizes his breakdown which will require yet another stay in rehab. And so, for the first time in months, she can lie back on her bed, and close her eyes and try to sleep with a clear and composed mind.

Crystal gently places the document on the side table. For a moment the lines on her face disappear; for a moment she forgets where she is – and in that moment, at last, she is who she has always wanted to be.

Blue skies and a warm breeze! What a splendid day!

He is on the coastal highway driving his father's favourite sports car – the red Porsche he has always desired but never been allowed to touch.

With one hand he holds a zol; with the other, as he draws in the pungent blue smoke, he guides the super-charged vehicle round the bends that follow the ocean cliff. The road is smooth and well designed but every now and again he misjudges the curve and almost scrapes the metal railings that line the side.

Yes, the bitch will pay for her brazenness, will soon beg for mercy. How blissful to know that the next few days will deliver him from all the frustration built up over the years since her cursed arrival. But damn her! As old as she was, why did she still make him 'itchy'? He takes another drag. Too bad she was soon going to be just a memory, just a footnote in his still to be written epic account of life in the fast lane. Yes, that sagging body of hers still promised sweet madness.

He puts his foot down and the red bullet guns round the last loop before roaring into the straight for home.

Crystal fills her glass.

'Trevor, my boy, as always, you were in too much of a rush. You missed the one thing you really needed to lay your hands on. Just imagine, if you'd been the one to find it, 'Deny and Stall' would have been your watchword. After all, there are plenty of legal sharks to keep a matter in court for years. Maybe long enough for me to join your father in the next world; quite a different world from the heaven you like – that heaven where needles never get rusty.'

She plays with the buttons on her blouse. Sitting opposite her on the patio, he watches her fingers; those slender, nifty fingers turning, twisting the pearl buttons round and around and around.

'So keep your DVDs, give them to whoever you like. They really are too tame for blackmail. And stop your other games – especially your trying to open my door at night. Just go away, go and find someone who will satisfy your very particular . . . needs.'

Crystal slowly sips the white wine; it provokes a delicious wavy sensation.

'Yes, go away, leave me to live my life and I'll be generous. Be responsible and nurse your monthly stipend and you'll live the way you've always lived. I don't bear grudges. Do you understand, my boy? I really don't.'

She watches him clench and unclench his fists; watches him fiddle with the gold bracelet that circles his pale wrist.

'I know how to deal with your father's ghost. And maybe one day you'll also learn to put him to rest and stop getting into scrapes, letting yourself down and having to run home for a bit of a cuddle.' She pulls a face. 'You're on your own from now on, Trev. Isn't that . . . cool?''

He blanches. Arrogant witch! If only the old man hadn't died when he had! They'd started to talk again, started to get close again; the pain of illness had begun to open him up and he'd been on the verge of seeing she was just a gold-digger. Hell, another week and he would have reversed whatever he had left her. Just another week!

'Poor Trev, despite the endless dramas, he still hoped you would amount to something. But let me not be mean – once and for all, to show how much I loved him, I'll cheer you up.'

Crystal slowly undoes the top button of her satiny blouse.

'You see, I'm not the monster you make me out to be. I know when to be kind. And . . . I have my own dreams, Trev. There's so much I still want to achieve.'

She undoes another button, and another.

'I'm not going to give you the pleasure of making me fail.'

She slips out of her blouse, unhooks her bra.

'Come here, my boy. My lonely boy who needs his mommy so badly he can't stop thinking about her and playing with his . . .'

Without taking his eyes off her breasts he spits, 'Get out! Don't make me hit you!'

'Hit? No, no, you mustn't *hit* mommy. No, no – let mommy *hit* on her little boy . . .'

Pursing her lips, pushing out her chest, she stands. Yes, this will be a day for celebration and for righting wrongs. But before she can reach out and pull his mouth to her nipple, he jumps up and runs.

The house had been quiet and he had been restless, so restless that even the prospect of sharing her company was better than sitting alone. The lawyer had told him they would meet to discuss the will in the morning. He had not said anything about her. After all, everyone knew she was dying of the same disease as the old man; and now, in its final stages, it had taken not just her good looks but her brain.

Trevor lies back, fingers the needle hole. He can feel the warm buzz take hold, the slow push that turns his limbs into floating castles. The night will be filled with triumphant dreams. And best of all is the knowledge that there is enough in the drawer for more than another hit.

No need to be worried, everything will be alright because everything is at this most important of moments just fine, just fine . . . just fine.

Funny that she hadn't tried to delete that last clause that turned everything on its head.

Better wait before going upstairs. He won't be knocked out yet although the shock will have certainly gotten to him and what remedy does he have? In the meanwhile, she can do no better than ask the maid to bring another bottle of cold white to her room, maybe even a few snacks, some pate, a little salad. Then it will be time to dress, something chic, something elegant to show off her figure.

The lawyer has accepted her invitation to dinner. They had met several times when he'd come to advise the Old Man. He had leered at her like they all did. Of course he was married but she would not disappoint him. Let him glory in her beauty. Let him desire to possess it. Let him demand of her anything he liked. This was the final lap, the last obstacle in the race.

Crystal admires herself in the mirror. Takes out a ruby necklace to replace the diamond, adjusts the amethyst broach. But she must not take anything for granted. Despite her still undeniable charms, the drunkest among fools can sometimes not lose his head.

Ah, that must be the maid with that special Chardonnay.

When he wakes in the morning, he feels refreshed, energized. The new homeopathic pills the pharmacist had recommended left no grogginess. And just as well – he has plenty to do and it will be surprising if she is still alive; after all, the amount she had drunk was more than any person could stand.

Bali – that's a thought! A few months in the East, a few months on the beach with the German hippy girls . . .

Even though Crystal had produced a slick forgery, experts would see it wasn't the old man's signature. But then, it would never get to that. Just as well the maid shared his dislike of the 'madam' – was there a natural hair or milligram of genuine tissue left in her body? – and he has had plenty of time to prepare the concoction. She would have suffered no pain. The internet articles all gave that assurance and even if that wasn't the case, there was no choice – after all, living organisms are sustained by the dead.

Now it was time to go up and check. Break the door down if necessary. But wait a minute – it's still early. There's time for another line . . .

She can't stop herself from laughing out loud. Ah, the lawyer – what a ninny! Didn't take half an hour and he was ready to make the necessary 'correction'. As for Trev, well, who knows if he felt anything different. Stupid idiot to leave his little white bags lying in the bedside draw. And even more stupid to leave his bedroom door wide open. And stupidest still to have been so zonked he couldn't wake up when someone slipped in and fiddled about. Fee fi fo fum, who smells the blood of a . . . Trevilsome mun!

Yes, and now for another glass of bubbly. Certainly well earned and definitely not the last. Although one shouldn't be over confident, right? One should take things nice and slow, one sip at a time, one little sip at a time . . .

DUST

Dina Segal

She stands alone in the wilting room, her back to a dented formica countertop. All the furniture is sagging and grey. Her single bed rests in the corner against a once-white wall, the drabness of years of head-resting above her pillow matching the murky patch of wall surrounding the light switch. The linoleum floor is scratched and cracked. A faded cross-stitch of a vase of flowers, once orange and cheery, hangs dusty and listless. Her couch has holes in the maroon leather, cracks along the arms, patches of darkness and scuffing. Dull loops of fabric that had once held the cushions in place now droop underneath it. She tries not to sit there anymore, finds it difficult to get up, and once had to sit there for two hours in an endless cycle of struggling, and then wheezing, before falling on her back, defeated. (Finally, a nurse had come in and helped her into bed. She had collapsed, exhausted.)

Now she looks down at her body, then around the room, and yet again she knows she is going to die. Turning around to face the counter, she switches the kettle on, and tries not to look at her flabby arm. Slowly she reaches towards the shelf above the kettle. Next to the red box of Five Roses is a saucer. Gripping the saucer in her fingers, she puts it gently on the counter. On it sits a dry teabag which she drops into a chipped mug. The kettle begins to steam as she lifts the sugar bowl. It is full of different coloured sachets. (Every time she has a cup of tea in the communal dining room she puts a sachet in her cracked leather handbag.)

She has always known she is going to die. Sometimes thoughts of dying are so overwhelming that she would have to close her eyes and force herself to think of other things. As a young child she had lain awake for hours, too scared to call for help, too scared to close her eyes. She had been taught in school that God had always existed, and that it was bad to ask what had come before him. He was always there in His Absolute Power. But what came before God? No, don't think that! If you die with such thoughts, you'll be punished. But something had to have come first. What did the void look like? Stop, stop, stop thinking that if you die, you're going to have to answer to Someone.

She tears open a white sachet, pours the white sugar into her mug, watches the kettle steam. Why did it always take longer when she watched it? She picks up a dry rag off the countertop and begins to swipe it back and forth, from mug to kettle, kettle to dreary wall. And she remembers the striped wallpaper of her childhood bedroom, how it had livened up the room; the two beds lying parallel, covered in cheery pink fabrics. She had shared that room with her sister. They used to lie in bed at night and tell each other stories: they had giggled and whispered, shared secrets and biscuits, dolls and desires.

Her sister had once been given a brand-new, white, summer dress. But this was during the iciness of winter and their mother had insisted she wait until summer to wear it; an act so cruel in 'child-time', with its many hours of small victories and giant defeats, until finally the weather was warm enough but the dress could no longer fit the growing girl. And so she got to have it. And her sister had watched with green eyes and pigtails as she had twirled around and the skirt flew out, that lovely, spotless, tight, little child – not realising the bumps and bashes and destruction ahead that would sag the skin under her chin, make her waist a flabby tire of stretch-marks, turn her heels to cracked stones, dry her feathery hair into grey strings and turn her smooth hands into bags of spots and wrinkles and so weak they were barely capable of lifting the smallest weight. (At least she doesn't struggle with the two hundred and fifty millilitres of milk. When did they change from pints? She can't remember.)

Her kitchen consists of the chipped counter, the kettle, the sugar, mugs and tea on the shelf above, and the swing-top dustbin below; and, of course, the bottle of milk on the counter. She insists on keeping it. Hates powdered milk substitutes. But the milk goes off so quickly. She picks it up and unscrews the blue top. Gripping the white plastic, she sticks her nose into the opening, sniffs. She remembers her grandparents from sixty years ago. How they had looked, how she had despised their feebleness. What were they like before time took away their vitality? Why did she only remember them in their dementia and frailty? Sometimes well-meaning children came into the home, sparky and gleaming and certain like she once was. They glow with pride at their altruism. They will surely spend the rest of the week aglow at their good deed of cheering up these ancient has-beens. They come in, fresh, unsullied, and she knows they will end up like her despite their well-mannered disdain for the reality of humanity. They think they are invincible, as she once did, as her long-dead grandparents did. But she knows, if only they'd really listen, but they won't. Her only value is as barometer for goodness in little girls and boys. Were they willing to give up an hour on a Sunday afternoon?

She tilted the milk bottle over the mug, spilling its whiteness over the waiting teabag and sugar. She always puts the milk, sugar and tea in that order. Just like her mother did. Her mother loved tea; loved making it in her favourite teacup then slowly drinking it on the stoep.

A sudden breeze ruffles the beige curtains. A gust of air has managed to climb down the concrete tunnel. Her view consists of exposed plumbing pipes and strangely she savours the unfresh air, wonders why she hadn't savoured freshness when she had had the chance. The curtains ruffle again and she hears footsteps squeak down the corridor outside. She can picture the worn sticky lino floors, cracked like so many of those in the rooms it passed. And she wonders about the footsteps. Could it be one of the carers squeaking past in bright, white, rubber-soled shoes? All those sulky women in stiff clothes who speak about her all the time – in front of her – as if she's stupid, or deaf. Or already dead. They call them carers but she knows they don't. She knows what they are really like. Barging into her room as they please. Pinching her if she doesn't move fast enough. Speaking through gritted teeth.

She picks up one of her three teaspoons. It is slightly dented and scratched. Where had it come from? She doesn't remember buying it. Perhaps it had a previous owner. While she glares at someone else's scratch on its handle, the footsteps move past her room. Is she grateful, or sorry? She often daydreams about visitors, one single simple visitor, someone interested in hearing her stories. She has so many stories. She remembers her childhood that passed her like water through a cupped hand. Her wedding. She had been so nervous. She hardly knew Harry before their marriage. He was a lot older than her but their parents were good friends. She was nervous because she had never been with a man. Her sister had hinted that it could hurt. What if he found her body ugly, like she sometimes did? She had to wear her sister's dress. What if he hated it? The war meant everyone was tightening their belts. What if she looked cheap and stupid? What if it looked second hand? Would the people at the wedding remember the dress?

The bubbling tells her that the kettle has reached boiling point. She unplugs it from the wall. She has heard that you can get ones that switch off automatically. Now she strains with the weight of it, nervous of the steam. The kettle shakes as she pours water into the mug. Boiling hot splashes speckle the formica. She puts the kettle down and wipes the spots with her rag. It dampens in places. She picks up the teaspoon and stirs the tea carefully. Watching the brown liquid swirl, she grips the teaspoon between her fingers and wonders about the other hands that had once also held it.

Her mother had told her that the dress looked beautiful, like it had been made for her. Her father's face was so proud. That was a day to celebrate. To hold onto. Both long dead now. Her sister wasting away in some similar hell of her making. She had danced with Harry; his hand on her waist. So confident. So handsome. He had steered her impressively round the dance floor. His suit was black and he had worn a satin waistcoat. And though she had kept tripping on her hem, he had smiled indulgently. That was the end of her childhood.

She watches the tea stop swirling then presses the teabag against the side of the cup with the spoon. Stretching her tired arm, she places the saucer on the counter next to the red box. Is this fit punishment for all her mistakes? She picks up the chipped mug by its handle, careful not to touch its hot sides. She turns round and shuffling in her slippers walks slowly towards the armchair. Eyes fixed on the mug's rim, she sits down. He body feels like it should have creaked.

At last. She is in the armchair.

Her hands claw around the mug while she stares at the wall.

AN UGLY NAME IS A CURSE *(Bitso lebe ke Seromo)*
Lungile Lethola

This Sesotho idiom roughly translates as 'an ugly name is a curse' for it is human nature to strive for greatness and triumph – no one wants to be a victim which is why I am yet to come across someone named as such: we only have victors. And so I am still very angry at my mother and grandmother (may their souls rest in peace) for giving me the name *Mohanuoa*, which roughly translates as 'the one rejected at birth'.

Throughout my adult life, in my efforts to make something of myself, the negative impact of this name could not be ignored. I have always been proudly South African; I even swore that I would never leave my country in search of greener pastures but that was before I discovered that in Sweden it is against the law to give your child an inappropriate name. To be born in a country so considerate and protective of its newborn citizens would have been a true blessing! In that instance I would have ended up with a sweet name like *Seithati, Moratuoa* or *Lethabo*: a name to assure me that the Universe has nothing less than an abundance of love and happiness for me . . . a name to give me a sense of pride and triumph over life's hardships.

When life's tides throw people with such beautiful names about, I am sure they always find calm. I cannot imagine someone uttering a sweet name like *Moratuoa* in an angry or depressed voice. The name itself demands peace, warmth, pride and joy. Whenever someone asks me my name, a dark cloud always descends no matter how happy I was before the question was asked. A thin, inaudible sound escapes from a dark place inside of me as I softly tell them, praying that they catch it first time round and not force me to repeat myself. The curse of my ugly name hits hardest when I have to audition for some non-MoSotho director – most especially a white one. They would add salt to my open wounds by mispronouncing it then asking me what it means, and then lick my already open and bleeding wounds by saying, ' *it's a beautiful name, such a nice flow to it'*. . . Screw that! I sometimes attribute my failure in the world of show business – where appearance and perception are everything – to my unflattering name: definitely too ugly, too long and hence unfitting for any production company.

Of course, one may argue that these companies come across many people with names just as bad as mine – and who have proved the infamous idiom wrong, just another myth. The Majakathata's of this world are high flying citizens who never had to beg for anything; instead they are known to be providers for the less fortunate. The Matlakala's turned out to be the opposite of rubbish. Then you have your angelic, peace-loving Mantwa's. And to make it even more frustrating and confusing, there are plenty of those blessed with beautiful names who are supposed to be icons of hope, love and everything good but instead turn out to be complete life wreckers, true agents of the devil!

All the same, I applied for another ID in an attempt to get rid of my name but thinking over it today, see that it was a total waste of money and time. A name sticks to you like a jealous lover, chappies! People from my childhood just don't know how to call me by any other name; to them I will always be *Mohanuoa* or '*Hanu*' as others affectionately call me (which affectionately shortened or not, is still inappropriate and embarrassing. It's like feeding me bitter aloe coated with sweet caramel). And so my life progresses at a snail's pace, I don't even see space for children in it but should I, by some heavenly intervention, one day beget offspring, names, like *Katleho* (success), *Bohlale* (intelligence) and *Tswelopele* (progress) would be top of my list to pave a prosperous way for my children and, whatever they turn out to be, I will at least be exonerated.

The elders always manage to fabricate some explanation for the ugly names they give us, especially in my BaSotho tribe where '*horeheletsa*' (naming a child after a relative whether long dead or still alive) is common practice. I don't care how dear a relative is to me, if they have an ugly name I am not naming my child after them! The tendency of naming a child after a natural catastrophe that the parents may have been caught up in round the time that child was born is also very popular – which is why we have names like *Mapalla* or *Pharela* (both roughly translated as 'famine'), *Medupi* (rainstorm) and *Maphefo* (nail biting cold). In most instances, when you dig deeper into the real core of these names you discover that the lame excuse about '*horeheletsa*' is just a cover up for something plain and simple like a dispute among parents or their families (or both), my name *Mohanuoa* being a perfect example.

Yes, I do have a relative from my mother's side with whom I share my name. But I believe the real motivation was what transpired between my parents when they discovered that the seed of their youthful lust had been sown and, as in most teenage pregnancies, their friendship was broken and the poor child, being me, had to be a victim, a lifetime reminder of how my father denied ever participating in bringing me to Mother Earth. At some point my mother must have realized the damage caused by my name (needless to say, some point far too late). And in an attempt to make things right, when I was 7 or 8 she announced, out of the blue, that she had another name for me, a very nice one; indeed, the only problem was that it was an English name and people in my community struggled with it until they simply gave up and decided to stick to what they knew best.

As I matured into an enlightened young woman bombarded with material about 'Black this, Black that', 'African this, African that', I deserted my melodious and very acceptable English name that had helped me leave the cocoon into which I had been born and integrate into a larger community. I adopted a Xhosa name with a more positive meaning than my original SeSotho name in the hope that people would warm to it and forget about *Mohanuoa*.

I am still hoping . . .

PINKY THE SIDE CHICK

Brian Khumalo

It is the night before his big day – his wedding. He does not care about spending the last hours of his 'freedom' boozing with his mates and inviting strippers for their entertainment. Instead, he chooses to be with Pinky. Though Pinky is not the bride to be, she is one of his side chicks, and because she is his favourite side chick, he wants to commemorate their last union (I mean, sexual congress) peacefully and undisturbed.

He has her favourite perfume on – Hugo Boss sprayed all over his body. He holds her delicately and they begin to dance to the same rhythm. Engulfed by each other's arms, they feel safe and float on in utter pleasure. She knows he will be wed tomorrow. She has known about the other woman for months now, but being his side chic has never been a problem for her. She celebrates it and accepts it. Once they both reach sexual ecstasy, they collapse on the bed. He rests his head on her breasts for one last time. Her heart beats even faster than before. He runs his big hands on her naked body, admiring her female figure.

'*Umuhle* – you are beautiful' he whispers.

He has always said this to her, but this time he actually means it and she can feel it as she looks into his loving eyes.

'If I am beautiful as you say I am, and if you love me as you say you do, then how come I am *umakhwapheni* (the side chick)?' she asks.

There is silence in the hotel room. He cannot answer her, not because he does not have the answer but the question came so unexpectedly. As the side chick she is expected to be the perfect escape – she must be seen and not heard. She must not have a voice or question his intentions with her. And so, just like that, he leaves her in bed and gets dressed. And she cries but her tears mean nothing. They have had their pleasure and now he must get ready for a new chapter in his life and one in which she will not be one of the featured characters. So she lies there in bed and even though she is heart-broken, deep down she knew how it was going to end – they always go back their wives and fiancés after they have had their way with her.

Admittedly, Pinky has been one of my favourite characters in this evergreen drama. With her colourful clothes and matching personality, she is often the main topic of controversy and is cruelly judged by her community for having several male partners and has to seem oblivious to the constant chitter-chatter at taxi ranks as well as the mean looks she gets from the taxi mamas. I guess you would be surprised if I told you that Pinky was the smartest girl at her school. She had effortlessly passed from one grade to the next, sometimes without even studying for exams. Then she tried going to university but it just was not her thing – being bound at another institution of learning just did not sit well with her.

However, this post is not about her intellect or her decisions thereafter. It is about her critical role as the *umakhwapheni*. I always admire Zulu for being such a descriptive language – *umkhwapheni* derived from *ikhwapha* which means armpit, a secluded area of your body, warm, yes but hidden. And so these women are hidden from public view and only left to fulfil their male's desires. If your wife, girlfriend or fiancé refuses to go out to watch that boring action film on Saturday then the side chick steps in and takes care of that. If she has a migraine and cannot do the dirty with you, have no fear for the side chick is a speed dial away. Once you're done, you hide all the evidence and carefully tuck her back in under your armpit. It's like that cartoon series, Pokemon. She is your Pokemon and when she has served her purpose, she returns to her Pokeball until you put her to good use again.

Now Pinky is a different side chick. Being raised by a polygamous father and a mother who bent over backwards trying to fulfil his everyday needs, she grew up with some loathing for relationships as such. She has tried being in relationships, once or twice but we all know how this story will end. He will shower her with compliments; pronounce every pick up line under the sun and she will smile and actually think he cares. Then once he has her at his mercy, he will take it a step further until he devours her. That is his aim after all – to use her body and move on to his next victim. And she will cry herself to sleep at night and blame herself for his sadistic temperament. And after this let-down, she will find it hard to love again let alone trust someone else while she battles with the emotions that he carelessly distorted. I guess it is true there is a very fine line between pleasure and pain.

But having said this, Pinky vowed never to be like her mother. She made a promise to herself that she would never yearn for a man or his love. And so she finds solace in being the side chick. It is almost like a dance. The man arrives at the ball with his wife. They dance but she complains and says her feet hurt. But he will be saved from any inconvenience because a Pinky will cut in and enable him to carry on dancing. His hands rest on her body and they move side to side. For that moment he forgets about his irritable partner in the background. Pinky comforts him and feeds into his needs. Of course, at some point, like all good things, the music will stop and he will go back to his wife and Pinky is left alone again, searching for her next temporary dance partner. Such is the life of the side chic but Pinky loves it. The men think they're in control when they shower her with gifts, even money. They think have power over her when she turns up at their command.

But Pinky learned a long time ago how to use her body to get these panting men. She is just as heartless as they are, posing the question: who really has control? The men have to come up with stories for their wives when they go out to see her. They believe the only way they can keep her on tap and safely away from their 'loved ones' is by spending their hard earned money on her and hiding all evidence of these secret encounters before they return to their homes. Pinky, on the other hand, enjoys this thoroughly. She takes pleasure in hearing the stories they tell their wives on the phone while she excites their private places. She loves tasting the lips that their loving wives kiss before their men leave for those long business trips. Behind those closed hotel doors she holds the power – unlike her mother she makes them beg for more until they are at her mercy.

It is the day of the wedding and Pinky decides to attend it. She dresses in a disturbing black outfit. From the look of things, you would say she was attending a funeral. Yes, today she is not the colourful character that everybody knows and loves. Today she is that black widow who lives down the road.

She completes her look with huge sunglasses and sits front row in the centre. It is a beautiful day to have a wedding. Though everybody in church is shocked by her choice of outfit, she does not care. The groom has seen her too. He gulps, starts shaking in his tight fitting tuxedo. But she does not stop the wedding when the minister asks if there is any objection to the marriage; instead, she pierces his heart with her presence.

What can I say? She has a slightly sadistic disposition. The new-lyweds step happily out of the church, and their friends and family joyously throw confetti over them. Pinky also joins in the festivities. She and her former lover lock eyes. He is overcome by a sea of emotion; she is cold as ice. Her intentions are not to ruin his special day but for those few minutes she wants to be the haunting image that will resonate forever in his mind.

Yes, she is Pinky. And when the couple celebrate their first night as wife and husband, and all the years thereafter, she wants his mind to still be making love to her.

THE TRAIN HOME

Shanice Ndlovu

Karina fumbled furiously for her keys; her bag was a horrid mess: a boiling pot of old banknotes, half-torn papers, crude poems and stories, candy wrappers and a lot of other things she just couldn't bring herself to throw away. A soft drop of rain landed on her forehead as she felt the smooth rectangular card at the bottom of the bag. She hurried into the station.

Safe and away from the rain, she grabbed her cellphone and shoved two red earpieces into her ears. Beethoven was always good on a day like this. She sat herself in the nearest seat she could find and tried her best to relax: just think about the ocean, she told herself. Book reports to submit and article deadlines to meet, she hardly knew how she was going to cope. Stacy, her best friend, always said that most of the problems Karina had were only in her head. And maybe the pretty blonde was right.

The struggle of trying to finish a book she had been writing for nearly two years was stifling her; typically, it was the difficulty in writing a final chapter that would enable everything to make sense. Those final words are supposed to be magical, aren't they? Explain it all – and at the same time make one wonder what kind of mind had conjured this type of magic. She had read endings like that, endings that simply made her care. But, truth be told, she was starting to question if she had anything of that sort in her. She couldn't just be a good writer that made you smile; no, she had to take your breath away.

The people on the train home were always the same: grey, middle aged men in clumsy trench coats, university students with their headphones on and various non-descript women. Then, before she knew it, the train made its first stop and Karina realised how warm it had become, and would have opened the window if not for the seat that was in her way.

The boy next to her was busy on his iPhone and seemingly oblivious to all else around him. 'Hi,' she would say, 'could you please open the window.' No, that wasn't right. How about, 'Could you please crack that open a little bit?' She almost laughed but quickly killed the thought with a rather awkward cough. This was an old habit – if she could help it, she always practised her conversations before speaking though in the end things hardly ever came out as they were planned.

Come on Karina, she said to herself, it's a window not a marriage proposal. He was dressed very well, she thought; his black shirt was buttoned to the last and went well with his black jeans. That jacket was quiet fashionable as well – not that she knew much about fashion in her routine blue jeans and sloppy coat.

'Hey . . .' she said; her voice so raspy and crude she felt embarrassed. For a moment she thought he hadn't heard until, almost in slow motion, he lifted his gaze from his iPhone.

'Sorry, what was that?'

'Could you please ummm . . . crack ummm the window. I mean, crack it open.' Goodness why she even bothered to practise was beyond her.

'Cool,' he said, and got up. 'That better?'

He stood there next to the open the window, running his free hand through his thick brown hair with its traces of gold like spun sun rays – not that she was staring or anything.

'Yes, that's better,' she managed to say.

At least she had responded quickly and not tried to say something witty which would have in all likelihood come out an atrocious mess. Now she was just content with settling into the awkward silence, for she had paused Beethoven and was watching the boy return to his iPhone. At close observation, he seemed to be her age really, if not a bit older – or was that just her mind trying to justify itself?

A few spatters of rain fell through the open window and landed on her lap. Within minutes larger drops began crashing in. Karina felt the urge to stand up and close the window but she was of average height and the window was too high. Should she ask him to close it? Goodness Karina, you are just pathetic, she thought miserably.

'The rain just won't stop will it?'

He complained – although the complaint was rather lost when it was said with a smile like that. He closed the window and dropped his iPhone into his fashionable jacket.

'Yes,' she said, without being certain what it was she was agreeing with, and then 'Thank you.'

That smile again; his eyes shone green like emeralds.

'I'm Joe,' he said.

His hand was warm and soft when she touched it.

'Karina,' she told him.

She must have looked hideous trying to decide whether a smile would be appropriate or not but it had come out before she decided it was.

'Interesting name,' he said.

She laughed. Goodness I have the weirdest laugh, she thought.

'Yeah, it's like Karen only . . . more exotic.'

In truth she was named after her great-grandmother who had also been a writer. 'A devious old poet who just refused to get into the ground,' her father had often joked. She tells this to Joe and he laughs too.

'So you're a writer?' She nods. 'What do you write?'

What did she write? She wrote poetry when she was sad, articles when she was broke and short stories when she was bored. She could have said that she had also written some historical fiction and that now she was writing a fantasy book.

'I write fiction.' That seemed like a reasonable answer. 'But I write articles for The Branch from time to time.'

'I thought you would be a poet like your great grandmother. You seem like one.'

Ah, yes, it's the natural curly hair and the lack of makeup. Or is it the dark caramel skin and the freckled cheeks? Either way she knew what he meant or at least thought she did and told him as much.

'No,' he laughed. 'It's that tendency to give a vivid description of everything. Isn't that the way poets are? People who find beauty in the world and put it into words.'

She smiled. Ah, she liked this one.

'You're right,' she replied. 'But it's not just beauty that can be put into words.' She stopped then added in a dramatic voice, 'I love you like all dark things are to be loved, in secret, between the shadow and the soul.'

'That's terrible.' He ran his fingers through his hair and grinned. 'But it's still beautiful.'

She pointed outside. It had grown dark and the city lights could be seen through the wet glass.

'It's stopped raining.'

'I visited Paris once and it rained all weekend. I mean if you're gonna visit Paris at least have the good sense to pick the right season.'

Was he trying to impress her? No, he didn't seem the type.

'I'm sure Paris is still Paris in the rain.'

'You are funny. Of course it is.'

'And I will visit it one day when there isn't so much to do.'

'Oh, busy girl! But you should. Paris would look good on you.'

He smirked and she was glad that her ears were safely hidden behind the tragedy that was her hair for they would be as red as beet juice.

'I'm sure it looks good on everybody then.'

That was really smooth Karina! Goodness she could be as thick as a brick. But he only laughed; he had a queer laugh.

'No, not on everybody,' he replied.

Then before she could tell him that he was imagining things, he asked, 'So when's your book coming out?'

Her book? How much should she tell him? Would he make more fun of her?

'Hopefully before the winter. It's just that I'm having trouble with the ending.'

'Yeah, they say endings are the hardest. But what exactly is the trouble you're having? Do they or don't they?' And he smiled.

Oh, my God! Despite his playfulness, he seemed genuinely interested. And because no one she knew had any genuine interest in her book troubles, she told him about her search for the magic, right down to the part where she took your breath away. It all sounded a bit ridiculous when said out loud but he did not laugh.

He was silent for a while, as if trying to process it.

Then he said, 'I don't know Karina. It sounds like you've spent two years creating this world and writing this story and now for the past three months you've been stuck in one place. Maybe, just maybe . . . you don't want to finish it.'

How dare he say that! Of course she wanted to finish it.

'This book has been a part of your life for a long time. When you publish it, it's not just yours anymore; it belongs to everybody who reads it. Maybe you don't want to give it away.'

No, that could not be true. Writing was vanity but part of that vanity was giving it to the world and seeing their reaction – wasn't it? She had not worked as hard as she had just to be selfish. No!

'I think you might be right. Maybe I don't want to finish it.' She stopped and he waited for her to continue. 'But not because I'm selfish. It's because I'm afraid.'

'What are you afraid of?'

'What if the world doesn't love it? What if it's not as good as I think it is?'

176

'What if it is? You won't know until you finish it and stop searching for magic that is already in you.'

'You don't even know me.'

'Sure I do,' he sniggered. 'You are Karina, named after your great grandmother. You write poetry when you are sad and you are confident and self-conscious at the same time. You want to go to Paris and you want to take my breath away.'

Suddenly the train stopped and the doors flung open. Joe picked up his bag from beneath the seat and shuffled to his feet.

'This is my stop. Hope to meet you again exotic Karen.'

His hand was warm and soft against hers.

'I look forward to that.'

She flushed.

He let go of her hand and again that smile, goodness.

Karina watched Joe walk out on to the platform and listened to the train wheels heat up against the track; she closed her eyes and laid her head back against the seat.

There was a bang on the window and she looked up. The sleeves of his fashionable jacket had been rolled up and his emerald eyes were on fire. Karina opened the glass right as the train began moving.

'I'll be waiting for that book Karina!' he shouted.

'Yes, before the winter!' And then, without thinking, she added, 'Hey, I found my ending!'

And, indeed, she had.

TWO SOLDIERS

Collins Chinhanho Thole

The drums of war were beating. They had been beating for some time. But when the war came, some people were reluctant to risk their lives fighting. Far away in the wasteland, in one of the villages which had a predominantly adult population, there were a few older girls and two or so distinguished young men. These young men were militant-looking in every way. Everybody knew they were ready to go to war, and everybody wondered why they did not do so. Several of their colleagues had gone away to join either the guerrillas or the Government soldiers. Now the few who had not yet run away to join the bush war would enlist in the army because there were no other offers close to home and they were hungry – but of course this became their crime against the loyal black community who thought they should be killed execution style.

At first, David Sango did not succumb to the temptation offered by either side. Aged twenty, an athletically built young man, he was not a coward but he had watched young men with whom he had gone to school being killed by the community mob after being accused of joining the wrong one.

One morning, an old man of the village questioned his ambitions. The two had met at the kraals where people penned up their cattle, and said to David:

'I guess there are only two sides to choose from in the war, boy. Either you're for us or you're for the soldiers. What are you still waiting for? Or don't you ever want to join up as have all the other young men in this village?'

'I'm still waiting for the right time,' replied David, not pleased with the enquiry.

'The right time to die or the right time to survive?' the old man mocked. 'Tell me, what's the right time for a young man to join the struggle for his own freedom?'

'No one waits for a time to die.'

'Be careful, my boy. The mob is watching if yours is the wrong motive.'

The mob? A huge group of people in the community who ganged up against young black men and women who joined the war on the

179

side of the soldiers. Orphaned from birth, both David's parents had accidentally taken poison and died, he had grown up in the foster care of an uncle and aunt who raised him as their own child.

The mob. Everyone feared the mob – and for a good reason.

The Government required every young black person to enlist and join the war on their side against their own people. David Sango loved girls and girls like money. Now that most of the schools in the villages were shut down due to excessive fighting, teenagers did nothing except roam the dirty roads and loiter at Growth Points without apparent purpose. The girls were young, loose and beautiful. They were black and they smelled of sweat and urine.

David Sango had set his eye on a particular girl but he was waiting for when he had saved enough money and the war was over. The present situation frustrated him. He wanted to go away and come back to the village one day wearing a top class army uniform and carrying a gun. This was all there was in terms of work those days and in the meantime there were many girls to seduce.

One day a truck full of soldiers on routine patrol pulled up on the side of the road just as David was walking there, going his way.

'Yes, comrade,' a black corporal said. 'Tell me, where are the guerrilla fighters operating in this village?'

'I don't know where they are,' David replied, smiling benignly out of habit.

'You only see them when you go to the night vigil in the mountain?'

'I don't know.'

Soldiers on patrol were a nuisance, especially black soldiers, he thought clenching a cold jaw. David knew many more questions were coming and braced for them.

'Your name, comrade?'

'David Sango.'

'You don't know?' The soldier pursued, adding almost that instant. 'If we give you a lift in this truck you wouldn't change your mind and tell us some truth?'

'Give me a lift? Where to?'

'To the police station.'

'Honestly, I don't know where guerrilla fighters are.'

'The last time you saw them was when you went to the night vigil, Isn't that so, Dave?'

'Yes.'

'Yes! Get on board, boy. You'll show us where you went for the night vigil.'

Then luckily one of the soldiers said, 'Oh, no, leave David now, Corporal. David, when will you ever enlist to join the army, eh, still busy chasing after girls?'

And David said to the soldier, 'I'm still waiting for the right time, sir.'

Noel Sango and Nikiwe, his wife of thirty years, had an eleven-year-old son. He was their only living child after three had caught a fever and passed on. Sumba and David slept in the same room, although David was much older. Sumba went to the township school which fortuitously was not yet shut down. Since the small town was adjacent to the community, the small boy went alone every day and returned home in the late afternoon.

Now it was David's obligation to milk the cows every morning. He usually woke up when Sumba went to school and took the cattle to graze in the wasteland. But on this day, close to noon, Nikiwe found the animals still penned up. She was alone as Noel had not returned from his early morning chore in the nearby mountain of cutting trees for firewood.

At first, she was flabbergasted. The cattle had started making a noise because their time to graze was overdue. They struggled and mooed, kicking up the poles that held the corners of the kraal in an attempt to break out. At that point she hurried to the room the young men shared to find out what had transpired. She pushed in the hard brown door, her eyes probing all over the room. The blanket on David's bed was gone. So was her husband's coat which always hung in a corner. Then, to complete the puzzle, David's small suitcase was not in its place beneath the bed. At that point she assumed the fool had gone to join the soldiers – for nobody carried a suitcase when going to the bush camps to join the guerrilla fighters. It was far and you travelled mainly through the night to avoid detection by the soldiers, so everybody travelled light.

'Oh, David!' Nikiwe cried out aloud. 'After all the trouble of bringing you up, you hit us on the back of the head!'

And she was correct in her supposition. Someone had seen David carrying a suitcase and hurrying away through the bush, and dashed to report this to the mob. And when Nikiwe went down to fetch water from the village hole, the people assembled there were busy discussing the subject.

They all sat on their upside-down buckets, arguing about something. Maude, a massive unmarried woman with five offspring, had addressed the gathering and arrived at the verdict that they would slaughter Noel Sango for his crime of making the wrong choice.

Then Nikiwe Sango had arrived and there was chaos as people scrambled to fill up their buckets and started to leave. Others were amazed or indifferent.

Every time somebody made this wrong decision, they had to face the wrath of the mob; but first the news was debated at the water hole. This was where all gossip was exchanged. It was at the water hole where minor village cases were tried; and it was at the water hole where the mob decided to execute someone in public for joining the soldiers.

The women gathered first. The men came later – they did not have to carry any buckets to collect water but came to finalise what the women had discussed. Although Nikiwe Sango was not supposed to know or hear anything, before Maude left, she had uttered a strident laugh.

'Better an Indian,' she said. 'But a black man like you and me joining forces with the oppressor? This clearly shows that as long as there is money, black people will never be completely united. How many white people have you seen yearning to be black or joining a black guerrilla revolution?' She laughed once again, struggled to pull her bucket out of the iron bars which protected the water hole. 'Put in some money and there will always be somebody ready to cut his brother throat.'

Nikiwe Sango was fortunate enough not to hear more for large drops of rain started to fall and, like the rest of the women, this chased Maude away. Poor David Sango would face execution when he returned to the village – the mob never forgets. Nikiwe thought about Sumba still at school. What would she tell him when the boy asked? In addition, there were all the girls that David had sacrificed by joining the soldiers. Would they still love him when they heard what he had done? Surely, they would participate in the ritual of his execution as required.

'You heard the story about the boy?' Noel Sango inquired from his wife as she put the bucket of water in its space at the back of the

182

hut. This time he did not look his wife in the eye as was his habit. Nikiwe Sango turned, sloshing water on the cow-dung rubbed floor. The sharpened axe in Noel Sango's hands dropped too. This indicated loss of hope in both persons.

The woman watched her husband with dignity, her fear increasing. She knew that she was again to be blamed for previously she had been answerable for every wrong made by the two boys. In the past, she had always apologised profusely and, impressed by this humbleness, Noel Sango had always smiled. However, this was a different matter. The boy had run away to join the soldiers and someone had to be crucified for it.

'What story?' Nikiwe felt beads of sweat trickling down her brow.

'Aha, so you haven't heard anything yet,' said Noel Sango irritably. 'Where is your son David? Isn't it you who sent him to make a fire in our eyes?'

She decided to lie with impunity.

'They said that he was taken away.'

'Taken away, eh? Who took him away?'

Noel was torn apart by both anger and confusion and in response Nikiwe Sango's voice turned into a plea of agony and sorrow.

'Some people saw a bunch of soldiers pull him away with them.'

'He took my coat, the useless rascal!' Noel Sango tried to control his voice 'You remember where I got that coat?'

'Yes, my husband, at the Wenela Mines in Johannesburg.'

'And now it is gone!' And he shouted out. 'Who can replace such a fine coat?'

But in truth what enraged Noel Sango more than the forfeiture of the coat was the threatening situation in which David had placed them.

At midday the sun unexpectedly appeared from the clouds but only for a brief while. During the course of that morning rumours of David running off to join the soldiers had been heard, collected and then re-invented.

The stories went like this: David had gone off to look for a lost cow in the forest. The soldiers had bumped into him and dragged him off. No, it was the guerrilla fighters; they had accused him of wanting to join the soldiers and whisked him away to their base. No, David was hiding in the bushes with a pregnant girl. He was ashamed of his fornication. No, David was alone. He was in some other trouble and couldn't face his family. So these were the rumours and there were more. Nevertheless, whatever the circumstances, the mob never forgot. They kept more secrets than the mafia.

Finally Noel Sango said to his wife: 'I hate to think what's going to happen to me if it's proven that David has joined the soldiers. Remember what we did to Jack Mabaso after his son made the same blunder? You women shouted loudest. We, men, threw gasoline soaked tyres over his body. Before that we had just witnessed Steven Masai's death. They cut his head and spiked it on a spear like a worthless Shaka Zulu sculpture.'

To which Nikiwe Sango replied, 'Steven Masai did not join any war. He died because his daughter accepted a ride from the bad guys and he would not let the mob touch her.'

'And they killed both of them?'

'And they killed both of them.'

Noel Sango dropped his voice. 'Now it's my turn because of David's unwise ideas. He thinks helicopters and tins of beef can win a war. Am I going to wait here until the mob knocks on my door?'

He was breathing his last few hours and the horror grew in his mind. They would spare his wife and young son, Sumba, but what would happen to him? Fortunately there was one way of escaping from all the shame and the fear: suicide. In a moment, plunge into the void. Yes, it was the only way out. But what would Sumba do? How would he manage this double tragedy? Sumba! My Sumba! No. He had no right to do anything so cowardly.

So he said to his wife 'I shall go away. You will explain to Sumba what made me run. Perhaps he will understand. And later on----well, you never know. I'm young and can put up a fierce fight.'

Nikiwe Sango nodded sadly. 'Where are you going?'

'For the moment, to GaRankuwa, near Pretoria.'

'To your brother?'

'Yes. You'll write to me.'

'Is the money in the house enough? What if you don't find him at the old address?'

'I'll go to Thari, the bus yard, and inquire about him.'

'But for all that travelling and job hunting, you will need cash. The last time you were there he asked you to buy food. Your own brother! Cooking for him did not satisfy him. He said a man needed to find work. That was a wakeup call for you.'

'What do you have in mind?'

'I thought you could sell one of the black bulls. The butcher indicated last week that he would pay a good price for the middle one.'

'Get my bag packed. I'll go and see the butcher now.'

The 11pm train was crowded with soldiers and ordinary people. David Sango, who had walked the 10 mile distance from the village to the station, had managed to find an empty corner and sank back into it, staring out, without seeing anything of the countryside gliding past into the slowly deepening twilight.

Around him people were talking. He heard a loud voice:

'Papers! Everyone, papers in hand!'

He reached into the inner pocket of his jacket and handed them over quickly.

The soldier was white and young. After staring long and hard at the image on the paper, he handed the documents back. (On the whole David noticed that white soldiers were less inquisitive than their black counterparts.) No further incident occurred and after several hours his journey ended at the Main Railway Station in Salisbury. A police officer in uniform showed him the road to the Tomlinson Police Depot. It was not very far so he walked. Apart from the small suitcase in his right hand, he had on his uncle's grey coat which hung loosely on his lean body making him look like a loser. But was this the case? Though at first he had dreaded that someone would come after him and send him back home, now it was different – he no longer even stopped to look behind him. He had gone too far. Noel would never find him. In any case, despite his promise to David's father that he would look after David as if he were his own son, he had never been a good father. In fact, there was reason to believe that Noel would be more worried about the disappearance of his beloved coat than by the loss of this troublesome dependent.

An hour later, David Sango stood in front of a red brick building. The words 'Tomlinson Recruiting Hall' indicated that he had reached his destination. He peered inside. Sitting on a long metal bench in a corner of a huge room was a man. The man was small and his beard was straggly and black. No one else seemed to be present. Though he seemed to be lost in thought, the man must have sensed that he was being observed because the steel bench creaked as

185

he turned to study the newcomer. The two stared at each other but no word passed between them.

David entered the building and as he came closer to the man, he realised just how haggard and filthy he was. No comb had passed through his hair and his clothes were as greasy as a mechanic's. There could only be one explanation: the man was a vagrant who had wandered in looking for leftovers and a place to sleep.

Keeping his distance, David said, 'Is this the recruiting office?' and rested the small suitcase on the floor as he began to struggle out of his coat.

'Office?' the man replied, before pointing to a blue glass door at the far end of the hall. Then he added, 'That is the office but it's locked and nobody's here yet.'

David started to read the small notice next to the door. The office opened at 8 o'clock. Through the glass door, he could see a clock on the wall. It was 7.39. After he had put his coat over the small suitcase, he looked the small man over once again.

'You also waiting to join up?'

The man again ignored him but after a while he said, 'I want to see these people. I want to ask if they can find something for me to do.'

'Something to do . . . in terms of a job?'

'That is correct. Sit down, my name is Temba, Temba Ncube.'

Taking the seat facing him, David gave his name and then inquired from Temba Ncube why he had come to join the soldiers in the city and not guerrilla fighters back in the village. Once again, Temba Ncube took his time to answer. But finally he said, 'I've made up my mind, pal, and I've no intention to change it.'

'You've surely made up your mind. I've made up mine, too,' said David. 'And that's very good of you not to change it – but that doesn't answer my question.'

Temba Ncube pulled out a packet of cigarettes, extracted one, lit it and began dragging nervously.

'The enemy wiped out my entire family and . . .' his voice suddenly quit him and he was very sad.

'I am sorry, Temba,' said David, offering a hand which the other grabbed and held tightly. 'I'm sorry. But . . . who did that to you?'

This time there was no pause in order to reflect. 'Guerrillas. For no reason, really.' Temba's eyes moistened. 'The bodies are still warm, David. Still warm.'

The recruiting officer knew why the two young men were inside the hall – they were hungry – so he did not ask any questions. Although he wore a nametag above the left pocket of his camouflage uniform, introductions were necessary. His name was Mark Avis and he was a sergeant. The other man with him in the office was a captain. His name was Ben West. For both David Sango and Temba Ncube these were the first white hands they had ever shaken and this made the two young black men feel important.

The two white officers informed them that before they had settled in Rhodesia, they had been mercenaries in several African countries. Because Temba Ncube did not understand English, Ben West spoke to him in Chilapalapa, a language invented by the South African Boers to communicate with their farm hands. Although neither David Sango nor Temba Ncube could make head or tail of most of what the two instructors told them, they nodded each time as if they understood for they instinctively knew they were expected to. After assisting the two black men to complete several forms, the officers arranged for them to be driven to Morris Training Depot, about ten miles away. And there, they started a new life.

The depot instructors equipped the newcomers with the necessary training gear and showed them where to sleep. Here they met hundreds of other men who were in different stages of training. Some went out to the shooting range every day. Others were occupied with road running. All recruits took their meals in one large canteen and did not have to wash the dishes later. This was amazing. David Sango thought about his uncle Noel. He wondered if the village mob had not slaughtered him. And he vowed to return to the village though he knew the mob never forgets.

Meanwhile Temba Ncube brooded over the farm where he'd lived. Life on the farm had not been easy. After harvesting potatoes all day, they slept on the ground under the stars. Joining the army was entry to a new world where at the very least you got your own little bed to dream in. Soon the farm seemed far away and his past was partially forgotten.

And so the days passed into weeks, and fortunately they were not separated but put in the same regiment, B Company, and ranked as privates. One night in the barracks, lying on top of their small beds while some of their colleagues played cards and others read letters from their loved ones, Private Temba Ncube and Private David Sango were going through a small photo album that belonged to the latter. Neither of the two had written letters back home because they were in hiding and feared to be discovered.

'And this here was my wife,' Private Ncube said, pointing at the ugliest black woman David had ever seen. 'She's dead now,' Temba continued solemnly. 'Some heartless baboon did it and one day we'll certainly meet behind a bush and shoot at each other.'

'Poor thing,' commented Private Sango before turning to the next page. Two little children stared out at him. They must have been twins. They sat on the floor of a round thatch hut without their clothes on and they seemed to be happy. They, too, were dead. Then, before they could turn to the next photo, the noise in the barrack increased before subsiding, then increased again before finally dying and leaving behind it a strange tranquillity. And without any order being given, all troops stood to attention as their commanding officer, Brigadier Thatcher, walked in – his step as fast as when he was with the British Special Forces. Another ambush, someone predicted; and he was correct.

'You're leaving for Hobe TTL in exactly thirty minutes. 3rd Brigade has come under intense fire and the guerrilla fighters over there seem to be well-equipped . . . so be careful.'

And with that, Thatcher was gone, walking away even quicker than when he had come in.

The community of Hobe TTL never talked. The soldiers kept up their patrols until exhaustion got the better of them. In the late afternoon, Private David Sango as well as Private Temba Ncube found themselves sitting in the shade of a small rural store. About fifteen members of B Company sat together with them, their weapons resting over their knees or on the ground before them. Cigarette smoke clouded the whole place and they discussed trivial matters in low tones. The October sun continued to bake the earth with untold vengeance.

For Private Temba Ncube, sitting down to rest was an act of pure cowardice. His desire was to hunt down the guerrilla fighters who had killed his wife and kids. To Private David Sango, war seemed an exciting adventure; he was more than pleased that he had joined. After an hour or so, Ncube inquired from the black officer sitting near him, when they would go back into the bush and flush out the guerrillas. The officer seemed to be hurt by this sad reminder of work. He ordered Private Temba Ncube to rest and shut the hell up.

'War is not a game,' he said, looking at the young man with a critical eye. 'War, even a war of words, is a serious demanding business!'

However, within a few minutes he gave the order to resume patrol and soon they were lost in the forest beyond the village. The sun was still hot and the going slow. The platoon sweated as they battled through the dense bush cutting a trail with machetes but there was no sign of the guerrillas. This went on till late afternoon when the officers finally decided they were following false leads and started them back to their makeshift base. The men were thankful; it had been an unrewarding day.

Suddenly, just as the sun was beginning to sink, a hail of AK47 fire was discharged from behind them. The forest seemed to burn all at once. Rocket propelled grenades and mortar rounds rained down on B Company. In the ensuing confusion, Private Sango and Private Ncube forgot to fire their weapons or to take cover. Their more experienced colleagues hid behind huge stone boulders waiting for the storm to end while Temba and David ran round the battlefield like headless chickens. And when the battle was over, Private Temba Ncube was lying in Private David Sango's arms. Six bullets had slammed into his stomach and he had not even seen the enemy.

While waiting for promised reinforcements to arrive, the survivors of B Company sat in small tired groups, eating from their supplies of canned beef, tinned beans and dried fruit. The men did not speak. You only know how much you want to live once you have been near death.

Brigadier Thatcher hopped into the last helicopter to leave the scene of the attack but only after warning his troops of more battles ahead. With five bodies lined in a row, the helicopter left the school playground flying towards the city. Private David Sango thought about Temba, now lying on ice in the back of the helicopter. He remembered the shell that had exploded against the tree where he lay with Temba in his arms. Sango's ears still echoed with a wooing sound when he spoke. From time to time his whole body shook until he fainted.

When he awoke several hours later, David lay in a military hospital bed many miles away from the battlefield. A man who looked very much like his uncle Noel stood by the ward basin talking to a group of sick soldiers. Now this man was a corporal; the insignia above his shirt pocket said it all. But if he was in hospital then he must have cheated death too. David looked closely: yes, it was Noel and that meant the two of them were soldiers – a corporal and a private. Then David noticed that Noël's army fatigues were bloodied and he could not stand up straight because of the heavy bandages wrapped around his legs.

At that moment Noel told the other wounded soldiers that he had just left his sick bed (in another ward) because hospital beds made people feel sicker. He then started telling them about his experiences. David was too weak to leave his bed and get closer to the group but he managed to sit up which made it easier to listen to what the man was saying. Why, indeed, had his uncle changed his village mob allegiance and decided to enlist with the soldiers? Was he not one of the first men to cast a stone at those who decided to do so? When did he repent and how in hell's name did he cheat his own death?

'We were on patrol in an area where there were many guerrillas. Several times we came under fire. Men died. Several were wounded, just like all of us here. But we had to keep moving back to base. Sometimes we came across little black girls who had been displaced by the war. They were not fortunate enough to see us first and bolt into hiding. We used these small girls but not before our superiors had first taste. And the onus was upon the last person to destroy the evidence by strangling and burning the corpses. We enjoyed these occasions. And why not? Our seniors taught us that there is no mercy in a war, brutality is very much a part of the game against terrorism.'

Each word the corporal spoke made a big impression on Private David Sango. He wanted to get closer. After much effort he succeeded in getting down from his bed and staggered towards the group. At length, he reached them, and paused. The men who gathered round corporal Noel Sango saw David first. They noticed his inflamed eyes looking at them sharply. Then Noel, too, turned to look at him swaying on the hospital floor.

He stopped speaking. There was immediate recognition in both men's eyes. Someone told him to finish the story. Another man also begged him to continue. But Noel was so delighted to have found his long lost son that he stood silent, quite overcome by relief. Only the night before he had jerked his thoughts away from a vision of poor David in flames! The women shouted loudest, screaming that the mob never forgets.

'By a miracle we survivors managed to stay together during the long march through deserted villages. Finally we set up camp in a graveyard by a church and primary school. Here we managed to dig trenches and collapsed from exhaustion. The distance to the town where we were to find our transport was too far for us to continue. And that was last Sunday. I think you know that our technicians had serviced all existing aircraft in preparation for a final major offensive against the advancing guerrilla fighters only to be ordered to stand down and not take our planes up. But the news came though. Cease fire. The ten year old war was finally over, and we had lost."

Corporal Noel looked into the eyes of Private David Sango. The men around them fell silent. Something was passing between the two men – something that no one gathered there had any right to know. As he struggled to get David over to his bed in the corner, Noel looked at the men who were his audience and shouted 'Perhaps we would not have won but we could have fought on.'

Sitting down on David's bed, trying to be comfortable, the Corporal said, 'You wrote any letters home, Private?'

David shook his head slowly.

'Corporal, I'm sorry. I did not. The mob could have found me.' Then he said, 'What about you, when did you join up?'

'The morning after you were gone.' Then, forcing a smile, he added, 'I lied to your mother that I was going south to find work.'

'I trained at Morris.'

'I trained there, too, and turned out to be the top artilleryman of the year. Then they promoted me and I was sent away.'

'Let's be glad for how this has turned out. After all we only live once.'

'Yes, soon the hospital will discharge us. The conflict is over and the mob has forgotten about us. I miss my boy and my wife.'

And so it was that the two of them, who for different reasons had betrayed their people's struggle, survived the war and returned home in peace.

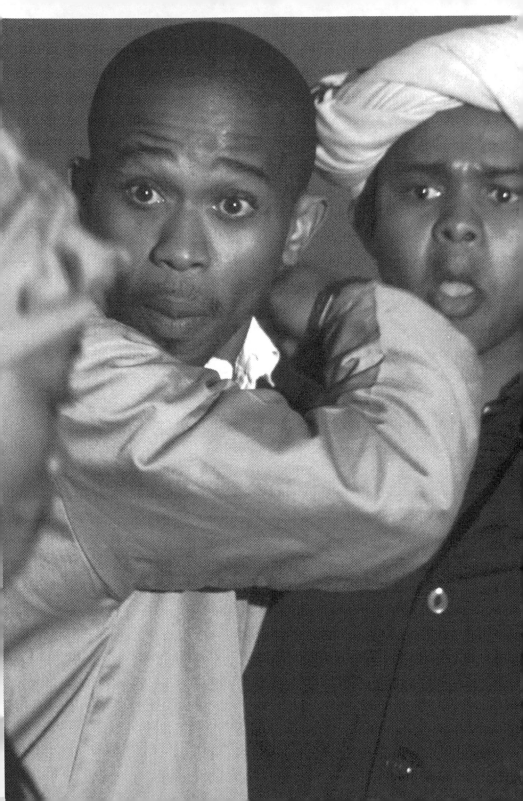

UTOPONIL
(A Breakthrough in the Treatment of Xenophobia)

J. Martin Labuschagne

There was a fluttering of papers and white coats as the new psychiatry students walked behind Professor Doctor Franz T. Smalberger through the Xenophobia wing of the Manto Tshabalala-Msimang Hospital. The professor stopped when he reached the reception area of the ward and waited as the students formed a semi-circle around him. They were ready to capture every word of this renowned expert – everybody except Marius Troskie. Marius was the most senior amongst the students and had grey patches discolouring his hairline. After a career as a doctor in the army he had decided, despite his age, to specialise in a field he has always been very interested in, namely psychiatry, but at that moment he was having second thoughts whether it was really worth it.

The learned doctor Professor Franz T. Smalberger spoke.

'Now, after we have been through the section for the criminally insane and you thought you had seen the worst of the mentally ill, we now come to the Xenophobic.'

All wrote down what he said.

'These patients are our most dangerous . . .'

'Well, Professor, do you seriously believe that they are dangerous?' interrupted Marius and provoked sharp glances from the other students.

'They might not be violent now, but they carry with them the propensity for the most horrendous sort of violence, comparable only to sexual violence, namely racial violence.' Professor Smalberger looked directly at Marius when he said the words 'racial violence' to bring the point home.

Marius quickly added another question: 'But Professor, is institutionalisation really a necessity?'

'Dr Troskie, it is not only imperative for medical reasons, it is also demanded by the authorities. As you will recall, after the proclamation of the 'Prevention of Racial Violence and Related Social Deviances Act' of 2035 it is a statutory obligation for all psychiatrists and other health workers to report any signs of xenophobic behaviour to the local police station so that the necessary court order can be obtained to remove such an individual to a safe surrounding for treatment. I want everybody to remember that it is not just good, sound medicine, but a legal obligation to report xenophobes.'

After this lengthy reply, the professor and Marius tried to stare each other down while the other students industriously took notes of the authoritative explanation. When it looked like everybody had written down what they wanted to, Smalberger continued: 'Let us now proceed to view the different treatment methods we employ at our facility,' and led everyone down a corridor which had numerous windows embedded in the walls.

He stopped at the first window. It proved to be a two-way mirror which showed into a room. Inside, two people were busy in some sort of session. One was a white man clothed in the standard light blue garb of a hospital patient. The other was a small Indian lady dressed in a short skirt; she was sitting cross-legged on a chair and appeared to be talking to him. He, in turn, sat with his arms folded, looking at the floor.

'Our first line of treatment is extensive psychotherapy to bring the patient to acknowledge the problem and to develop insight into the harmful consequences of the disorder. We have found that cognitive behavioural therapy is the most effective therapy. The patient is shown the irrationality of his fear and assisted in forming positive experiences of people of other races.'

While the students were scribbling away, Marius just shook his head. Professor Smalberger glared at him. When it appeared that everybody had finished writing, the doctor said: 'Follow me'. He walked to the next window. In this room, a group of white men were sitting in a circle listening to one of them speaking.

'As a second line of treatment, we encourage our patients to regularly attend group-therapy to help them integrate their psychotherapy into their daily lives. You see, we find that although the CBT is initially successful, when the patients are released back into civil society they tend to relapse into old behavioural patterns. So there we have created XA – Xenophobe Anonymous – to act as self-maintaining, self-perpetuating support groups for people suffering from this disorder.'

A Chinese student put up her hand. 'What if the second line is also ineffective? What would the next step of treatment be?'

The professor raised his eyebrows. 'Well, there is a rather controversial procedure which has proven to be the breakthrough we have long hoped for . . . despite the opposition of many human rights organisations.' Smalberger smiled. 'Please follow me so that I can demonstrate.' And with that he led his flock down the corridor to its far end where he paused before a set of swinging theatre doors and announced: 'Ah! We are in luck. There is a procedure in process at this very moment.'

They entered another room where there was again a two-way mirror. On the other side lay a surgical theatre with a bed in the middle; the bed faced a television that was mounted to the wall. On the bed lay a white man dressed in a green frock. His hands and feet were tied to the frame of the bed while his head was held in place with a set of straps around his crown, chin and neck. It appeared that his face was directed at the television monitor which at this point was blank.

A set of wires were attached to his ankles, his abdomen, his hands and face; the wires were connected to a large machine with numerous lights apparently indicating whether each wire was active or not. Next to the machine was a console with a computer screen. A man in a white jacket, presumably a doctor, was typing away entering commands while other staff clothed in surgical masks, were attending to the patient. A nurse entered the theatre with a trolley on which lay a set of different metal syringes. One of the staff took a syringe, tapped it to dispel any bubbles, and unceremoniously injected the patient who gave the impression of being half-asleep. The patient's eyelids immediately started fluttering but soon settled into a rigid stare.

'Now that the preparations have been finalised the main procedure can follow,' commented Professor Smalberger as the students watched the drama unfolding before them. All the theatre staff suddenly looked at the television. A few images appeared – at first out of focus and then slowly clarified so that the screen read: Phase 1.

'The patient has been sufficiently drugged to make sure that he will feel the minimum pain and that he will be able to withstand the whole process.'

The staff left the theatre room. Only a nurse and the doctor operating the console stayed behind. The nurse kept busy with the machine monitoring the vital organs of the patient. The doctor sighed and pressed a button. A set of pictures started flashing on the screen and with every picture, a simultaneously shock was inflicted on the patient. His body gave a light jolt as each image appeared. Marius could make out most of the pictures: swastikas, Prussian crosses, raised white fists, an old South African flag.

As if Professor Smalberger could read his mind, he suddenly said: 'The patient is shown a whole complex of images associated with or-directly depicting racial hatred which is then accompanied by a shock to cause a natural aversion to them.'

A hand went up among the group. A Jewish lady asked: 'But Professor, the patient is sedated? How can he form an aversion response to the images?'

'Oh, that is the beauty of the treatment. The response of aversion is inserted subliminally. The patient would have no memory whatsoever of the painful shocks but would have a different attitude after phase two has been complete.'

'Phase two?' asked another student.

'Yes, the follow-up phase where we reprogram the subconscious mind to have a positive appraisal of the specific race for whom the patient has a phobia.'

'And how is that achieved, professor?' asked a third student, this time a person of African-descent.

The professor looked genuinely delighted to be given an opportunity to explain, 'Well, the reverse of what is done here, is applied. The patient is shown a set of pictures depicting the race he fears and is fed a set of pleasant stimulations via electric current.'

Everybody looked impressed as they scribbled down their notes.

Then Marius suddenly asked: 'But what if the fear is based on reality?'

'What do you mean?'

'Simply: what if the fear is due to a traumatic experience with people of other races, say black persons, and his phobic reaction is a normal defensive strategy towards any future danger?'

Everybody seemed shocked by his peculiar suggestion.

'I still don't get your point,' the professor insisted.

'It could be that the patient's so-called fears are, in fact, natural and rational responses to threatening situations. These sensations might actually be necessary for the organism, in this case our human patient, to cope with potential dangers. Has anyone actually checked into the grounds for his fear? Maybe shock-reflex treatment is not knocking sense into the patient but knocking sense out of him.'

'I see where this is going, Doctor Troskie, and I am not going to allow it during my lectures. Please come and see me afterwards in my office,' Professor Smalberger said sharply, and lifted his finger as a warning gesture. His delight in explaining the process to the students had disappeared and a surge of irritation transformed his whole demeanour. The remainder of the lecture was conducted in a very-toned down manner as he imparted the wisdom of psychiatric sages to the young student minds.

When everybody had dispersed, Marius was waiting for him. There was an uncomfortable air between the two men. 'Kindly follow me to my office,' the professor commanded and started leading the way. They walked through the maze of corridors and finally arrived at a nondescript grey door personalised with Smalberger's name.

'After you,' said the professor and let Marius enter.

Marius wasn't surprised by the office – it looked much like his own. There was a bookshelf with a collection of books and files and other paraphernalia used by the psychiatric establishment. What was interesting though was the copy of a painting depicting the Tower of Babel. Marius frowned at this – trying to place its meaning with the rest of the office. The professor sat down behind his writing desk upon which a human skull was standing. He gestured to Marius to take a seat. After Marius was seated and a few seconds passed, the doctor spoke.

'So, Doctor Troskie, how can you possibly deny that Xenophobia is a delusion?'

Marius cleared his throat and began: 'Well, doctor. I started having a few doubts a while back. Say about three months ago. I was working late one evening at the hospital when I drove home at about 4:30 the morning and on the way I was hijacked by three black men at a stop street . . . '

'So . . . ?' Professor Smalberger was frowning.

'Thereafter, I was fearful and hateful towards black people in general to such an extent that it influenced my relationship with my black colleagues. I was rude to them and generally irritated by their behaviour. I started analysing my change in conduct and concluded that I was forming a defence mechanism against black people in order to protect myself physically against another assault. In other words, I realised that my fear was based on a real experience and therefore a valid response . . . '

'Surely, Doctor Troskie, you can't be serious.'

'Why not? All the behavioural literature acknowledges that a fear response has some basis in reality and therefore a natural reaction.'

'It is not the same thing,' the professor insisted.

'How can it not be?'

'Doctor, I can't believe you are thinking this, never mind saying it. Remember the Nazis? Remember the massacre of six million?' (He emphasised the words 'six million'.) All this was due to the xenophobia that you want to defend. Imagine how many lives could have been saved had the disorder been identified earlier. The Holocaust would simply never have happened.'

'But that is not what I was intending, I simply wanted to question the validity of . . .'

Smalberger cut in, 'Well, that will be the outcome of your fear if it goes undetected and untreated.' The doctor jabbed his finger at the desk. 'It could lead to another round of Apartheid, not to mention the surge of attacks in Great Britain on Pakistani youths in the summer of 2023. Remember that?'

Marius shrugged now feeling embarrassed by his proposition.

'You must be aware that the xenophobic disorder manifests itself also as a denial regarding the classification of Xenophobia – as if your mind is denying the delusion of racist violence.' Professor Smalberger added.

Marius sighed deeply. 'I don't know professor, it's just that lately I doubt the validity of the disorder . . . '

'You are suspicious of the definition of the disorder?'

Marius was reluctant to answer, but the word slipped through his lips, 'Yes.'

With the self-assuredness that only an academic can have, Professor Smalberger nodded.

'It sounds like a text book case of xenophobic denial coupled with a recent traumatic experience causing deeper suspicion. Are you aware of that?'

Professor Smalberger sat back in his chair almost triumphantly while Marius looked down sheepishly.

'Yes, I am aware of that.'

'Are you currently being treated for this?'

'No, I am not.' He kept looking at his hands.

Again the professor nodded and pulled a script pad closer. He started writing and when he was finished he presented it to Marius, who took it reluctantly.

'This is a prescription for Utoponil,' said the professor.

'Utoponil?' Marius was perplexed.

'Yes, it is a new and still secret inhibitor. It will help you ease your fears for . . . you know, for blacks and other races. I am taking them myself.'

'Do they work?'

'Like a dream.'

'Thank you, professor,' said Marius.

And both men smiled as Smalberger took out a small box of pills from his top pocket and offered Marius a glass of water with which to wash them down.

IDENTITY

Jacqui Greenop

Her parents were too shocked to speak. The clock chimed the quarter hour. A deep gurgling sound seemed to follow on from the fading dongs. She looked from one to the other: who would speak first? Her mother seemed to be making throat-clearing noises; her father was a statue, steely blue eyes staring straight ahead.

'He's very dark, you know.'

'It's called olive skin.'

'Mmm . . . this island that he's from. Where is it exactly?'

'Why don't you just say it, Ma.'

'Say what my child? Don't get so uppity.'

'Say it, Ma. Go on, say it.'

'So many of them coming over here now. To work on our mines. Lettie says they're very good at growing vegetables. Some of them are even opening up market gardens. Ag, I know they call themselves 'European', but I don't know my child. Why are they so dark?'

'Say it, Ma. I want to hear you say.'

'Calm down *meisiekind*. I just want to tell my friends his nationality . . . this man you're planning to marry.'

'We're done planning, Ma. The date is set, the church is booked.'

'But that's not possible! I haven't spoken to the dominee yet.'

'The 'dominee' is Father Da Silva and the wedding will be at the Troyeville Catholic Church.'

'Oh, my God!' Is this wise? It all sounds very . . . papist.'

'Get used to it, Ma. I'm going to be a Catholic now, like my husband, like all the other people on the island. Your grandchildren will be Catholics. And we're not going to grow vegetables. He's a qualified welder . . . a damn good one. He fought for our country, was even taken prisoner, dammit.'

'There's no need to swear child. I just want to tell my friends and family who you're marrying.'

'Ag, Ma, just tell them I'm marrying the man I love.'

They decided to speak English since that was the language all their mutual friends used. A fresh start appealed to their spirited natures: somewhere away from here; a different community on which to stamp their brand. So they planted four of us down in the English heartland of the country. As our awareness of ourselves in the community developed, we learnt to open our vowels, lower our voices and restrain our gestures. These people valued understatement and control. Steadily I chipped away until I fitted the space they made for me. I mastered their language, even became expert at it, chose to earn my living teaching it back to them. Such a perfect fit, many asked which part of Britain my parents were from. Fitting in was about surviving. But I knew, all four of us knew, that at home things were different. We ate different food and my parents spoke differently. Our house was louder, more colourful, somehow busier and fuller than those around us. The only kids from school in church with us on Sundays were the Irish immigrants. None of these things was advantageous to fitting in.

At some point, wriggling in and out of the space they made for me began to chafe. As a young adult, starting to look outwards, I began to see little cracks in our parochial community. As the cracks widened and the light poured in, something began to dawn on me: our community was not so cosy. I realised that I disagreed with quite a number of their values. As I switched on to the wider world, I saw they were downright bigoted. What a varied smorgasbord existed out there! My parents became more interesting. And so the identity thing reared its head at a very early stage.

In my dreams I wander free, on my own, floating on a buoyant breeze. Clocks, watches and cell phones do not exist. I always knew that time was an arbitrary construct. My feet touch lightly on fine sand fringed with sea grass. On, over the hills, atop a kopje, looking down on the veld. A bank of black cloud masses on the horizon, then bursts. That ozone fresh smell as the first heavy drops churn up the dust. A perfume I wish I could bottle. I dance, I sing – not very well – but it feels good. I find a shallow cave and write and write and write.

In my half-waking hours, in those fleeting if-I-could-have-my life-over moments, I am an aid worker somewhere in Africa. I know there is terrible cruelty and inhumanity, an overpowering smell of desperation. But that doesn't form part of this gilded fantasy. This is all about satisfying work, a simple hut, simple food and huge glorious chunks of time to read and write. In the wide-awake world, however, there is no simple, free-floating, detached spirit. Now a mother and a wife, three additional souls have become embedded in my being. To excise them would require cutting. It would cause pain, be bloody.

My shape has expanded to hold the children cut from my belly. White neoprene belly hanging over a stretched pink white scar. My being still holds the child who leapt back into the stars before sucking in oxygen. Imprint of a son, shadow of a boy, eclipsed by the breathing flesh of those two who made it through, were plucked out safely. Greedy mouths, greedy hearts, hungry heads. Your cries, your demands are my music – my *raison d'être*. Your needs define me.

That journey we took together, my child, through the dark night in this restless city, driving from place to place, a sanctuary to keep you safe, to save you from yourself. One goal in mind: please God let him see just one more sunrise. That journey etched in my heart. And then, having survived the night, on seeing you pale and frightened, I wanted pluck out those demons and beg them to rather reside in me.

I am also bound to the trunks of those precious trees in my arbour that were cut down too early. Kim, shot in the head like a rabid dog – an unfathomable deed. Even though I tease out the strands till they become scraggy and jagged, I cannot find the why. And also Mewêe, little bird, your beautiful cheekbones irreversibly stamped into the metal of the sports car you loved to drive at the speed of the wind.

Daddy, the day before your spirit left us was even worse. I wasn't ready when you told Paul and I to look after Mommy, to make sure she stayed in the house she loved so much. A ragged cut tore my body in two on the inside – left and right – releasing heartsick and dry heaves into the open cavity. A solid lump stopped my answers to my family's curious questions, their faces misted by stinging salt water.

Then there was the grey spongy tumour that came to live with me for a while. I became that vile thing till it was chemo melted and nuked, then cut from my breast. The nauseous stumbling journey back to life defined me. To a life amplified, brighter, more focused, more joyous, just more of more – another chance.

I see a glittering diamond held up to the light. All the facets – dark and light, love and hate, pain and sorrow, joy and fear – form one brilliant stone.

THE NEW HOUSEWIFE

Hyun-Jung Anna Kim

Saturday, April 5

Dearest One,

Spring is here. Almost. I don't know whether to put the winter clothes, the hot water bottles, the humidifiers, the electric blankets away for you or not. Last night it was chilly. Tonight it is much warmer. Tomorrow they say it will rain . . .

We met when I was twelve. Well, not really. You know I am in one of those moods. Like funny and sad at the same time. You know this mood. And you know just how to push my buttons and make me mad. And I know how to get mad.

My mother asked me on the phone the other day if everything is alright between us? She said I sounded funny on the phone. And that's what I said. It's all I said. She and my Dad (as usual in the background) got quiet, and then did not say anything more about it.

When I first came to your house – nine years ago already, can you believe it? – I was so naïve. I almost said 'innocent' but that is not the right expression, is it? Though I was still young, and it's true, spoiled in some things, in some ways, I did not lead a sheltered life before I met you. You know this.

When you said you wanted me to be your wife, and to live with you in your country, despite my past, my parents all but pushed me out the door, and into the plane. They did not care that you were much older. They did not say it, but I know they were thinking, 'this is her chance, maybe her last chance' – at happiness, at safety, at finding a home; her own family.

I was clutching the ticket you bought for me. I picked it up at the airport counter, as you said to do. The ticket to my new life; a new beginning.

My old life packed into three suitcases. All they let me carry on this big journey.

I had never flown before.

I was afraid; yes, really scared. And excited.

I could not believe it. I was in the clouds.

Me, a poor, divorced woman, who could not have her own children. No fine education, like you. Married once to a poor bastard, scrubbing that sad apartment of his that never got shiny no matter how much I cleaned it. Scrubbing other people's houses and raising other people's children for grocery money, pocket money. So I could get my hair done now and then, save for a dress, and don't have to ask him for money all the time.

He hit me once so hard I fell under the table, twisted my ankle, for keeping that pocket money.

That was my life. You know this.

After giving that man seven years of my life, I found out he left me for a piece of ass who got pregnant. Does he even know if that's his child? I saw them together one day in the shopping market – that is how I found out. Him – at the market!

You saw me in the photos my cousin took. She promised she would not show them to anybody. We were only playing, and I did not take them seriously.

But they changed my life. You saw them. And then you looked for me. And you found me.

We wrote letters. I kept them. And sent each other more photos . . .

I went to check the internet every single day. Your e-mails made my whole day and nights. They were full of you, my every day and every night.

And then one day, finally, I came to you. You sent for me. I had to fly through the clouds to give myself to you.

I gave you my life. And you received it.

My new life. I trusted you.

THE MATTER OF MY GRANDFATHER'S GHIA

Rudi Benadé

In the west boardroom of the offices of Meyer, Mendelsohn and Maggit, as the second hand swirled round and the wood-panelled walls slowly oxidised, we, three interested parties, took our place at the grand oak table for the reading of the last will and testament of Johann Van Der Walt. I'm talking about myself, his grandson and sole heir, and the Bartholdys, Elsabie and Abraham – all of us sweating as the Free State heat fell like a woollen blanket on the proceedings.

Now the Bartholdys were a cabal of oblong figures. I had met them briefly once before and now, as then, they were draped in what were either frock-like shirts or shirt-like frocks. It was difficult to discern where Abraham ended and Elsabie began. Though nominally they were male and female, I could see no distinguishing features and at best the landscape of bulges and crevices underneath their faded navy-blue garments could be described as androgynous so that at worst one might even question if they were indeed mammals.

Unfortunately the purpose of their presence at this reading will remain obscure to you a little while longer as the rather long-winded Messrs Meyer and Mendelsohn themselves presided. (Maggit, though his name persisted on the letterhead, no longer practiced.) Mr Meyer was a plump fellow who struggled intermittently with the expansion of gas and gastric products; he blushed like a bruised tomato. Mr Mendelsohn, on the other hand, existed in the temperature-controlled microclimate of his own steely resolve. And while, we, the assembled were silent in anticipation, he produced a glottal bark that cleared his throat and could have emptied the room.

'I, Johann Van Der Walt,' he read, 'domiciled and residing at *Drie Riviere, Vereeniging* declare this to be my will, revoking all previous wills and codicils.'

The thing, the what-sit and the what-what-what, the this, the also and the that-that-that, all were then distributed with due process and the services of Meyer, Mendelsohn and Maggit would have seemed to align to the idiom of currency in exchange for fruit preserves, if not for the problematic final item about to be addressed.

Mendelsohn's reading-glasses perched on his nose like a mantis. He peered over them and said: 'And now we come to the matter of the two Karmann Ghias.'

My grandfather had two 1962 Volkswagen Karmann Ghias which he was, to my grandmother's constant annoyance, eternally restoring. In the five years in which I knew him, neither were in running condition at the same time; more often than not, neither was operational. When ordered from Germany, parts, if they could be found at all, would take four weeks to arrive. Within that time, if the first car was missing a part, the simplest solution was to harvest the said from the second.

Upon sighting the winner of the 1963 Cape Derby, my grandfather had the first car painted the chestnut brown the beast was born with. *Colorado King,* as he was called, went on to win the Durban July, also in 1963. This victory my grandfather also considered worthy of commemoration, and painted the second the same shade.

Uniquely, the two vehicles only possessed between them, two plates (one front, one rear) and one registration disc. These were shuffled from one to the other and provided my grandfather with the stock quip that, in the eyes of the state, though not those of his wife – there existed in his garage only one vehicle. This, he would go on to say, in a hush behind a bowed hand, was the reason for both his admiration for the rule of law and my grandmother's need for prescription spectacles.

Now strictly speaking, the second car was not my grandfather's. This much I know, and there exists no legal document denying the fact. The convention for establishing an agreement of ownership in *Drie Riviere* consisted of eye-contact, a steady handshake and the threat of being badly spoken of in the church foyer on Sundays.

The second car was, in fact, the property of one, Arno Van Heerden, the local butcher.

Van Heerden, as I understand, solicited my grandfather's services as a mechanic for the restoration of the rolling chassis of a 1962 Karmann Ghia and, for this purpose, made him a fifty percent upfront payment of a bundle of forty R20 notes. The chassis itself, and Van Heerden's word, would serve as deposit. My grandfather was also promised a leg of lamb every Friday for the duration of the project.

'As you are now aware,' continued Mendelsohn, 'Johann Van Der Walt was in possession of two of these vehicles, and it is agreed, by his grandson, that one of these rightfully belonged to Arno Van Heerden, here represented by his daughter and son-in-law, Elsabie and Abraham Bartholdy.

'In Mr van der Walt's own words: *My 1962 Karmann Ghia I give to my grandson, along with all the spare parts and associated incidentals (manu-als, papers, etc) in my possession. Any other vehicles in my care, not belonging to me, are to be returned to their rightful owners. Any debts their owners owe at the time of my death may be waved, although it will not be possible to return deposits.*

'As no special mention is made of the second Ghia, the task of identifying its owner is of utmost importance because the bulk of your grandfather's estate, with the exception of expenses and debts, has been donated to charity, and the Ghia amounts to the only tangible asset assigned to his heir. It is also the only pre-residuary item specifically catalogued for distribution. In other words . . .' and here Mendelsohn, seemed to take pleasure in adjusting the temples of his glasses and allowing his cool grey eyes to flash behind them, '. . . it is the only thing he gave anyone, and he gave it to you. But . . .' And this time his pause was accompanied by a scratching of his Adam's Apple and a movement of his other hand just below the table. 'There is a problem. The vehicles are identical in appearance and we are struggling to identify which belongs to whom. In this regard, we must assume both engines had been replaced since neither matches the engine number on the registration papers in your grandfather's name. The VIN numbers, located in the front wheel well, have either been removed in the process of rust repair or are unintelligible following the accident.'

'The accident?' I asked.

'Yes. Were you not aware?'

'I didn't know it happened in the Ghia.'

'Unfortunately, yes. One vehicle is ruined, the other in perfect driving order. The question remains, how are we to determine which is which?'

I thought my grandfather had been in the Daimler. I could not imagine his driving the Ghia out of Vereeniging, not for the distance of over one hundred kilometres. The Daimler was his regular vehicle and certainly the safer one. Perhaps he considered it appropriate to drive the Ghia to an appointment which would deliver that illusive final motor part that promised to complete the repair. Perhaps he thought it necessary for it to be present at its own birth.

The Karmann Ghia was really a Beetle, mechanically speaking. The body, which would be described with lascivious adjectives –

voluptuous, full-figured, shapely, buxom – was styled by Luigi Segre of Ghia and hand-built by German coach-builder, Karmann, but grafted onto the chassis, engine, exhaust system, transmission, driveshaft, wheels and suspension of the ordinary Beetle.

Those familiar with either vehicle will remember that the extent of protection in the event of side-impact was limited to a double-hinged door and two coats of paint.

I remember driving in the car with my grandfather on a Sunday. He would be wearing his tweed driver's flat-cap and he would light his pipe and tell me to roll down the windows. His smoking was prohibited in the house – a self-imposed ban he instituted in reverence for the delicate female nose. He would not even smoke in his library for its proximity to my grandmother's sewing room. However, I certainly had no problem with him smoking and liked the smell of his tobacco because it meant I would get to change the gears.

When we drove together, he tried to teach me to listen for the pitch of the engine revving at five thousand before shifting the ivory gear knob down and to the right. Instead, I would take my signal from the way he would raise his two bushy eyebrows like a vaudevillian stage villain.

Somewhere in the undercarriage, the teeth of the gears thrust into place and we would carry on our merry way, his one hand to the wheel whilst the other still cupped the pipe to his mouth.

'Oupa, why don't I ever get to change gears in the Daimler?'

'The Daimler is automatic,' he said. Except he said this in Afrikaans, *outamaties,* which sounds exactly like *ou tamaties* – 'old tomatoes' – leading me to believe there was some wooden crate mechanism doing service in the otherwise high-end vehicle. 'And because the Daimler still belongs to the bank.'

Having said this, Oupa was meticulous in taking care of all the cars and of his other properties and instilled in me an obsession for washing the fleet on Saturdays. The hosepipe ran from a wall at the back of the house, in front of which slept a gutter made from an erosion in the earth. The ground sloped toward it so that when I crossed the gutter the first time, it woke with a trickle but by the time I was done washing the Daimler and both Ghias, it was alive with a river bursting its banks. This muddy terrain had to be crossed several times in the execution of my duties and caused me to leave large brown footprints all over the yard and the kitchen and earned me a brisk pinch of the ear from him and the threat of the wooden spoon from her.

The Bartholdy's folded their starchy arms.

'I don't care if it is the exact same car or not,' said Abraham, the slightly more potato-shaped of the two. 'The fact is,' he waggled a tuber at me, 'he owes us a car and the working one is the closest we'll get to it.'

'I must remind you that you have no legal claim here,' said Mendelsohn, calm but firm. 'There is no conclusive evidence as to what transpired between Mr Van Der Walt and Mr Van Heerden.'

'The evidence is sitting right in front of you!' said Elsabie. 'How many of my father's lamb chops did it take to make this boy?'

How sweet of her to remind me of those delicious meals! But how stupid because Mendelsohn pounced without mercy.

'Exactly! For how many years did your father send chops to Mr Van der Walt?'

'I don't know. Maybe . . . fifteen.'

Mendelsohn smirked. 'Week after week for fifteen years. Why didn't he fetch it if his debt had been paid?'

Here Elsabie started blubbering, 'It's just that he was very busy with the business . . .'

'Yes, a very busy business. Madam . . .' Mendelsohn smiled triumphantly. 'Your father left that vehicle with Mr van der Walt for almost two decades and you have the effrontery to . . .

I couldn't believe it! Was Mendelsohn trying to prove that even a small town lawyer knows how to browbeat witnesses?

I chimed in: 'Mr Mendelsohn, please. I've asked them here because if there is any way of establishing ownership I'd like us to try. My grandfather would have wanted to have his debts settled.'

'Yes, yes, quite so! That is certainly what Mr Van Der Walt would have wanted.'

At last the hitherto silent Mr Meyer re-entered the meeting. Without further delay, he put forward two possible ways to establish ownership and argued for and against each possibility.

'We could determine which vehicle had the greater mileage – Mr Van Der Walt's is likely to be the one with the greater mileage on account of his using it more frequently – although the lack of reference and the fact that both cars were bought used make this impractical.

Or we might take stock of the parts and see which were ordered in the period before Mr Van Heerden delivered his vehicle to Mr Van Der Walt. I understand some of these will be found in both cars but perhaps we could consider the car with the greater amount of these parts to belong to Mr Van Der Walt. An arduous task, of course.'

'As I see it,' said Mendelssohn, and he took off his glasses to rub his eyes. 'Mr Van Der Walt's Ghia exists in some proportion in both cars. It can be said to be both working and wrecked. This is also the case regarding Mr Van Heerden's Ghia. However, its portion in the wreck must be considered useless and irretrievable while the other portion currently exists as spare parts in Mr Van Der Walt's. I'm afraid gentlemen and lady, my duty as an attorney is only to the contents of this will. I must therefore grant both vehicles to Mr Van Der Walt's grandson. Now please, let's wrap this up before we all evaporate into a tizzy,' and watching Meyer's cheeks puff up with a suppressed burp, added, 'I fear it may already be too late for my colleague.'

I stepped into the foot well and sat down. The seat remembered. I could feel its depressions shifting from his to my body. Every inch bore testament to him and was an extension of him. His maintenance of its water and oil was like trimming his fingernails or combing his hair. I grabbed the adjustment lever and slotted it back but not before being filled by an uncomfortable suspicion that I was erasing my grandfather. Everything I did in it would make it more mine and less his. But what joy! It was all there: a dashboard – built before the proliferation of plastic – of chrome and ivory; the spindly steering wheel he had only gripped with his fingertips; the radio dial still set to 88.9; the smell all Ghias carried – of felt and leather and time.

But then, suddenly, I knew it: this was not my grandfather's Ghia. There was something missing, something which told me, unequivocally, that this was not the car of a man who took his hat off when entering someone else's home; who used a shoehorn to keep his Brogues crisp, and not for vanity but to display respect for others; a man who, had he been here today, would have been wearing his best suit, even in this heat, because it was Sunday.

Truly, there could be no doubt that this surviving car was Bartholdy's – in all the years that my grandfather kept it, drove it, fixed it, cleaned it, swapped parts for it, I knew he never considered this Ghia to be his because he would only smoke his smelly pipe in the car he knew to be fully his. And yet, here I was at the wheel and poor Elsabie had lost the battle.

There was nothing to be done – in honour of my grandfather I took out his old pipe, pressed in a wad of tobacco and, as I drove off to visit my latest girl-friend, lit up the neighbourhood with a big, Van Der Walt smile.

He wakes up

Billy Rivers

He wakes up at noon, no, that's not really true, he tells himself this, that he's lying, that it's past noon and he needs to be honest about the hours he's keeping – with himself if no one else. 'Lazy' his voice croaks to the cracked ceiling. He shifts, rubs gummy eyes, and groans – feels like someone worked him over with a sledge hammer. This is what he gets for trying to be healthy, a good little man going to the gym, wailing on those pecs. Throwing back heavy blankets, he puts his feet to the floor and stands. A series of pops accompany the movement. Shaky steps carry him to the kettle. He flips the power then the switch, stares at the coffee jar, chooses a tea bag instead.

After a long piss he goes back to the kettle and makes himself a mug of tea, sips it, wishes it was coffee. The light outside his window is that distinct kind of orange, the type you get this time of year – almost spring but still chilly, especially in the basement. He grabs that dressing gown, the one he got in the charity store, and puts it on, still amused by how much it cost him – about as much as a garage pie. It looks like someone died in it.

He sits down at the desk, turns on the computer, takes another sip, grimaces, opens a Word document, wonders what to say . . .

The fridge hums its electric drone. He usually turns it off at night because it's so close to his bed. The noise always wears at his senses, fills his head, drives his teeth together. Yet he never notices the hum unless he's trying to think, or sleep. In the morning he switches the power back on to boil the kettle and keep the milk fresh. Now he gets up, turns the power off again, sits back down.

Quiet now. But no words come. What kind of mood is the bitch, creativity, in today?

The phone rings. He answers. The line's bad, no signal in his bunker, his fortress. He goes outside, feels the rising heat of the day. The line clears. He recognises the voice. Has a conversation. Hangs up. Standing in the driveway in his underpants and dead man's dressing gown, he feels something for the first time in weeks: and the sensation isn't welcome.

But enough bad news and the scale finally tips away from the mundane. Good to have that haze clear, be able to think again –

at least 'just about'. He starts to construct a bomb, some powerful combination of thoughts and feelings violent enough to blast away the remaining fog. He puts the phone in his pocket, grabs his keys, goes for a drive.

Moving helps.

He rolls through the suburbs, past high middle-class fortifications. All manner of growing, eating, beating, sleeping, and fucking going on behind them. The suburbs look dull because they are dull. He wonders why black people are the only ones to walk around them when it's mainly white people living here. On occasion he's seen a lone Dutchman on a two legged mission, sometimes a kid with long hair and a Heavy Metal hoodie. The only other whites who put foot to pavement usually have an iPod strapped to their arm. They seem to be running from something. It's rare to see them break a sweat.

His foot goes down and the car picks up speed, casting him further into a metropolitan nightmare.

He always thought he'd spend more time doing this when he got his wheels. Jump in and drive. No destination. Have an adventure. Find something new. Just explore Jo'burg. Eat something good. See and maybe even grope a pretty girl and for the smallest of moments, fall in love, then get back to the business of living.

Traffic put an end to that dream: the dead zone of the commute. The navigation of taxis and impossibly fast busses, the stink of their engines, the po-faced housewives in their gas-guzzling monstrosities rolling fat asses to Woolworths, the grinding noise of yet another spiky haired dipshit cranking up the volume of generic house-electro-pop, all that auditory sludge crawling over the airwaves, spreading out over the sea of bastards.

He realises he's driven to Sandton.

Turning the car at a roundabout, a Bentley cuts him off. He lays on the horn hard. Sticks a dead-man-dressing-gowned-arm out the window, and razes his middle finger. 'CUNT!' he screams.

He sees a street-side vender on the sidewalk; she's got what he needs. He pulls over, starts rummaging around in his ashtray for change. With a handful of coppers he gets out of the car and is immediately aware of the heat beneath his bare feet and the cool breeze blowing against the sweat clinging to his exposed chest and belly.

He stands in front of the vender; she looks back at him blankly.

'One Courtley, sisi.'

'Fifty cents, my baas.'

He drops the change into her hand and takes a white filtered cigarette. Standing there bare foot, in underpants and a dead man's dressing gown, he smokes and watches a pair of pigeons fuck.

When he's done he gets back into the car, finds an old Clash CD and sticks it in the player. Starts the car, cranks it up, heads for the highway. It doesn't seem so bad up there, high up on the N1 South, traffic moving fast, green suburbs spreading out to his right, good music.

He starts to relax, starts to think without the fog. Feels good to be moving forward, even without a destination. He heads to a side of town that has colour; a little more dangerous, a little less bland. The great Jo'burg balancing act. The better the bar, the worse the area. The more fun, the greater the danger.

Less shining buildings, more dilapidated wrecks with superior character and better bones. The old part of Newtown. He catches himself wondering at their monetary value – a compulsion coming from his upbringing. Raised by builders; which is why doesn't hate cell phones, just people who talk on them.

He drives around for a while, feeling out the pulse of traffic – as the taxis do – getting into the lanes that move faster just as they start to, pushing past lights well into the orange. More often than not he fails but it feels good when he doesn't. Eventually he finds himself under the N1, in that rare nook of the city, the one plastered with three story testaments to the spray-can. The graffiti reflects the city's temperament, captures a portion of her soul.

He stops here. Just sits in his car watching as the colours stretch out for two blocks. Eventually paranoia seeps in, takes root. He gets to feeling that something's going to happen. Something bad. Maybe someone's going to stick a gun through the window, blow his head off, leave him stretched out on the sidewalk in his dressing gown and underpants. Leave him there for the career dog rapists that prowl this city at night. He's convinced it'll happen and so very badly doesn't want to die looking silly.

He starts the car and heads back to the suburbs.

The day's getting clammy, even though it's almost over. He looks forward to the coming rains, something to wash the dust and smog away, a grand Highveld thunderstorm to split the sky with jagged light.

The thought brings a memory, he's lying on his back, half-drunk,

21 years old, heavy rock guitar blasting from the doorway to the rooftop, rain freckling his face as he gazes up at the sky – good times with good friends.

The sun sets to his left, pollution and high altitude refracting the light into a rage of colour. A pumping of joy, at keeping pace with his home town, sits at the back of his teeth like the onset of two hits of ecstasy, good ecstasy, the kind you get from Nigerians at the Hilton in Hillbrow – definitely a risk worth the payoff if you're brave enough to go inside.

He gets home, cuts the engine, goes back into his basement.

Another cup of tea. Another wish that it was coffee. Another long stare at a blank word document.

His fingers hover for a moment over the grimy letters; then he types:

'He wakes up at noon . . .'

THE PARLOUR TRICK

Estelle Van Der Spuy

Vy was a neck man and his date had the most beautiful one he had ever seen. His right eye followed the contours, rested on the intricacies of the French plait; his left eye, being glass, did not.

Vy was short for *turksvy* – his hairstyle resembled the thorns on a prickly pear. Chantelle saw that his lower lip was cracked; he moistened it regularly with the tip of his tongue. White stuff had gathered in the corners of his mouth. She mentally cursed Yolanda for setting up this blind date with her cousin.

Vy put his hand in front of his mouth for a soft cough, stretched his arm and allowed it to come to rest on the backrest behind Chantelle. Chantelle shifted forward and fiddled with a shoulder strap. Her empty coffee cup had gone cold; it would not be rude to plead an early meeting in the morning.

'Let me show you something.'

Vy got up. Chantelle suppressed a sigh and leaned back in her seat. Vy put a square box in her hands – it was surprisingly heavy.

'I found it in one of those antique shops on Queen Street.'

Chantelle lifted the lid.

'You need to use it with this.'

Vy jerked something from his sleeve – a length of fraying black velvet.

'Look.'

He lifted the object from the box. His fingers brushed against her hands; his nails were bitten to the quick. He swept the cloth over the cold roundness and revealed the crystal ball cradled against the blackness in his hands. He lifted it like a chalice. Chantelle leaned closer; she expected to see her own reflection but found herself staring into Vy's right eye. The dull green of the glass eye was trapped in the globe and magnified. She cleared her throat.

'It's so interesting – I've never actually seen one of those, but I really need to get going. There's a team meeting tomorrow at eight.'

'Wait, listen to this . . .'

Vy took the box from her hands. He fished out a scrap of paper. Chantelle looked at her watch. He read:

'The blackness will roll away and latent memories and visions will appear in the glass . . .'

He stared through the glass at her; all Chantelle saw was the blackness of the velvet.

'What do you think; would you like to try?'

Vy thrust the ball at her; the smell of brandy lingered on his breath. She took it; the velvet was warm. Only then did she notice that Vy had dimmed the lights. Inside the ball, candles flickered; Chantelle felt dizzy; a warmth covered her neck and face.

'Let me.'

The ball rolled to the ground; the velvet covered one bare shoulder. She felt the bluntness of his nails under the other strap. His hands were on her neck. His right eye was glassy too.

And soon she knew that the bristles of his sparse beard were pricklier than they looked.

Extract from THE POLITICIAN

Colin Jiggs Smuts

This is my story. You see, I was born in an awful ghetto, in the lower part of Bossies, nickname for Bosman Village, where they have private houses, council houses, matchboxes and train houses. I suppose I was lucky, we had a matchbox. My mother died when I was ten years old. Even before mom died, they used to fight 'cause my dad was always drunk. They would fight about his whoring. Shit, I can still hear my mother screaming at him. But he would beat her up and tell her, it's his house and he's the boss, she must be careful, he wears the pants, he's not a moegu!

I was the eldest. I used to comfort my three brothers and sister. We were all so scared of him, that he might come into the room we shared and beat us up – which he did quite often. Though he hasn't been well over the last few years even today I hate him for what he did to my mother and us. Man, when I get panicked calls from my brother who stays with him, I drop whatever I am doing and drive out to the Northern Cape to help out. But whenever I arrive, and see the bastard alive with his woman – I don't know what number she is after my mother but she seems to stick with him – the old hatred comes alive and I want to strangle them both. Of course I like to impress him. I love the way the kids and whole neighbourhood gather around my BM and admire it outside his matchbox in that small country bumpkin town and say 'Meneer's se groot seun is hier, die groot man van Joburg af, vat weet Madiba!' Ja, even my father who is a drunk and a womaniser from Johannesburg, impresses these poor country people as a sophisticated person from the big city and is referred to as Meneer!

Ha, ha. You know he's lucky he's my father. If he wasn't, I would have finished him off like I have many of my enemies. But I still hate him! You see he deserted us when Mom died. He couldn't handle it. He wasn't even at the funeral. Aunt Mable, my mother's sister, and her family moved in with us. Her husband had deserted her. In fact, he never even married her. I later learnt that all her five kids were from different fathers. They stayed in one of those train houses below the railway line. You know, those houses you come through the front door into what they call the dining room with a partition in the middle and the other room is the kitchen with a coal stove and the back door.

There's a toilet and the only tap for the house in the yard, which is bigger than the whole house. And that's it. I know of families of over twenty people staying in those train houses. That's why I hated apartheid and what it did to our people. But even more I hate those fucking bourgeois coloureds who thought they were white and stayed in private houses in the top part of the township. Fuck, I hate them although I'm above the lot and now I like to show them I am the BAAS like my father used to say to my mother. And I love it when they, and the white liberal and boere businessmen, gaatkryp me when they need something or want favours. Ha, ha. You see, I'm a politician now. I'm the guy in charge!

It's like my aunt and cousins. After two years, she took over our house. I think she slept with a clerk at the council housing office and got my one brother committed to a place for delinquents in PE (where he still stays). It was part of Aunt Mable's plan to get rid all of us and take over the house. My brother, Sam, was not a bad guy, just liked hanging out with the mense, and now and then stealing something from the shops, no big deal. But one day they caught him and some of his friends at the local supermarket and instead of standing up for him in court, she helped condemn him by telling the magistrate that he never listens to her, is rebellious, mixes with hooligans, and how she's struggled to bring him up and make a decent person of him since his mother died and father had deserted the five children. That bitch sealed Sam's fate! Lucky he's a big guy now, married and all with kids but he won't come back to Johannesburg although I asked him to. And now that I am a big time politician I've flown down to see him. Hey, man, was he impressed. You see showed up at his place in my fancy wheels and I stayed in the Holiday Inn where I entertained him and his whole family. Jesus, you would swear I was Jesus Christ Superstar, they all thought I was Santa Claus come from heaven. It's the best, Oom Shaun! Those kids showed me genuine reverence! You see, I'm a councillor now in the Metropolis, I have an expense account, a huge salary and unlimited travel. I've made it! But back to aunt Mable, she treated my sister, my other brothers and me like shit. We never got enough to eat, we were slaves to her and her kids. She's lucky I'm not vengeful. Otherwise I would have her kicked out of our house that she stole from us and let her lie in the gutter where she belongs, the bloody alcoholic bitch!

But like I said, the real people I hate is whites and those fair skinned coloureds who think they are white. Ha, ha, but I've been showing them. Man, these people are gullible, especially if you play real black victim. I have to laugh sometimes but in my position, I give them shit, I tell you. All my life I had to play up to these people, you know even in the church pretend you're a good Anglican. But I got those priests right. I used to collect, my broer, all the way to Matric! Ha, ha! You know I must watch myself. I'm only telling you this. If I said it to other people, especially that arse-hole Rams who I conned into believing he was my father figure and I was his second son, they would go mad. And you know what, old Walter my buddy who's now an MP in Parliament, and dark like me, we fucked all the fair coloureds in Bossies plus all those stupid white liberal women who thought we were township revolutionaries. You know, we even married two of the fairest girls in Bossies. Ha, ha! And these women, just like their families, thought they were larnies.

But to be honest, I couldn't have done it if we didn't meet up and work with Tanya. Hell, that woman was a master. You know she can control: her husband, her family, politicians, man, you name it – she's a master. She even has the president eating out of her hand. You see the three of us worked together very closely in the old days and even now. She used to tell us to support her cousin who we all thought was going to be the main man. But when he fucked up, we all thought she would switch her support to another cousin who's also a politician. But she hates him. So who took over the mantle? Why, us two and her, and have we three not prospered ever since? After all, we did do the work. You know, she's the most popular person on the regional executive and gets the most votes every year at elections. She even has personal access to the president. Hey, man, it's a pity with this African thing. If our Tanya was black enough, she would have been the first woman premier in the country. But right now the three of us are going to go places. I tell you, my man, our next goal is to make it in national politics.

The art of the matter is to study people and to know how to make them believe you agree with what they are saying, and so gain their confidence. Once you've done that, you're home and dry. Hey, man, people are so gullible, it's unreal. Take the Anglican Priests. They thought they had me. I did everything they wanted me to do: I was a boat boy, a server, read sermons – the works. So they financed me right through high school. It's a pity my three other brothers and sister didn't know how to handle them and the bourgeoisie – if they'd done that, they wouldn't be such a burden on me now. (But really, not my sister that much although I have to dry her tears every time her husband messes her around – which is normal. And my one brother in PE, he doesn't bother me. It's the other two who keep getting into kak.)

Malcolm, the second youngest, has already had several busts and done time. I think he's queer. Once my wife came home with the children and he was prancing around the house in her underwear. She went mad and threw him out. Shit, did this create a storm in the street! They were laughing about me the councillor with his wife throwing out his moffie brother in panties and bra. Well, I sorted it out. I told her off, like she can't create a skandaal like that. After all, he was only having fun. Damn, I had to fetch him from the local shebeen and bring him home. Ria, my wife, can't tell me what to do even with her whole play-white family, after all, I support her, I'm the baas! The youngest, Arthur, has also been bust and spent time in prison. I've tried to get them trained in some skills and jobs, but they always fuck up. I even tried to con Rams into running a computer course for community workers and told him, they and their friends were working in our community project in the township and needed computer skills. But it didn't work. The computer teacher saw they were barely literate and couldn't even speak English, let alone understand what a computer is. But she could have tried. I mean really teach them if she was interested in genuine grassroots development. But all the bitch did was intimidate them so badly in the first workshop that they hardly showed for the next lessons, were either late, hadn't done their homework or just dropped out. Of course this woman complained to Rams from the start and the whole project just fizzled out. Fuck her, the white madam. She could have tried harder. I mean these guys were from real deprived backgrounds. She didn't have to come over so heavy with her larnie attitude as if she was teaching white university students at Wits. Rams hauled me over the coals for wasting valuable resources and especially this bitch as a resource person who had agreed to do the workshops for free. He wanted to know how I could claim to be bringing community workers for training who were actually dropout crims not interested in anything but a freebie and how to pull the next con. Of course, I accused him of being a bourgeois coloured who doesn't understand the grassroots working class and didn't see through the computer lady being a white racist! Well, he didn't fall for that shit and I was careful not to try another con like that with him again. So now I have Malcolm and Arthur staying with the old man in the Northern Cape. I mean he is supposed to be some type of mechanic and driver. It's his turn to take some responsibility and teach them skills and find them jobs. Why must I always carry the burden? Let him also see how they've turned out through him deserting us – the fucking old lecherous, drunken bastard!

You see, we black people have suffered at the hands of the whites and these play-white coloureds and rich Indians. There's a lot to redress for what they've done to us. But you see with Madiba we have to be patient. He likes these exploiters. They always treated him well. I mean sometimes I like to call him an Uncle Tom but I won't do that at a party meeting. Luckily we all know that when Thabo comes in, things will be different. Then we'll really be in charge. For now we have to tolerate these whiteys who accuse us of nepotism, overspending, lack of transparency and being incapable of governing. But fuck them, they only looked after themselves – we are looking after all our people. You know, they even complain that we never work full time and that what is called our allowances is double a normal salary. After all, we haven't inherited big businesses like them where they took the fifteen thousand a month allowance and the entertainment allowance as something of a freebie for doing service. I mean, we devote all our time to this work and our only income is the allowances for attending to business and entertainment. I mean we are the biggest metropolis in Africa, we have to entertain all these groups from other countries who want to invest in our city. We can't go on like paupers when we meet these people. These whiteys didn't go on like that when they were in power. Of course the fact that all our travel on council business is paid for helps. And of course the cellphones. Oh, by the way I have to admit the pussy on offer, it's lovely. But paying for all our travel and the cellphones is absolutely necessary. We are on call twenty-four hours a day. I mean, we see to our people at all hours of the day and night. And there are always crises. So we're only doing our duty. Not like those reactionary white fart arses and their black lackeys. Yerra, man, but when you in charge do those fuckers gatkryp you! And you know, we keep trying to change things but these reactionary bastards keep frustrating us. And the press, they were never so vigilant when their white brothers were running the show and we were suffering!

You know, I used to envy those fair skinned coloureds. I used to wish I was fair like them with straight nose and hair. But now I'm glad I look like a darkie with cruz hair and flat nose. A lot of the brothers think I'm a darkie too. Man, I have now even remembered who my darkie ancestors are, I mean as my mother and aunt told me. Before I used to play that coloured line and say my grandfather was from Mauritius and my grandmother was white. I mean, as Rams, that fucken stupid fucker who likes his whisky and his own ideas, would say, 'Man, if your grandmother was fair and married a black man, it means she was mixed and therefore black. And after they invented the colourpeans, she became a coloured and ultimately your grandmother would say she was from Germany or some other European country. He told me that most of the boere and larnies in this country are from the same origin as us. And even the so called darkies. He said we all related. We all mixed. He told me the Bantu speaking people came here about two thousand years ago, they were the iron age people and they conquered our people, the Khoi. And after they introduced all their wonderful discoveries, like smelting iron, cultivating the land and animals, especially cattle, our ancestors showed them our religion, that the medium to God was through the ancestors, the Amadlozi, which proved more powerful than theirs. After all they were invaders in our country. But our spirits were stronger and they adopted our religion. So we had conquest and absorption. But when the whites came here, just like before in our history and culture, we helped them because they were starving and suffering from those white diseases they brought from Europe. We got them better. Then we gave them land, sheep and cattle and showed them how to till the land in our country. We also allowed them to take our daughters as wives. I mean, fuck, this Rams arsehole used to say, the only substantial number of white women to come out here was with the 1820 settlers. And those were very few, despite what the official history of the system and the SABC try to show. Moreover, that was after more than a hundred and fifty years of white settlement, albeit mainly confined to the Cape. And what did we get for it? he used to shout. Dispossession, rape, plunder, desolation, poverty, apartheid! Anyway that man is unambitious, he just wants to talk and drink and likes his own ideas, totally worthless, although now and then he wants to boast about his prowess with women. But I listen to him and think, oh, you old timer, if I must tell you of Walter and my conquests, you'll know what womanising is all about!

You see, I grew up the hard way. It was only when I met Walter, and after that when he introduced me to Tanya, that my life really started to change. I mean her husband, Tim, was deployed to look after and control Rams. But the useless bastard couldn't even do that. You see he's a fair-skinned, play-white coloured, too, with lots of money. And he couldn't take Rams lording it over him, being his boss, when he was personally richer than him and a lot of those straight-nosed, straight-haired coloureds. In fact, he had a shit load of money. He didn't have to work. But Tanya insisted on it, otherwise they would look bourgeois. They even stayed in a council house, although in the type that was the top of the range that the council built. But Tim hated that he couldn't flash his wealth like the rest of the coloured larnies who built their own fancy houses in a special coloured area on the western side of Johannesburg on the fringes of what now is commonly known as Soweto.

After the Boere kicked out those people they identified as white, Jewish, Indian or African, they found no coloured businessmen of any real capital substance they could sell the land to in order to develop 'private enterprise' and show the Non-Europeans the benefits of white civilisation. Hey, I'm lying – there was one exception: a doctor who still runs a questionable practice. And so, they created additional businessmen, one of whom was Tim's father, an upholsterer in a factory, who overnight became a millionaire landlord, compliments of the system. The other was a friend of his who was a carpenter in the same furniture factory. The two of them owned little township cafes run by their wives and children while they worked at the furniture factory and that made them capitalists, or at least two people who the Boere could identify as engaged in private enterprise. The system offered the two of them and the doctor huge tracts of confiscated property with buildings and tenants intact at rock bottom prices. Between the three of them, they ended up the biggest landlords in the coloured areas. The upholsterer and the carpenter even became Joburg's first coloured hoteliers – like the system had to have these ethnic hotels for accommodation of 'ethnic' visitors from other parts of the country and show this as 'progress'! The Indian dudes saw the gap and quickly opened up their joints using the system funding for their own ends. It didn't matter to them if you dug jazz or were left wing, just as long as you paid. The coloured dudes didn't have that sophistication. And the doctor pulled out. Although he drank, as a so-called follower of Islam, he couldn't be seen to be a partner in a booze selling establishment. Got to maintain standards you know and keep up with appearances! But Tim's father and his buddy were the perfect fall guys. The system got their Uncle Toms, all coloured, with a white dude in the background to run the hotel for them. The benefits were enormous. Besides owning the only legal bottle store and drinking establishment in the area, they were allowed to supply all the shebeens, which helped their profits enormously, all illegal by the way, under the watchful eye of the system. In fact they were also taken on their only overseas trips ever, compliments of the biggest liquor chains in the country which were all controlled by the same monopoly with their overseas counterparts as hosts. And these white owned chains invested heavily in these ethnic enterprises set up by the system, quite often gaining full control of most of them through their own ethnic nominees who they employed. And they tell the TRC that they never collaborated with Apartheid but were opposed to it and did 'their best' to advance the economy. Yeah, selling out had enormous benefits for collaborators of all persuasions!

But what really fucked Tim up was the way his old man changed his life style when he stopped being an upholsterer and became a businessman. He suddenly became this flamboyant character and was hardly ever at home. He was now a company director and had to take care of business. Rumours started to surface that his father had other women. His mother became distraught and started to drink quietly. His old man had sold the shop and now her duties were just keeping the house neat, looking after the children and seeing to the Big Man when he came home. The more Tim's father got busy and never came home, the more his mother descended into alcoholism. This started to have a terrible effect on the children. But all the old man did was shower gifts on them during his rare visits and ignore the fact that his wife was out her mind with alcohol. Then, after a while, he just stopped coming home and set up house with his mistress and even had two children with her. The old lady grew worse and became totally erratic. It was at that time that Tim met Tanya. I think he was fifteen years old. He needed a mother figure to replace the one who was disintegrating in front of him. He was the eldest in his family and Tanya was the only female, besides her mother, in a family dominated by her father and eight brothers. She needed someone to dominate and Tim wanted to be dominated. It was perfect. In fact, she has been the over-riding figure in his life ever since. He saw to the other kids while their mom descended into alcoholic madness and his father's indifference increased. He needed someone to lean on, to help him, to tell him what to do and Tanya filled that role. He also developed a very uptight and brusque approach to his old man, taking care of business and his siblings and his sick mom but never allowing himself to be sentimental.

Ja, you know he can be admired, but he had money – not like me who had to survive by my wits. That's why he's so weak and is so dependent on Tanya; if she had to leave that guy, he would collapse. Even so, it wasn't all roses – that woman was so busy and was away most of the time, both locally and overseas. Hell, I used to admire how she could travel. Of course, Tim would look after the kids and the house and take care of domestic matters. He didn't mind, after all he was used to it, he had been doing so all his life. Even if she was not part of an official delegation to attend some meeting – wherever it was – and she wanted to attend, she would get there by paying her own way, or rather by getting Tim to fund her and stop pleading poverty. And she would end up the star of the meeting. So much so, that everybody would think she was the delegation leader. Hey, that woman can talk, man, and impress people. Both the internal and exiled national leadership thought highly of her – not forgetting the foreign embassies. As a result, she would have hitches here and there, mainly from the local women and other politicians who couldn't compete with her. Ha, ha, now and then if they got the move right, the regional or national lot that were anti her and us, as we were all part of the same team, would insist on a meeting in our area to test the views of our constituency. They thought they would be trapping Tanya and us by showing that we had no mandate and did not represent anybody. Ah, man, it was easy to counter. Even if it was a weekend, we could get people in. If our talks didn't work, Tanya would organise bread from Tim and we would hit the shebeens and Walter and I would organise the men and Tanya and Rachel the women. We would promise them booze afterwards but on condition that they came to the meeting and praised us as we spoke and especially Tanya. Shit, it worked like a charm. You know these elitists don't like to come and meet the people and shake hands with them and talk about their problems. Naah, they like to sit on stage and watch from a distance. The way those people used to khuza us and especially Tanya, we overwhelmed those bourgeois who were the cabal. They really were impressed and thought we had the best run and most popular township organisation. Hell, we just made sure that we paid the shebeen owners to supply enough booze, dagga and mandrax and some pap and vleis for those who had supported us to bomb their minds for the evening! And it worked so well that those arseholes who hadn't attended the meeting but checked the rewards others received for supporting us, would come in their droves when we called another one. They treated the three of us like gods. Shit, we were their saviours and Tanya, the Rain Queen, was the bringer of all things good.

But, let me tell you, man, it worked even better when we met that self-opinionated prick Rams who thought, and still thinks, he knows everything. You see, that ou was into the big bucks with the embassies. He knew how to write proposals and budgets and list the infrastructure needed and all the other admin shit that whites and overseas donors like to hear. Tim had confirmed this when he worked for him as a bookkeeper. But he had failed to organise the guy, and Tanya said we got to use what he got – we got to get our hands on the bread to use it for the revolution. 'That ou Rams is too pap, he just want to use it on education and to teach kids how to dance and act and draw and useless things like that. Comrades, what have the comrades of '76 said? Freedom Now, Education Later!' She enlisted the support of her cousin who was a part time artist and knew Rams. He had also left Uncle Tom politics some while back and now had a smart job as an affirmative action supervisor in a Yankee furniture factory who had applied the Sullivan Codes. She had first wanted to approach her other cousin who also knew Rams but decided against it as she felt Rams might have some reservations against him as he was still serving on the Uncle Tom city council. You see, Tanya and her family have always been involved as they felt they had to use all the loopholes that were open even if some people called it selling out. 'But my family,' she would assert, 'have always been concerned about the community and have always tried to do their best on their behalf, no matter what the obstacles were, even if it meant being branded a sell out!'

Well, the plan was set. Raul, her cousin, would befriend Rams through their common dabbling in the arts. We formed ourselves into a civic organisation making Raul the chairman. Soon Rams and Raul became buddies – with that aspirant Princess Di wife of his and the kids at his side. Jesus, that woman was dumb; and when she had a complaint about Raul, she would run to Tanya. And Tanya knew her cousin was fucking around but she would soothe our local Princess and soon they were together again and all was forgiven. I'm telling you, I admire that man, the way he could handle his women. Shit, I've learnt a lot from him, like how to play them. Even if they found out about each other, they still loved him and slept with him. Tanya also felt her cousin, who was older than her, was a master.

But ou Raul was sharp. He checked out what the prick Rams was into and played his cards right. You know, that ou can speak, charm and impress people. I'm telling you, all types of audiences love him. That's why I say me and old Walter have learnt a lot from him. Tanya too, but it's in her blood. Me and Walter had to train ourselves. Pretty soon ou Raul, working with Rams, got himself elected as chairman of the arts outfit that Rams set up. He checked ou Rams' connections to money were somehow connected to the party and shifted his politics. He even told Rams that he was an atheist like him. And to prove his point, he told Rams he had given up his Islamic religion to marry the Princess who was an Anglican, and they got married in church (which I am not quite sure is the truth). He even opposed his long time buddies on the committee from the BC and helped Rams screw them off the committee. And he befriended this white woman writer (whom he hated until then) because he said Rams checked her real bad. He and his family spent weekends and all their other spare time with Rams and his family. And this ou Rams likes to drink and talk, can't keep a secret, that man. And he had this access to the bread, and we had to find a way of getting to it. And that's where the civic came in so handy.

Now we did have one to two hiccups with this strategy. Rams and his project had mounted a drama presentation exposing the tricameral parliament and the elections for it. The performance, which was followed by a discussion with the audience, was touring the townships. They were working through civic organisations in each township. Each civic was responsible for organising the venue and publicity and mobilising the local community. As we had formed our 'civic', we were requested to host the performance in our area. But they had chosen a Friday night which was problematic as people normally got paid that day, and had money in their pockets, and preferred drinking – they were loath to go to a church hall and see a political play and hear speeches about not voting. Besides, not many of us would be speaking, only Raul welcoming the group; there would be no toyi toying etc. And over and above all this, it was early days and we had not yet mastered the art of getting our local audiences in. We soon learnt that a day in the week – when they're broke – is easier. Shit, besides us, only three people showed up. We explained that, as we were a new civic, it would take a while for the community to understand how important these issues were and that as a predominantly working class community, Friday night was a bad night as people preferred to let their hair down and jol. But Rams and company claimed that most of their gigs were held on Friday nights in areas just like ours and in some even more poor and depressing than Bossies. Besides, many in the cast held day jobs during the week and could only perform on Fridays or the weekends.

It was decided to cancel the show but they offered to help with the canvassing and spend a Sunday with us doing a door to door number. Of course, we declined their offer and stated that we had enough manpower – they were just not all there that night. I mean, we couldn't have them coming into our area and checking out the scene. And two weeks later, when we managed to muster fifteen people, we had quite a job persuading Rams and his cast to go on with the show on the basis that these fifteen people would persuade many others in the community when they joined us in our door to door canvassing. You see, the UDF had just been formed and civics had to do most of the work. We explained that immediate numbers are not what counts but that over time the message must get through. Well, they went on, and of course we told other civic and political groups how the hall was filled to capacity with over fifteen hundred people who couldn't all get in. The civic was a brilliant idea actually because that was to be our entree into the UDF.

After the performance we had a strategy meeting. Through his moving in the art and political circles with Rams, there was the possibility that Raul might be offered a job in a major NGO. Besides, that Rams chap needed closer working on. Tim wasn't succeeding as planned. So it was decided to deploy me as he was looking for a programme assistant. I had been working as an unqualified teacher at the local Anglican Church school. I had been a bright scholar at school and a great soccer fan. I was always number one in class. My work was always ahead of the rest and my reports excellent. In 1981, my matric year, the coloured students in the Transvaal went on strike. It was our late entry into the struggle. Walter and I soon became student leaders. He became chairman and I was secretary of the Super SRC which was set up to direct the strike. Sadly, the strike didn't last long. It was isolated and only taking place in coloured areas. There was no linkage to the students in Soweto. But though soon crushed, it brought a consciousness of the struggle to many coloured students. It also brought us to the attention of the security police who detained us together with a lot of other students. However, to our surprise, apart from sjamboking students during demonstrations, they were not harsh to us during detention. Nor were they interested in who the leadership was. Rather they warned us that we were making a grave mistake in challenging a government that was doing its best for us and protecting us from the barbaric kaffirs. In fact, we were going on just like the uncivilised and ungrateful savages who hated us and wanted to kill us too!

Well-being, the Chairman and Secretary of the Super SRC, had a lot of very good spin offs for Walter and me. It brought us to the attention of Tanya and a whole range of groups involved in the struggle – from the Indian Congress, Cosas, Azapo and the BC student groups to the Soweto student formations, even the SRC at Wits and the BSS. I suppose here at last was some sort of political grouping that could be referred to in Bossies. Suddenly we were in! And from then on we were invited to so many meetings and parties, juslike it was lekker. We were big time now. And what's more, it was the first time Walter and I had white pussy. Shit, those white liberal lefty chicks really thought we were main time revolutionaries and they couldn't stop putting it out. But Tanya was the master. She called us together and explained we mustn't be taken in by all these groups and offer them our knowledge, support and allegiance. We must build our own support base and use them – not allow them to use us.

Walter and I were not sure about this. We were suspicious of her as she was a high buck and had never taken notice of us before. We told her we would think about it and let her know. But she kept contacting us, inviting us over, preparing nice meals for us. She would take us to our meetings and pick us up afterwards. She would also take us out with her and Tim and he would pay for everything. We started spending a lot of time at her house, discussing things, watching TV or learning how to work her computer – they all had computers in that house even the two kids. Hell, they had bucks. I used to wonder why they stayed in a council house when they could afford to build in 'private' areas in Bosmont or Fluerhof. And when she got to know of my unhappy home circumstances – of staying with my aunt Mabel and nine children in the house – she said I can't study for matric in such a situation and offered me her maid's room to stay in for free. You see their maid stayed in a Wendy House, also at the back of the house, as Tim used the room as a storeroom. Of course that was an offer I couldn't refuse. So I stayed there for several years until I got married. It was the first room I had to myself and I really grew fond of it. Ja, that woman was good to me. She fed me, clothed me, gave me money – alles! But Tim hated having me around and from the start treated me like I was some piece of trash. He also resented having to take his stuff and store it at one of the properties he owned. And on top of that, he had to paint the room out and furnish it for me even though Walter and I helped him with the painting. What the hell, I didn't take notice of him – Tanya was the boss, not him. He used to insist that I do household chores and help with this and that. But if Tanya wanted to speak to me or wanted me to go with her to a meeting or something, then fuck him, he had to do whatever he wanted done by himself, ha, ha!

When I come to think of it, Tanya was a very restless person. She liked to be on the move. She knew a lot of people in the Labour Party 'cause Raul and his brother were big in the party. She would often decide on a visit to one of these sellouts and take me with. This would upset Tim but he had no say and had to look after the kids and take care of business. Besides he had the maid to help him and that was a big plus. Tanya had organised the maid so that she did the cooking, cleaned the house and saw to the kids – the whole works. Tanya told Tim the trips were networking, she had to keep in touch to know what people were busy with, it was important for her career. As for her job, she would just ask for time off or most times tell Tim to phone in and say she was sick. In any case, she didn't need the job – they had enough bucks. So travelling with her was the first time I saw Durbs and Cape Town and other parts of the country. In fact, it was the first time I ever travelled. Sometimes we would just visit some relatives of hers in the countryside who ran some cafe or trading store. These trips were short, normally just a couple of days, at most a week. Poor Walter couldn't come. With his family of eight brothers and sisters and strict parents, he couldn't take off so easily. Tanya would ask me if it's okay to be out of school and I would say no problem, I would find out what

I had missed and quickly catch up. I was always ahead anyway. But ou Kleinbooi, the reactionary fucking senile principal, didn't think so. I suppose if I was one of those straight-haired, fair kids, it would have been different. He was always treating me like I didn't belong, like I was in the wrong school, that I looked more like a Bantu than a coloured. He was very prejudiced against us coloureds who were dark skinned with fuzzy hair, as they used to call our hair, which was ridiculous because the man was a dark skinned, straight haired, short little Hottentot bastard who had married a fair coloured woman who produced fair skinned kids and so Kleinbooi went on as if he and his whole family were white! He was always against me, never praised me for my good marks or prowess in representing the school at soccer and athletics. Everything I did was always wrong. And when Walter and I led the strike at the school and got onto the Super SRC that was too much. He berated us at troublemakers and the cause of all the unrest and warned us that we would not bring down his school or cause trouble there! The fucking bastard took his revenge. He refused to allow me to write the matric exams, despite the fact that I had registered, due to my lengthy periods of absenteeism. I explained and Tanya backed me up with a letter that I had to visit my very sick father in the Northern Cape and had to help find my missing brother who had run away from the reform school he had been sent to in PE. As the eldest child, it was my duty. None of this helped. Of course Kleinbooi didn't buy the story about my sick father and missing brother. Bossies is so small, everybody knows each other's business. It was known that I didn't even know where my father was at the time and if my brother did manage to run away from reform school, the only place he knew and would run to, was Bossies and in no time the cops would know he was there. Tanya even pleaded with a Labour Party connection of hers in the Department of Education to no avail. They stuck by the rules that if you missed a certain number of school days, there was no way you would be allowed to write the exams. But I was different, I would have walked it. They would not even take into account my earlier term reports that Tanya showed them. Fuck it man, I was a brilliant student. They didn't realise my talent and how cleaver I am. I also had this dream of becoming a medical doctor. In fact I had told the teacher who did careers counselling at school that my ambition after matric was to do a degree in Medicine. He had advised me that it was a tough course to get into and that I would need outstanding math's and science marks to make the grade. He also told me about how to go about applying for a bursary. But I didn't bother. I knew that I would have to find a job in order to help my other brothers and sister. But it was a dream I would pursue later, I told myself. Kleinbooi also made it clear that, as I was eighteen, I would not be readmitted the following year to repeat my matric. You see, with the turmoil in my family I had missed a year or two at school from being posted from pillar to post among the aunts and uncles after mom died until we settled with aunt Mabel. Kleinbooi told me I could to go to the trade school or one of the private colleges in town. It was easy for him to say so. But what could I do with no money and so many obligations. He also added that he was not going to allow his school to become like Soweto schools where big men and woman in their twenties are still doing matric and beating up teachers and threatening principals. We are not Bantus here, we coloureds have standards and are civilised like white people. The fascist black straight haired coloured who also thought he was white! Pity we didn't have the power we have now, we would have put all those reactionary bastards in their place!

But I was creative like that, Rams likes to say about himself. I invented the story that I wrote the matric exams but that, between Kleinbooi and the Department, they refused to release my results because of my involvement in politics. Hey man, and it worked. I have got away with it for years. I even added that as a result, I could not take up my studies at Wits Medical School who had accepted me. Jesus, thanks to my convincing manner and the fact that there were many cases at the time of the department refusing to release the results of students they considered 'political', nobody had gone into it and realised it's a bit inventive. And I mean, after all, they were all convinced that I had done my matric, so what harm is there in it? Besides I have gone on to do a diploma and a degree at Wits University, howzat?

You know I was helluva good at soccer too. Several teams from the National Professional Soccer League wanted to sign me up. I was the best ball player in the school team and later for my team, The BV Spurs, better known as the Bossies Spurs. Hey, you had to see how the mense praised me when I was playing, especially the girls. Ah, man, just like now with politics, it brought me many cherries. But you know those fair skinned, straight haired coloureds and Indians from Sacos threatened me. They said I would be a sell out if I took up one of the offers from the professional teams. But it was an exciting offer for a poor, deprived boy like me. The glamour, the pay, hey, it was difficult. I wanted to do it. It would have been my ticket out of the ghetto. It was all right for those high and mighty Sacos people to talk, they had money and were well off. So they got the priest, Father Bernard, to speak to me. He hinted that my bursary might be affected as the other brothers and sisters on the committee might not take too kindly to me taking an offer from the NPSL. I spoke to Walter about it and he suggested it might not be worth it, especially if I got buggered up with a knee or some other injury and would be out and left on the dust heap as a has-been; nobody would check me then. I took his advice and stupidly declined the offers. Fuck, I was so glad when the National Sports Congress came into being and fucked those Sacos bastards!

So what am I to do? I can't go back to school. I can't write my exams. I won't get a matric. That fucking Tim bastard is moaning to Tanya about him supporting me and demanding that I pay some rent for the room and a contribution for the chow and staying there. Fuck! Meanwhile Walter had written his matric and had applied and was accepted by the Bush College in Cape Town and would soon be off to do his degree. I mean even that ou was well off. He had a mother and father and family. Me, I had nothing – except aunty Mabel and the worry of my brothers and sister. And Tanya wasn't working at the time and that made that stingy bastard exploiter of a husband more befoked. He raved about having to support her and her meatball. He had a cheek calling me a meatball! I mean, fuck him. I was her friend, her companion, her adviser and now and then her lover. But fuck even here, Walter was first. I hated Tim and still do! Ha, ha, you must see now that she is main time, she has a lover and it's very public. In fact, he is a married ou but he and Tanya go all over together and even, now and then, with Tim in tow. And this ou, is a darkie boy, nogal. But he's got position in the business world and in the Party. Now and then Tim likes to joke rather than show how kak he feels at a function when ou Lappies, that's the guy's nickname, has his arm around Tanya in full view of everybody, so he says, 'This ou sees my wife more than me!' When he really feels humiliated, he starts talking about divorcing her. But that will never happen, he's too pap and dependent on her.

And now Lappies goes all over with her so often on official occasions which is really on holiday they call him Mr Tanya. Ha, ha, I love it. And ou Tim still has to see to the kids, the house and take care of all the shit, man, Tanya is a master, I tell you!

SUBMISSIONS
Botsotso journal & website

All submissions are welcome. Please email original, unpublished work in any South African language and be careful to keep a copy as we cannot be held responsible for loss or damage to manuscripts and cannot return work.

Simultaneous submission of the same work to several magazines/publishers is not acceptable. However, should you wish to withdraw work from Botsotso kindly inform us timeously. All work received is considered by the editorial board but due to the high volume of work received we are not always able to respond to each contributor. As such please bear with us if you do not receive feedback!

No payment for published work is offered as our budget is very limited but selected work will qualify you for a complimentary copy of the magazine. Copyright of all published material remains with the writer/artist but the proceeds from the sale of Botsotso magazine are used for new projects. As a non-profit entity we are struggling to achieve financial self-sufficiency – a very difficult goal to achieve as the "market" for new, original South African writing (especially for poetry and short fiction) is extremely limited.

Please remember to include your contact details: name, postal and email address, telephone number.

Botsotso magazine appears irregularly as a number of important variables have to be satisfied – quality and diversity of submissions, funding, time to edit – but we do attempt to produce at least one edition a year. Some work is included in both the electronic and hard copy versions of Botsotso but we reserve the right to publish in one or the other as circumstances allow.

botsotso@artslink.co.za
www. botsotso.org.za

Printed in the United States
By Bookmasters